PRAISE FOR *The Last River*

"[*The Last River*] belongs to the realm of Jon Krakauer's *Into Thin Air* and Sebastian Junger's *The Perfect Storm*. It is gripping, insightful, thought-provoking, and it delves into the mindset of extreme adventurers and into the soul of whitewater paddling." —*Albuquerque Journal*

"Suspenseful . . . " —*USA Today*

"With his riveting account of the [Tsangpo River] trip, Balf has supplied a smart introduction to the daredevil lifestyle of river runners." —*Fortune*

"Todd Balf's saga of an assault on the 'Everest of rivers'—the fabled Tsangpo—is a rich and troubling story about the dark side of America's infatuation with extreme adventure. It's a must-read for anyone who loved *Into Thin Air*—or who might be contemplating that next first descent on a killer river." —Erik Larson, author of *Isaac's Storm*

"Crisp . . . a well-rounded view of the expedition." —*Seattle Times*

"*The Last River* is high adventure and fine writing. Todd Balf is a splendid storyteller. For anyone captivated by *The Perfect Storm* or *Into Thin Air*, *The Last River* is your kind of book. It is every bit as riveting." —Kevin Baker, author of *Dreamland*

"A tale that rivals Jon Krakauer's *Into Thin Air*. . . . Balf is a consummate craftsman in not only reconstructing the events, but in examining the motivations that propelled these adventurers to take on the deepest gorge on the planet." —*Toronto Globe & Mail*

"A flowing, well placed narrative." —*Seattle-Post Intelligencer*

"A well-balanced tale in which the technicalities of exploring and paddling share space with ruminations on man's spiritual quest and mortality." —*Publishers Weekly* (starred review)

"Fascinating . . ." —*Dallas Morning News*

"A sober grabber for the adventure-reading legions." —*Booklist*

The Last River

The Tragic

THREE RIVERS PRESS
NEW YORK

Race for Shangri-la

by Todd Balf

For Patty, Celia, and Henry

Published by Three Rivers Press, New York, New York. Member of the Crown Publishing Group.

Random House, Inc. New York, Toronto, London, Sydney, Auckland
www.randomhouse.com

THREE RIVERS PRESS is a registered trademark and the Three Rivers Press colophon is a trademark of Random House, Inc.

Originally published in hardcover by Crown Publishers in 2000.

Printed in the United States of America

Design by Lauren Dong

Map illustration by Rodica Prato

Library of Congress Cataloging-in-Publication Data

Balf, Todd
     The last river / by Todd Balf.
     ISBN 0-609-80801-X
         1. Rafting (Sports)—Brahmaputra River. 2. Rafting (Sports)—
Himalaya Mountain Region. 3. Brahmaputra River—Description and
travel. 4. Himalaya Mountain Region—Description and travel. I. Title.

GV776.81.H54 B24 2000
915.49204'5—dc21

                                                                00-031421

ISBN 0-609-80801-X

10 9 8 7 6 5 4 3 2 1

First Paperback Edition

Acknowledgments

Thanks to Kristin Kiser for her editorial guidance. To Esmond Harmsworth for his encouragement, and to Patty Adams, Tom Balf, Eugene Buchanan, and Daniel Coyle for their manuscript input. Thanks to Jon Gluck of *Men's Journal* magazine for his original editorial direction, and more general support, and counsel; to Alex Bhattacharji for his research assistance with the original magazine article; and to Terry McDonell. Thanks to Bill Breen and *Fast Company* magazine for my temporary leave from usual duties to complete this project. Thanks to Rachel Pace, to David Smith for his copyediting, to Jillian Dunham for fact-checking, to Alex de Steiguer for her photography, to Brad Anderson, and to all my family for their energetic help and especially Nancy Balf, who generously offered her transcription skills.

Finally I'd like to thank Connie Gordon and expedition team members Tom McEwan, Roger Zbel, Wick Walker, Jamie McEwan, and Paulo Castillo for their time and detailed recollections. Thanks also to several in the whitewater community: Jan Nesset at *Canoe and Kayak* magazine, Lisa Fish at U.S.A. Canoe/Kayak, Jason Robertson at American Whitewater Association, and Bruce Lessels and Edward Wilkinson at Zoar Outdoors. Thanks to expedition experts Lukas Blücher, Arlene Burns, and Peter Knowles and to Cathy and Davey Hearn, Evelyn McEwan, Norman Bellingham, Joe Jacobi, John Weld, Andy Bridge, Lecky Haller, and Ryan Bahn. Thanks to Laura Deakin for her concise tutorial in molecular chemistry.

LHASA

LHATSE

TIBET

Friendship Highway

Mt. Everest
29,000+

Himalaya

NEPAL

BHUTAN

INDIA

Wan Lin, 1998

The Last River

Great Falls of the Potomac, August 1975

PREDAWN, THE POTOMAC RIVER. BOYHOOD FRIENDS WICK Walker and Tom McEwan, now in their late twenties, and a young tagalong, Dan Schnurrenberger, stumble around their island campsite gathering up gear. They don helmets and spray skirts, grab paddles, and furtively slip into the swift but familiar current. The plan is simple: Before the park service is up and about—the Virginia side of the Potomac is part of Great Falls National Park—before anyone is up and about, they will paddle upstream a mile and a half to the base of Great Falls, then climb and rope-haul their boats to an overlook where they can scout the crux move of the seventy-five-foot drop one last time.

Great Falls is a twisting, rock-jammed stretch of whitewater where the immense western river–sized volume of the Potomac abruptly plunges off the Piedmont Plateau to the coastal plains. Nobody has ever run the vertical falls. The conventional wisdom is that nobody will run the falls. As it is, some seven park visitors each year drown in the rapids. Most of them slip off the gorge's high cliffs and are swept into the fierce whirlpools at the bottom of the falls. The thrashing currents can hold a person for a long time. Some victims are never spat out.

And yet Walker and McEwan, hotshot local whitewater racers, have been toying with the idea of a run down Great Falls almost as long as they can remember. Day after day they'd train at O-Deck Rapids and look the short distance upstream to the pounding, mist-shrouded cascade. Could they? At some point the pair began to believe something fundamentally different from what a million or so residents in metro D.C. and every single boater on the Potomac believed—they could. Not only could they run it, but they'd show everyone that their endeavor wasn't the reckless act of thrill-seeking idiots but the work of shrewd, utterly rational individuals. After all, they weren't day campers out on a dare. Walker, fair-skinned and block-chested, was a decorated military officer stationed at nearby Fort Belvoir. McEwan, a dark-complected six-footer, was married, with a child on the way. They'd show that Great Falls was an objective that could be professionally trained and planned for, something they could study and know until the craziness had been wrung from it.

In the years preceding that Sunday in August, they put the falls under their peculiar microscope. As far as they knew, nobody had ever boated off a major falls. They mapped the river's holes and eddies and drops at a myriad of water levels, then they went out and played guinea pigs at nearby, presumably less sinister, waterfalls. From West Virginia to North Carolina, they boated off increasingly high drops and even swam into the thrashing maelstrom at their base.

In one episode McEwan didn't get flushed out for almost a minute. Part of what they were doing was river morphology—understanding the chaotic behavior of a river at its wildest. Part of it was survivalist training—keeping it together when every mental impulse screamed for hitting the panic button. Each experience added up to a kind of blueprint for what to do, or, more accurately, what not to do when boating off a vertical fall. By the time they scrambled up the cliffs above the first twenty-five-foot drop, the "Spout," they had a sense they'd done their homework, cracked the code. Moreover, they had a belief that they'd come to understand Great Falls (and, by extension, any other similarly monstrous and mythic river) for what it truly was—rocks and water, as Tom put it. What it WAS. Not what their fears or other people's fears told them it was. And what it was was runnable.

The river cascades seventy-five feet in two hundred yards and is defined by three distinct drops. They'd put in above the bottom falls and run that first. Then the middle and bottom together. Finally it is time to do the complete top-to-bottom run. The day is lightening and time is running out. Soon the park rangers will be wandering about. First sight of boaters atop the falls will no doubt cause a convulsive response involving a phalanx of pissed-off fire and rescue squads. Tom McEwan moves fast, but he's not rushing. He slides into the boat's cockpit, fastening the stretchy, girdlelike spray skirt around the lipped oval opening to seal him in—and water out. Then he peers ahead to a point where the river's course drops completely from sight, and launches his twelve-foot fiberglass boat into the abyss. McEwan, Walker, and Schnurrenberger run the upper rapids just as they drew it up. They ferry hard left at the first eight-foot drop, zigzag through the bouldery middle rapids, and then approach the Spout, the final cataclysmic drop. Miss the hard left move, and the current will pile-drive them into a massive hole studded with rocks and ledgy outcroppings. A boat can easily become vertically pinned in the subsurface rock pile. If the boater's hands are free, maybe he can pull his spray skirt and maybe he can swim out. Only a few years earlier McEwan had been in a similarly grim scenario in the Linville Gorge, when he'd managed to exit at the last moment by upthrusting his knees with such desperate force he emerged with the splintered deck of his boat hanging off his spray skirt. More likely the thundering whitewater simply pounds the life out of whoever is beneath it. There is little to no rescue option. You have to save yourself. In a minute, maybe a little more, it will all be over.

But nobody misses the move. The trio dig their paddles into the current with a hard right sweep stroke. The boats pivot—almost in midair, it seems—and skip across the lip of the falls. Then the world drops away and they're falling almost three stories. Exploding into the pile below, each disappears momentarily and then bursts free to the surface. A moment later they're safely tucked into an eddy. They don't whoop it up as though they've cheated death. Rather, there's the sense of satisfaction that they are up to the unknown. Utterly fit for it. Then they paddle away, not bothering to tell anybody about their feat for several years to come (and to this day they refuse to say which of them ran the falls first). This makes the tale of the run even better when it does finally surface. And then the mystique about it—and about them—grows. Tom and Wick become local legends.

But the Great Falls was a mere prelude, a training trip for a major whitewater expedition Walker and McEwan had planned for the Bhutanese Himalaya later the same year. After Bhutan the duo had in mind an even bigger, more audacious objective: a monstrous and largely obscure river in southeastern Tibet called the Yarlung Tsangpo. It appeared to have the largest drop of any river in the world. It traveled through a gorge that was one of the most remote places on the planet. According to a book Wick Walker had unearthed, there were reports (in the sacred texts of a particular monastery) of some seventy-five waterfalls in a virtually unexplored and fabled stretch of about twenty miles. The suggestion of a real-life Shangri-la in those same gorge depths captivated them. It was the Everest of rivers. Undone and unopposed. Of the few river runners who were familiar with it, almost all believed its volume, gradient, and remoteness made the Yarlung Tsangpo beyond the means of what humans could do in a boat. Maybe not surprisingly, Walker and McEwan weren't so sure.

To solve a problem which has long resisted the skill and persistence of others is an irresistible magnet in every sphere of human activity. . . . The possibility of entering the unknown; the simple fact that it was the highest point on the world's surface—these things goaded us on. The problem aroused no invidious comparisons; it was intimate to us as a team and personal to each of us as individuals. There was the challenge, and we would lay aside all else to take it up.

—SIR JOHN HUNT, EXPEDITION LEADER OF THE FIRST SUCCESSFUL ASCENT OF EVEREST

McLean, Virginia, September 1998

AS TOM MCEWAN DRIVES ALONG THE I-495 BELTWAY, A THICK mist begins to fall. It's unseasonably warm, and rush-hour traffic is heavy and getting heavier. His wipers skitter haplessly across a cracked windshield. The 1980s-vintage Rabbit isn't exactly a pleasure craft in the rain. In big downpours the water kicks up through the rusted floorboards and rushes in the hole in the passenger-side door where the handle used to be. After years of service transporting him to rivers up and down the Eastern Seaboard, the beater is on its last legs. But then that's pretty much been the case forever. Tom could probably scrape the money together for something better, but he won't. He has a stubborn allegiance to things that look hopeless.

With the expedition team's departure tomorrow, he's en route to a final meeting tonight at Harry Wetherbee's house. The local D.C. forecast calls for more rain, more humidity, and a big band of thunderstorms. Passing over the Potomac where it flows wide and smooth, he knows the water level is high for the Spout, probably three feet and then some on the Little Falls gauge. The one time he ran it at these levels, he got hammered, he and his boat stuffed to the deepest, most ear-throbbing part of the hole for half a minute. Normally it's a relatively safe run at this time of year. One more postscript, maybe, on an El Niño year that just won't quit. Elsewhere things are much worse, of course. In California houses are falling into the rising Pacific. In East Africa the rains have unleashed a disease epidemic. And in Asia several Himalayan rivers have crested their banks, killing thousands. As he pulls into a long slopeside driveway, Tom sees Roger Zbel's four-by-four truck and thinks about the call Wick Walker got a couple weeks ago. "Hey, Wick," began Roger, alarmed by the rumor of widespread flooding in Tibet, their expedition destination, "this isn't gonna be some kind of suicide mission, is it?"

Harry's nice neat suburban house in McLean, Virginia, is bursting at the seams. As the de facto headquarters for the "Riddle of the Tsangpo Gorges" expedition, Harry's low-slung red-brick house has been ground zero the past several weeks for a swarm of UPS carriers. Winging in from all points is the esoteric stuff of a Himalayan whitewater boating expedition: two tons of freeze-dried food, medicine supplies, solar panels, helmets, dry suits, climbing ropes, thermoplastic boats, and an assortment of high-tech communication gadgetry. It's all crammed in Harry's basement, to be organized (with the exception of the boats) into twenty-eight seventy-pound cargo bags and schlepped to Dulles International tomorrow for shipment to Kathmandu. For Harry, a close friend of Wick's and a retired U.S. State Department operative whose posts included the USSR, Ethiopia, and India, the voluminous deliveries are a bit disconcerting. He's accustomed to maintaining a low profile. His house, in the wooded Chesterbrook section of town, is on a cul-de-sac that's so tiny, it's sometimes left off local maps. God knows what the neighbors think of the hubbub. As with most things he's done, he can't really talk about this either. Everybody on the expedition has sworn an oath of silence. Their itinerary, which will theoretically bring them to the most remote corner of Tibet, might be suitably dramatic to impel the Chinese to scuttle their mission, Wick fears. Most of the team members—there are eight in total, four who will paddle the river and four to patch up and resupply the four on the river—are hardly used to this sort of intrigue. Nobody balks, however. Wick is a retired lieutenant colonel whose U.S. Army background is reputed to include a few covert foreign operations, and he and Harry have deep expertise in this stuff. If they say it's better not to broadcast the fact that they're en route to Tibet to paddle through a fabled and unexplored region closed to foreigners for the better part of the twentieth century, then they're probably right. In fact, Doug Gordon, one of the team members who will be paddling, tells his Seattle-based mother so little she ends up querying a local paddle shop for details. "My son is going to a place called the Tsangpo Gorge," Diana Gordon declares. "I think it might be dangerous, have you heard of it?" The paddle shop owner, like 99 percent of the world, has never heard of the place.

Tonight's agenda is to double-check gear and break the ice a bit before tomorrow's marathon flight. Most on the team know one another. Those who don't shake hands and jump right in. It has already been a long journey for some. Paulo Castillo, the trip videographer and a sponsor-arranged hire, got the call to join the team only a few weeks earlier—about the same time he was returning from a three-week expedition to China. He's just in from his home in California. Roger Zbel, his wife, Nancy, and their three-year-old daughter, Cari, have made the hilly interstate drive from their home in western Maryland. The trip is relatively short, but the journey feels long. A legendary local paddler, Zbel has always longed to go on one of the expeditionary trips Tom and Wick are famous for, but this is the first time he's been asked. Doug Gordon, on temporary leave from his Ph.D. work at the University of Utah, is the only one not here. Having just returned from an overseas academic conference, he's trying to steal a few more hours with his wife, Connie, and their two preschool-age boys, Tyler and Bryce. Still, the feeling of being in one another's company is overwhelming. After months of uncertainty about whether the trip was going to come off—and in the case of the trip's organizers, Wick and Tom, both now fifty-one, it's been almost twenty-five years in the planning—everybody feels a pump of adrenaline just rapping on Harry's front door. Done are the days of trying to get the lay of the land by yet another volley of E-mails. For the first time things seem absolutely tangible. They've got tickets, they've got permits, and they've got a shitload of gear. The last to arrive, Jamie McEwan, grabs his big brother, Tom, and gives him a bear hug. "Man, we're going to Tibet."

Wick looks on with a fond smile. He's short and stocky and has a big, horse-toothed grin. He has an easy Southern manner about him and a confidence that isn't brassy but isn't hard to miss, either. It has been years since he and the McEwans have been bound for the same stretch of river. He has witnessed other McEwan reunions where the two former Ivy League standout wrestlers lowered into a ready crouch and began to throw each other around. On the one hand the rumbles had a kind of Kennedyesque, boys-will-be-boys charm to them; on the other, he was never quite sure they wouldn't rip each other's heads off. "C'mon over here for a second, you guys," he interrupts, "I want you to take a look at something."

The long-delayed maps arrived yesterday. As everyone knows, these aren't just any maps. For months Wick has been pleading with Denver-based Space Imaging, a sponsor, to get them satellite-shot space imagery maps of the Tsangpo Gorge. The state-of-the-art, newly declassified technology, until recently available only to U.S. and Russian governments, was long ago seen by Wick as a critical tool to the exploration. Good to a resolution of five meters, the map set includes overview images of the entire gorge in addition to enlargements of areas the river team suspects to be most treacherous. Space Imaging analysts, or what the company calls "sky archaeologists," annotated the maps with close-ups of sections where they detected especially violent rapids or waterfalls (there are many). Finally they further refined the images by overlaying them with digital elevation data to create a 3-D profile of the expedition route. The photography, says Wick, is surely the most accurate and detailed information anyone (at least anyone planning to set foot in the gorge) has ever had.

With the maps unfolded on Harry's basement floor, all eyes shoot to the same place: a contorted stretch of blue folding back on itself. Variously called the inner gorge or the Great Bend, it's the deepest, darkest part of the river gorge, a place where no westerner, or perhaps anyone, has traveled at river level. It's a spot of Buddhist myth and considerable Western lore. Over the past century everything from a Niagara Falls–sized cascade to some version of the fabled Shangri-la has been said to be ensconced within it. (The fictional Shangri-la imagined in James

Hilton's *Lost Horizon* was loosely based on early and incomplete trekking explorations within parts of the gorge.) Of course, the high-tech maps cannot replace the human eye. The images are shot from an orbiting Indian satellite four hundred miles away. That said, what they show is still numbing: "Look at that crease," says Wick, pointing out a cumulus-shaped gash of white in the steepest, most hairpinned part of the river course. "That's new."

It's a huge hydraulic event. Hunched more closely over the poster-size map, Roger, Tom, and Jamie—the paddlers, minus Doug—are agape. There are also two huge falls that precede it within the paperclip-like bend they inelegantly but accurately dub "the Thumb." The space-imagery maps show that their classified mid-1970s topo map—which they'd acquired using Harry and Wick's contacts, and upon which they'd based all their planning heretofore—is grossly and dangerously inaccurate. It doesn't even show what they have now dubbed "the Crease." Until this moment the working game plan was to boat the section where the Crease has popped up. What other lethal surprises are in store? Wick acknowledges that they'll need to scrap the old game plan and get over there and see what they can see. A day away from leaving (and after years of research), they're back to square one. On the flip side, though, there's the seductive realization that they might be on the brink of a startling geographic discovery. In a subsequent call to the expedition's major sponsor, the National Geographic Society, McEwan excitedly offered that it "looks to me like there's probably a one-hundred-foot waterfall in there."

The meeting breaks at 10:00 P.M. with plenty more packing to be done. Jamie heads back across the Potomac to his dad's place. Wick, who lives near Pittsburgh, stays with Harry. Roger and Nancy are en route to a local hotel. Hours earlier Roger had dropped by his dad's home in nearby Manassas to take him out to dinner. Roger wanted to explain what the trip was all about, how dangerous it was, and to let him know in so many words that there was a chance they might not see each other again. "That sounds like a really fantastic trip, son. I know you'll have a great time," said Walter Zbel, with not even a whiff of paternal reprimand. Roger's dad didn't understand the gravity of it all, but Nancy does. She was with Roger at Harry's and saw the maps, the Crease. Worried to begin with, Nancy now knows exactly what Roger and his teammates will be dealing with. As Roger accelerates onto a tunnel-black country two-lane near Harry's, Nancy waits to hear him say something like, "The trip doesn't add up and I'm not going to go through with it." But for reasons she can't really understand, he doesn't. He's going.

≋

WHEN TOMMY CALLED WICK TWO YEARS AGO TO SUGGEST THEY look into the Tsangpo again, Wick had to pause. For as long as he could remember, the river had topped their wish list. Back in the early seventies, Wick was already consumed with the Himalaya, studying maps and old Victorian-era narratives, and doing what few river runners back then did: looking for remote, brawling rivers that dropped out of the sky. Initially he'd designated Bhutan the place, not Tibet. He'd put together a bold expedition in which he, the McEwan brothers, and three others would be the first paddlers to enter the reclusive Buddhist kingdom, where they'd record a dazzling first descent on the Wong Chu, a river that plunged out of the shadows of 25,000-foot peaks near the country's northern border and dropped to the lowland jungles of India. The much-delayed American Himalayan Kayak Descent eventually came off in 1981, but the jittery Bhutanese government didn't let the team do what they wanted to do, restricting them to a comparatively small and far less juicy portion of the river. Their fantasy of darting over endless waterfalls—the whole reason why they'd pushed the envelope back at Great Falls to begin with—went unrealized. But in the preparations for Bhutan, and later while on the ten-day trip itself, Wick heard more about the Tsangpo and its hundred-mile-plus section in southeastern Tibet where the river sliced between a pair of five-mile-high peaks. It was bigger, steeper, and more remote than the Wong Chu or anyplace else. Denied the realization of their dream in Bhutan, Wick and Tom quickly made new plans. In 1983, when their information about the river was only rudimentary, the pair slapped together a proposal and applied for a travel permit at the Chinese Embassy in Washington, D.C. They never got a response— luckily, Wick later thought—but a Tsangpo expedition came up now and again, and he and Tom never really stopped thinking about it.

As the century was drawing to a close, others were consumed with thoughts of the Tsangpo, too. Tom's call confirmed what Wick already knew: "People are getting in there," Tom said, vaguely adding, "We oughta go over there and spend some time poking around." Yet Wick's situation was a hell of a lot different from what it had been back in the 1980s, when he and Tom dreamed about Tibet. Whitewater hadn't been a major part of his life for years. He'd been one of the country's foremost canoe racers in the late sixties and early seventies. Named to the inaugural U.S. Olympic team in 1972, he'd retired from competitive paddling after an eleventh-place finish in the Munich Games, then had quit altogether when his knees went on him in the late 1980s. In fact, of late he'd busied himself running a small thoroughbred breeding program out of his farm in western Pennsylvania (and doing the occasional odd job for the Pentagon, whatever that meant). The horse stuff had its own kind of draw. Each year the farm produced one or two lucrative offspring with Triple Crown–quality lineage. With any luck, one might be a winner. The horse business got to Wick in a way that paddling used to. He'd begun competing again when Tommy phoned him. Not in paddling, but in beginner's-level "eventing," an equestrian discipline combining dressage, cross-country, and show jumping. On his seventeen-acre hilltop spread, he'd made a ring with jumps. On weekends he'd find himself not in the hail-fellowship of boaters, but with a gang of prepubescent girls who could kick his ass. But Wick was having a ball. Those who didn't know Wick better and mistook the decorated former Green Beret for a one-dimensional type would surely be shocked by his interest in the cultivated world of English riding. Tommy knew Wick, though, and thus wasn't surprised. That said, he didn't figure horse jumping had a chance next to the Tsangpo.

McEwan was right. Walker bit. He wouldn't paddle, but he would draw up the assault plan. He was a logistical genius. He had worn several intriguing hats in a twenty-one year military career, from a Special Forces command post searching for MIAs in Southeast Asia to a security role at the U.S. Embassy in Islamabad, Pakistan. In the latter post, his last international assignment, he'd taken the opportunity to travel extensively in the country's most remote and mountainous regions, eventually producing a "frontier" guidebook to paddling in the Himalayas, the Hindu Kush, and the Karakoram. The gossip among his old paddling cronies was that he'd had a hand in planning the U.S. invasion of Grenada. Whether that was true or not, overseeing a mission to deepest, darkest Tibet would be a hell of a challenge— no easier today than for the British military expeditions that first attempted to explore and map the region more than a century ago. With his keen sense of history, Wick couldn't help seeing some parallels between himself and Tommy and the parade of eccentric, turn-of-the-century characters that had found themselves drawn to the exotic landscape. Let Tommy have the whitewater, thought Walker, who'd retired from the military in 1993. Masterminding a top-to-bottom exploration of the Tsangpo Gorge would be damn fun.

Running through Tom's balding and bespectacled head was a little doubt about whether he was still fit for this type of adventure, but not a lot. With the lean build and the perpetual training routine of a marathoner, he wasn't so sure he'd lost a step at all. The 1973 U.S. National downriver champion might be nearing fifty, but whatever he'd lost in strength he made up for in experience. In part, because of the radical improvements to paddling gear, Tom figured he was running harder whitewater now than two decades ago. He hadn't lost a bit of nerve or passion. If anything, he seemed hungrier and more animated than ever.

Tom was beginning to specialize in winter trips to Mexico in which he'd expose affluent D.C.-area boaters to the wonderful world of whitewater exploratories and the Tom McEwan way: a sort of Outward Bound meets Bad News Bears approach in which vans broke down, wallets were lost, food was an afterthought, and communication was impossible since nobody spoke Spanish. But the whitewater was fantastic and Tom's instruction exquisite. The contrast between Tom's on-water expertise (in twenty-five-plus years of river trip guiding, there'd never been a fatality on his watch) and his seeming incompetence off the water baffled many. Tom just had remarkably bad luck when he traveled, some smirked. Others suggested it was all part of an intentional program, a let-things-fall-apart affair orchestrated by Tom for the express purpose of letting others taste the fruits he so enjoyed: the part where you come out in one piece and alive. Oddly, or maybe not, the trippers seemed to emerge from the experiences not ready to sue, but energized, even transformed. There was nothing scripted about a Tom McEwan outing. Nothing sure.

Tom's teaching and guiding career began at Valley Mill, a legendary outdoor day camp in Germantown, Maryland, founded in the 1950s by his parents. In the early seventies Tom returned to teach at the sixty-acre riverside camp after some post-college wanderings and a failed bid at making the U.S. team for the Munich Games (the same Olympic squad his brother Jamie and best friend Wick had made). Tom got married, built a house on the property, and raised two children. Soon his whitewater program, part of the daily banquet of sports activities at Valley Mill, became the camp's signature attraction. Kids of rich parents were exposed to a dare-and-be-dared world they'd never imagined. They ran wild rivers, jumped off high bridges, and slept in ditches when they weren't doing the first two. They never complained.

Tom crafted a system that challenged everyone's comfort zone—counselors', kids', parents', and his own. The object was to create ultracompetent whitewater boaters. Thus the first thing a ten-year-old camper often did was swim rapids. At a higher competency level they jumped into the deep end of the swimming pool with their hands and feet tied in plastic tape (drowning proof was one of Wick's contributions, according to Tom). Or they had to execute an Eskimo roll—the technical move in which a boater rights a capsized boat without exiting it—in crashing whitewater. Each time they passed a test, they achieved a new level of competency and wore a sticker that showed their rank. The whole system was driven by one thing: everybody wanted to be like Tom. The ultimate achievement was the season-ending "red shirt" award. The red shirt, which only one or two might be graced with, signified that a camper had achieved the required proficiencies and then some. You were, in a word, hard-core. Or, put another way, you were fearless. The program had its detractors, but it spawned some of the most accomplished whitewater racers in the world. McEwan's view of how things were done was enormously influential. He figured teaching was his legacy, and he planned to take control of the family business with his brother and two sisters when the time came.

In the mid 1990s, about the same time Tom and Wick began to pursue the Tsangpo expedition in earnest, Tom learned that his sister had been designated president of Valley Mill upon his father's surprise wishes (his mother had died in the mid-1970s). A bitter family tussle ensued, with Tom joining his nephews' rival business two mailboxes down. The family spat coincided with Tom's rapidly disintegrating marriage of two decades. Tom's wife sided with his sister, and soon thereafter the two separated. In a strangely formal way, Tom calls the whole episode one of the great disappointments in his life. Tom probably would've wanted to go to the Tsangpo regardless of the upheaval, family friends thought, but the mess at home certainly didn't prompt any deep second thoughts. If ever there was a good time for a wilderness experience, as Tom euphemistically termed his death-cheating epics, now seemed the time. He and Wick—former high school classmates at Bethesda's Landon School and self-styled voyageurs—not only had the opportunity to knock off the big one, but to team up once more. Each man welcomed it.

≋

IF FRIENDS WONDERED HOW A FARAWAY RIVER MIGHT BORE SO DEEPLY into two men's consciousness, they really only needed to look at a map, any map. Technically comprising the upper portion of the

1,700-mile-long Brahmaputra River, the Yarlung Tsangpo begins as a glacial trickle on the auspicious flanks of 22,028-foot Mount Kailas, in southwestern Tibet. (Buddhists consider Kailash, from which three other mighty Himalayan rivers originate, to be the universe's cosmic center.) Adding voluminous bulk on its long due-east course across seven hundred miles of high, dun-colored Tibetan plateau, the broad Tsangpo is a mostly docile presence, maintaining a respectful distance on its parallel swath past Everest and the other Himalayan giants to the south. By the time it flows into and through northeastern India, first as the Dihang and later as the Brahmaputra, the river spreads Mississippi-wide again, most impressive for its immense discharge into the Bay of Bengal and its cultural sweep en route. Along the Brahmaputra's banks are three nations—Tibet, India, and Bangladesh—and three beliefs—Buddhism, Hinduism, and Islam. The fact that it is known colloquially as the Great River hardly seems surprising. A large measure of its lure, both for Wick and the explorers on foot who preceded him, had to do with the only exception to the Great River's otherwise civil meanders: its abrupt and well-hidden path to the sea through the Himalaya, the greatest mountain range in the world.

Some three hundred miles southeast of Lhasa, the capital of Tibet, where the river dives through a knot of towering peaks, was where Walker aimed to go. Ancient local hunters, apparently venturing no farther than the mouth of the gorge, imagined the waters tumbled into a huge hole in the earth somewhere within the mountains. Modern surveyors put a finer point to it. The gorge was defined as a 140-mile stretch running from Pe to Medog (the latter being the last major village before the politically disputed India/China border). This steady flow of off-the-scale "foam and fury," as the early-twentieth-century British explorer Francis Kingdon-Ward called a piece of it, plunges some 10,000 vertical feet, running beneath snow-capped Himalayan peaks, past verdant jungle (home to red pandas, leopards, and rare horned takins), and through the Tsangpo Gorge, with its vast depth (three times that of the Grand Canyon) and its razor-thin width (its sheer, mossy walls, which rise as high as 2,000 feet, are a mere sixty feet apart in places). With a volume of 10,000 to 100,000 cubic feet per second, depending on the monsoon rainfall and snowpack melt, the river drops at a dizzying average rate of sixty-five feet per mile. In the gorgiest part of the gorge, the drop is close to three hundred feet per mile. (By comparison, the much wider Colorado River falls eight feet per mile in the Grand Canyon and flows at an average rate of 10,000 cubic feet per second.)

Running the Yarlung Tsangpo through the Tsangpo Gorge was the definitive whitewater exploratory challenge. There was nothing on the planet that compared with it. Though neither Wick nor Tom would allow himself to say it aloud, others did: The Tsangpo was the Everest of rivers, every bit as mysterious, myth-laden, and malicious as the unconquered summit was when Sir John Hunt's expedition arrived at its icy doorstep in 1953.

As Walker and any other river runner could easily infer from the numbers alone—material that Walker was able to get his hands on fairly early in his research rounds—the technical challenges had to be immense. What they could run and what they'd have to walk around was anyone's guess. Not that there was any shame to walking parts of the river. As Walker would patiently explain to non-river-running friends, a first descent didn't actually mean doing an end-to-end run on the water. On the Tsangpo (as on numerous other rivers ranging from steep creeks to big-volume classics like the Indus, which flows from Kailash through

Pakistan), that would be impossible; the power of some of the rapids and waterfalls would bury even the most formidable paddler. Even the main current—what boaters call the "action" line—is too fast and powerful at certain water levels. (A big-volume river, hurtling along at up to twenty miles per hour in places, can easily snap a paddle in two like a twig.) To experts like Walker, what a first descent on a deep canyon river actually means is to make the initial end-to-end foray by paddling as much of the river as possible and portaging the rest, using expert trekking and mountaineering skills. As subsequent runs are made (and knowledge about the river's profile is disseminated), the number of portages invariably lessens. While every other major whitewater river in the world had been tackled in this manner, the Tsangpo hadn't. Not nearly.

When Walker drilled down farther, he began to better understand why. In terms of *both* paddling and portaging, the Tsangpo was monstrously difficult. River rapids are rated on a scale of I to VI, with Class I categorized as moving water with riffles and Class VI being the outer edge of what's safely runnable by the world's best paddlers. On big-volume rivers the scale isn't terribly useful, however, given the many added hazards and complexity of the water. The classic stretch of Colorado River whitewater flowing through the Grand Canyon has its own "Deseret Scale," a one to ten grading system that better matches the broad inventory of rapid types. The parts of the Tsangpo that were believed to be runnable presented a seemingly infinite variety of exotic wild-water phenomena, from Class VI-plus to channel-clotting, house-sized boulders to standing waves twenty-five feet high. The few who had paddled portions of the river (amounting to no more than ten miles of the gorge's easiest, most accessible stretches) said the current was deceptively complex to read, the surging main channel far more treacherous than it appeared from shore. Even eddies, the calm recovery spots behind rocks and along banks where the main current rushes past and paddlers can grab a breather, were fiercely volatile and absurdly powerful. Crosscurrents sloped off the exploding mess in the middle and surged crazily into the banks. In the narrowest 90-degree chutes, the river slammed headlong into cliffs and reared up steeply on its end. Walker's team might run a rapid, then find themselves in a place where they couldn't go forward, couldn't go back, and couldn't crawl out. These so-called no-return zones would require a kamikaze descent into the void, a game of whitewater roulette in which the possibility of surviving was slim at best. Because the gorge was so pinched in spots, the river saw minimal sunlight. Where the rushing glacial meltwater pierced the main river, the water never got warmer than the high thirties. Everywhere else, even where the gorge opened to allow a dose of sunshine, the water was in the forties and low fifties. Even in a dry suit, they'd survive maybe fifteen minutes in the frigid river. The remoteness of the gorge meant living out of a boat for weeks at a time. It also meant the chance of getting emergency help was nil. Commercial helicopters didn't fly there, people didn't live there.

The portages they'd need to make to get around the unrunnable sections were equally daunting. They couldn't merely transport their hundreds of pounds of boats and equipment across dozens of miles of pebbly river shoreline. Rather, they could anticipate full-on bushwhacks of several thousand vertical feet out of the densely vegetated, rain-sodden, leech-infested gorge, onto a steep ridge, through high-alpine passes, then back down the river via cliff rappel. Even river-level portages were fraught with danger. Most of the riverbed boulders, having only recently been deposited, were prone to rolling. Many were the size of city buildings. Geologically, the entire river valley was phenomenally unstable. Almost directly beneath it, the Eurasian continental and Indian–Australian tectonic plates banged against each other, in the same thrusting geological phenomenon that adds two inches of northeasterly growth a year to Everest. (The river predates the fifty-million-year-old Himalaya, the Tsangpo maintaining its course by boring an ever-deeper gorge as the mountains were uplifted.) In 1950 the biggest earthquake on record was centered in the gorge's midst, destroying all the villages in the area and sweeping many into the river. In subsequent decades smaller quakes and huge slab landslides regularly altered the riverside topography. Trails scratched into the terrain by local hunters routinely vanished in a season or two.

In the fall of 1997, Wick and Tom took the biggest and most sensible step either of them could think of: They went to Tibet to see the beast for themselves. In the interim Wick had gathered every scrap of hard info he could find and had drawn up a preliminary blueprint, but they both knew it was lunacy to attempt anything yet. Wick, Tom, a Himalayan adventure travel operator named Jon Meisler, and Harry Wetherbee and his wife, Doris, took what they called a random sampling within the gorge's core, starting at the Tsangpo/Po Tsangpo confluence and fanning out in two parties upstream and downstream. Tom and Wick's machete-wielding charge brought them to Chu Belap, a fearsome spot in the river where the twisting whitewater dropped precipitously out of view, vanishing behind pinched canyon walls. From their then-current map, Tom and Wick had anticipated the deadly drop; in fact, that was why they walked to where they did, hopeful that they could locate the big drop, then march upstream to see what *could* be boated, if anything. What Tom surveyed over the next four or five upstream miles turned out to be a trip-making sight;

contrary to widespread belief, a long stretch within the unexplored heart of the gorge appeared to be boatable. The dis-
crepancy was explainable: Apparently the river's steepness was
concentrated at Chu Belap and much farther upstream at the
other known drop, Rainbow Falls. In between the two, the river
blessedly leveled off. "Overall we looked right in the center, right
in the heart of things, and even though we didn't see but five percent, every single bit we saw was doable," Wick said.

Beyond that bolt of gratifying news was the fact that their
overall logistical strategy, which Wick had systematically designed back in Pennsylvania, proved out well in the field. The
portable satellite telephones worked, and support routes were
confirmed. Their hunch that October offered the best low-water
window appeared correct. They returned from the monthlong
journey elated; not only were they right on the money, but they'd
gotten the jump on an apparently growing pack of Tsangpo-
minded boaters, becoming the first to scout a remote stretch of
the inner gorge. Tom, who wasn't sure how his stamina would
hold up at that altitude, came away pleasantly surprised and
ready to take on the role as river team leader. To the horror of his
local guides, Tom even plunged into the glacial river water and
swam within yards of its rampaging current. "We took some long,
hard hikes," Tom told friends upon returning. "It's funny, I'd
wake up every morning and be so sore I wasn't sure I'd be able to
get through the day. But I found out after an hour or so of strenuous hiking, I could keep going somehow. Every day it played out
like that. The place was incredible."

Tom's age had been a bigger issue for him than he'd like to
admit. But the quirky cycle of exhaustion and renewal made him
feel as though he'd be able to hold up under the month-plus

stress of hard paddling and harder-still hiking. Mentally he felt as though he had the quietness within, a certain balance; he wasn't crippled with doubts about leaving home, or blasé about coming back. Few fifty-year-olds could ease into the unknown as he could. One adventurer his age, doing a roughly analogous extreme undertaking (rowing the world's oceans) and feeling similarly drawn to the call of the wild, broke into buckets of tears every time he went to sea. The oceanic distance he voluntarily put between himself and those he loved seemed at once essential and devastating. Middle age, with its heightened awareness of mortality and its natural intolerance of risk, seemed to hit him head-on at the moment he most wanted to wish it away. Tom defied the odds this way: He didn't show any signs of battling the little voice that told men his age to bike a little slower, ski a little calmer, and stay rather than go. He wasn't doing what he was doing because of his age, but because, as the trip indicated (both to him and evidently to Wick), he could do it.

With the trip now slated for October 1998, Wick and Tom had a thousand things to put in place to get back to Tibet: a team, gear, permits, money, sponsors. The scouting trip had answered "yes" to the project's broadest questions: Was it possible, and were they the guys to do it? But Wick still had to assemble the team and orchestrate the detailed, step-by-step tactical strategy that would safely get them to, through, and back from the gorge. Naturally, Wick approached it like a military exercise, the object of which was to neutralize the strengths of the opposing river. His ability to foresee every contingency and seize upon every available (and sometimes not available) tool was a source of continual wonder to Tom. A typical Tom-engineered Valley Mill project devolved into a kind of Charlie Chaplin routine: A kid would be asked to dig a ditch, but he'd have no shovel. Tom would direct him to a shed, but the shed would be locked. And the key missing. The next step? Calling a neighbor for metal cutters . . .

Before leaving for the Tibet scout, Wick and Tom had tipped off Jamie and Doug and a few others about their plans to take a look at the river with an eye toward running it. When they returned, they began contacting the same inner-circle comrades and describing what they'd found out. The guys on their shortlist weren't extreme paddlers in the popular sense, boiling with attitude and begging for notoriety. They didn't need whitewater heroes out to taunt death. Everyone's approach had to be measured, mature, and rational. They needed guys who could not only endure extremely stressed-out living and working conditions, but who could get along and even have some fun with each other while doing so. "This can't be a trip," said Tom, "where anyone starts to lose it after being out five days. I've been around campfires where the tension is desperate—you're wet, cold, hungry. Somebody drops a piece of food and everybody's eyes are riveted on it." They needed individuals who weren't afraid to walk—or paddle. They had to be a team, but they had to be prepared to save their own hides. In assembling expeditionary teams for big, intense rivers there is a common rule: The harder the river to run, the better the friends you need.

Jamie McEwan, forty-six, had tagged after Wick and Tom as a boy, had been with them in Bhutan and Canada, and was still on top of his game. He was also one of the best-known whitewater racers in the United States, having won a bronze medal at the 1972 Olympics in Munich. Doug Gordon, Jamie's best friend and a former teammate, was an equally obvious choice. Gordon, forty-one, had also been on several expeditions with Tom and Wick, including the Santa Maria in Mexico and a testing ten-day descent on the Aguanus in Quebec. He and Jamie not only knew Tom and Wick's sensibilities, but they'd been active of late, running hard rivers in British Columbia. Shortly after the recon, Tom asked each of them, and each signed on, contingent on the trip getting funding and final permits. Jamie and Doug, who now lived several thousand miles apart, couldn't imagine a better excuse for an extended reunion. Their friendship didn't live and die with athletic conquest—it was much more complex than that—but just the same, the two of them loved disappearing into a big canyon and having at each other. Tom and Wick's debriefs with them included gradient figures and seasonal water levels, the x's and o's of a big-water run, but also drew upon an alluring set of images that neither Doug nor Jamie could believe: the waves of unbroken jungle, the singsong sunrise chants of Tom and Wick's Monpa hunter-guides, the bellowing wildness of the river. Even the most innocuous parts of the river landscape, certain boulders or caves, represented places of worship and mythological importance. This was the biggest canyon, in the biggest mountain range. Theirs would be a first descent of historic importance; somehow, both Doug and Jamie's lives seemed to be flowing toward it. The expedition might also be a chance, thought Jamie, to try to "live out what Bhutan should've been."

Finding a fourth (and final) river team member proved tougher than they imagined. Roger Zbel signed on late. Initially, Walker and McEwan approached the usual suspects, many of whom were ex-racers like themselves who'd joined them on one adventure or another. Several were asked and several declined. Most cited conflicts with work or at home—eight weeks was a long time to be gone—but privately, several felt the risk level was too high. Though they thought Walker and McEwan were reasonable men, they didn't think the river itself sounded reasonable at all. America's most accomplished whitewater racer, Jon Lugbill, politely refused, as did another inner-circle friend, Andy Bridge, though he initially appeared ready to go. "When Tom called me and told me what they had in mind, I remember thinking that the rivers' statistics were just too much," says Lugbill, a seven-time world slalom champion and a fearless river runner in the eighties. "I pretended to be interested, but only because I didn't want Tom to think I was a wimp." What truly worried Lugbill, the father of two, about the river wasn't even the river but himself. Sooner or later, he figured, his competitive side would get the better of him and he'd challenge a rapid he shouldn't. John Weld, who, like Bridge, was a Potomac River student of Tom's, also declined after mulling it over for weeks. Tom, with whom Weld had pleaded to hold a spot open for him, was surprised. Jamie offered the spot to Lecky Haller, another world champion slalom boater and former teammate, but Haller also declined. "I don't do that," said Haller, almost apologetically. Then Bruce Lessels, a close racing friend of Jamie and Doug, opted not to go. "I guess Bruce is the only one of us who's being responsible," Doug told Jamie.

Fresh on the minds of everyone who said no, and even of those who said yes, was a tragic incident that had occurred a few months before the scouting trip. On June 25, 1997, along the White Salmon River in Washington state, a blond, superfit racer named Rich Weiss had tried to run a big vertical waterfall and died doing it. The fatality shocked the racing fraternity of which Tom, Jamie, Doug, Wick, and their prospective Tsangpo teammates were an avid part. Weiss, a thirty-three-year-old two-time Olympian, was considered one of the most versatile athletes the sport had ever produced. He was a state champion wrestler and a national-team-caliber freestyle skier. He was also brilliant, a

Ph.D. who had his own engineering firm. The fact that he'd died in whitewater, because he'd apparently careened off-line at the worst possible moment, ran counter to a long-cherished belief among racers, that guys of his talent and precision and guts didn't miss the moves they had to make.

Plenty of whitewater paddlers had died before, but no prominent American racer—the crème de la crème of the sport—had ever died running rapids. Weiss's wife Rosi, then six months pregnant, had been waiting for her husband at the take-out when a paramedic and a sheriff came along to tell her he was gone. News of the death seemed to have a particularly intense effect on Gordon, who was among the hundreds to attend the highly emotional funeral in Steamboat Springs, Colorado, and who later arranged a memorial fund for the family. Gordon later wrote, "It has been easy to ignore the increasing number of river deaths. *That wouldn't have happened to me . . . I'm better than he was . . . I'm smarter than that,* are the subconscious thoughts which many, including myself, have had. . . . Sorry, folks, but that won't cut it any longer. They don't come any better or any smarter than Rich Weiss. Will I teach my son to paddle? Absolutely, and I wager Rich would have also. The joy, the satisfaction, the personal growth I've experienced through paddling and the spectacular places I've seen are well worth the risk. But let's not pretend the risk isn't there. It's there and it's very real, and if we don't do everything we can to deal with it and minimize it, then we've missed a very important lesson."

At the time of Weiss's death, Doug's wife, Connie, was pregnant with their second child. The whole thing was just too close for comfort. Suddenly risk and death had barged into everyone's lives in a particularly real way. Prior to Weiss's death, the more vivid fear among racers of his ilk wasn't dying in whitewater but putting up a slow time. In whitewater slalom racing, similar to ski racing, boaters must zigzag through a series of hanging gates. Touching one—"blowing a gate"—is a time penalty. Norm Bellingham, a D.C. native and student of Tom McEwan's who would later win an Olympic gold medal in flatwater kayaking, used to make a risk game out of gate-running when he worked out. Touch the slalom gate on one of his runs and he died. In all the times he challenged himself to a "death" run, he never died once. Death was a game, losing was real. Now it was the other way around. Among paddlers in other parts of the country, in particular the few dozen who took on big wilderness rivers, the chilling sensation of mortality wasn't entirely foreign. But for the community of racers who'd been classically trained at camps and clinics and who'd competed the world over and who had faith in the steadiness and sureness of every single stroke they took, Weiss's death meant something much different. It entered a doubt into the equation where there really hadn't been much of one before.

Echoing in everybody's minds were Gordon's words: If it could happen to Richie, it could happen to anybody. Each and every one of them had been on similarly challenging rivers. By the end of 1997 the news was even worse: Fifteen expert paddlers like Weiss had died running rivers, more than ever before in the sport's history. In June Dugald Bremner, a superb adventure photographer, died when his boat was pinned on the Silver Fork of the American in California. The same month, Joel Hathorne disappeared on a steep creek in Idaho, neither he nor his boat ever to be found. In August, Chuck Kern was killed when his boat became wedged under a boulder in the Black Canyon of the Gunnison, Colorado. The roster of victims was long and getting longer, and worst still there seemed to be no good explanation why.

SEVEN MONTHS LATER THE TRIP WAS IN PLACE, BUT THE MONEY wasn't. Given the extreme costs associated with the expedition, it was doubtful they'd go without support. In July, National Geographic called Wick to tell him they wanted to sponsor the team. That joyously received news was almost immediately swallowed by a new threat. The reports of severe flooding in Tibet—at first unsubstantiated—were now verified. The major news services were all running stories detailing the massive flooding problem throughout China. Laying the blame on the global El Niño phenomenon, the authorities said the countryside was experiencing its worst floods in fifty years. At first the most severe damage seemed limited to the upper Yangtze, another massive river several watersheds to the east. But by late August, China's emergency relief organizations were reporting flood crests on the Lasa and Niyang Rivers, two major tributaries of the Tsangpo. According to a preliminary assessment, 14,000 hectares of farmland were flooded, 2,000 housing units had been damaged, and more than 4,000 animals killed.

What was going on in the gorge area was agonizingly difficult to comprehend, since the area is subject to its own peculiar weather system and nobody was there to monitor it. (For most major rivers in the world, water level information is readily available, but the Chinese withhold the Tsangpo's, perhaps in part because Tibetan freedom fighters once regularly crossed the river from hideouts in India to ambush occupying troops.) The team's Lhasa-based travel agency assured them the situation in the Tibetan capital, some several hundred miles northwest of the gorge, was fine. Attempts to get better information mostly failed. Just days before the trip, Gordon called a river-running meteorologist friend from Colorado State University to ask if he had any idea how the snowpack size was being affected by the record El Niño year. Gordon's friend wasn't able to collect much information in the short time frame, but from what he could gather, the Himalayan melt-off was liable to be far worse than normal.

At the same time, Wick called Steve Currey, a Salt Lake City commercial expedition rafter who was said to be planning a run, too. Currey, a veteran of Asian whitewater rivers, was adamant: Don't go. His sources, and they were good ones, he added, told him the water level was hideously high. But Walker wasn't sure what to make of Currey's advice. Was it legit, or was it a bluff? After all, Currey had also long dreamed of a first run on the Tsangpo and had actually been in D.C. recently, pitching the National Geographic Society for $600,000 worth of sponsorship.

Of course, high water in the gorge would radically diminish the team's chance for success. When they'd scouted the river the year before, they'd estimated the flow to be a reasonable 15,000 cubic feet per second. The formula for river volume is to multiply the river's width times its depth times the current's velocity. Most experienced river runners don't need to do the math to know that a big increase in volume (in the Tsangpo's case, due either to its flooded tributaries or to the melt-off) results in a change in velocity. In fact, for every doubling of the current's velocity, the force exerted by the water quadruples. Their whole plan was predicated on seeing a much different river (ironically, and also because of El Niño, they'd probably seen the river at an anomalous low in 1997). It was as if a mountain-climbing team had prepared for 14,000-foot-plus Mount Evans in Colorado and suddenly found itself looking up at something twice as tall. An Everest, in other words. Two or three times the water volume meant that the trouble index would bump up exponentially. The portages would be more difficult and more dangerous. The speeding current meant that any mistake that pushed them into the middle of the river could be deadly. Finally, it meant that even the easiest of rapids would mutate into breaking monsters. What were normally little standing waves might be two or three stories high. There'd be absolutely no letup.

And there was one other troubling hindrance: They still didn't have a permit to travel within the gorge's most sensitive zone, near the Indian border—the bottom third of the run. The problem was serious. There was little to no chance they could sneak the section. If they were caught, the penalties would be severe, something that might be especially sticky for a person with Walker's military background. Simply put, without permission to complete the run, they'd have to abort near a small village called Kapu, then climb out of the gorge over a 13,000-foot, snow-covered pass. Walker wasn't particularly worried about climbing out, but he knew that the local porters he'd be employing weren't going to have any of it. They didn't use the high passes in winter, and were highly unlikely to change their habits for a handful of Western visitors. Without the porters they'd be much slower (especially at the tail end of the trip) and much more prone to whatever Mother Nature chose to throw at them. Not ideal, any of it, Walker granted, but they'd just have to move quickly, making good time down through the gorge so they could be at their exit point no later than November 15. Before that date the passes would likely be clear, and the porters wouldn't mutiny. And maybe with any luck, once they got over to Lhasa, they could grease the right palms, break the impasse, and get their permit.

For a trip that had been in the planning for years, there seemed to be—what with the bad maps, bad weather, and permit hassles—a lot of "we'll deal with it when we get over there" items. Then again, if you could dot all the *i*'s and cross all the *t*'s without leaving home, what kind of exploration would it be? If they postponed, they had a whole other set of problems. For starters, one of the other river teams rumored to be heading to Tibet might beat them to the river. Also, some team members might not be available in six or twelve months. (Because of the severe winters and monsoon summers, spring and fall were considered the only seasons to go.) Gordon was particularly doubtful. He'd be finishing up his Ph.D. in the spring, and was already under consideration for several university teaching jobs. Hard as it was to get away from his post now, it would be impossible to dance off from a new job at a new university. And Gordon figured to be the team's best big-water paddler.

Right up to the last minute and the meeting at Harry's house, Wick and Tom madly assessed and reassessed; their judgment was being tested in a way that wasn't at all like scouting a rapid. In the case of any risk-laden rapid, you read the water, selected a line through it, and in the space of a few seconds, got to know whether you were right or not. "Read it and eat it" is how boaters phrased it. With this one they couldn't really know what they'd done until they got there and back. Ultimately, Wick and Tom went with their tried-and-true method: Let's go take a look, they agreed. They might not get the whole thing done, but they'd do a piece of it, maybe the most important piece.

Early evening on September 22, the scramble of eleventh-hour phone calls, E-mails, and second thoughts is over. The troops are all assembled at the British Airways gate at Dulles International, the gear checked all the way through to Kathmandu. About the only thing left to decide is whether to have their last stateside meal at Concourse D's Pizza Hut, Vie de France, or Panda Express. Having arrived on a connecting flight several hours earlier, Doug has thoughtfully brought his chessboard along, ready to clobber all comers like old times. His confidence and friendliness instantly impress Roger. The bottom line is that they are a band of old friends and potentially new ones flying off to an exotic sliver of the world, bound for a river that for one reason or another they ache to see. At the moment there isn't a doomsday vibe and not a grim face among them. The satellite photos made some of them feel nervy last night, but nobody looks as if he needs to be dragged onto the plane. Ahead are six weeks of aching muscles, endless river, and lovely fear. Paulo later jokes about it a little bit. Who was anybody kidding, he asks. It would've taken a shooting war to keep them all at home.

Flowing like a damned soul between the hot hell of the heart of the Himalayas and the cold hell of the windswept peaks that overlook the gorges, [the Tsangpo] became more and more turbulent, and at the same time the landscape became harsher and the rumbling of the water more threatening.

—FRANCIS KINGDON-WARD, SHORTLY BEFORE BEING FORCED
TO ABANDON A YEARLONG ATTEMPT TO BECOME THE FIRST
TO SURVEY THE RIVER TO COMPLETION

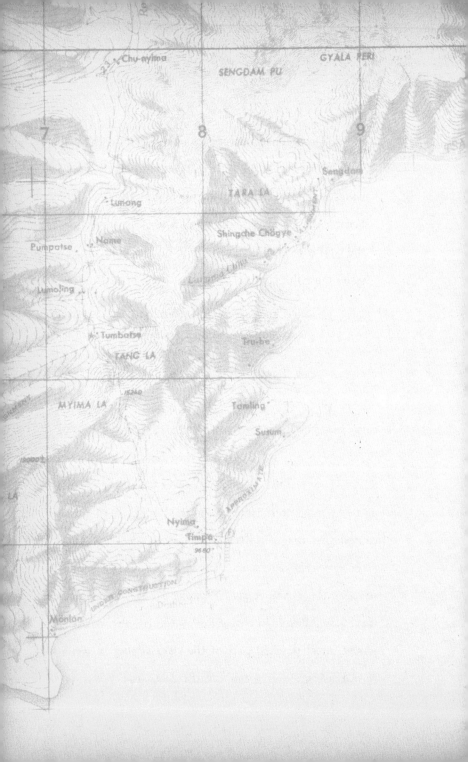

Tsangpo Gorge, Tibet, November 1883

Obscure as the Tsangpo is for the majority of westerners today, it wasn't always that way. At the turn of the century—the tail end of Britain's golden age of exploration—the Tsangpo was as buzzed about in fashionable Victorian adventuring circles as Everest. In fact the Tsangpo Gorge, and the mammoth waterfall it was rumored to possess, caused the imaginations of both stolid geographers and Fleet Street hacks to soar. "This interval," gushed writers in the *Proceedings of the Royal Geographic Society,* "must include some grand development of fluvial topography," the unexplored, most pinched part of the river veiling "a scene of wonderful sublimity—one of the last, and perhaps the grandest, of nature's secrets." So certain were they of the existence of the Lost Falls of the Brahmaputra that the Royal Geographic Society's president, Sir Thomas Holdrich, took the next logical step, writing in 1906 of a newly touristed and trekked-over Tibet that might include a "spacious hotel for visitors and those who enjoyed the outdoor life, right opposite the waterfall."

The slim evidence for a great cascade lay in the recollections of one of Britain's last surveyor-spies, an illiterate tailor and sometime guide from Sikkim named Kintup. He was recruited and trained by the British government to pose as a traveling pilgrim while surreptitiously carrying out detailed geographical surveillance in the frontier regions north of the Himalaya (places where Englishmen were expressly forbidden). The subterfuge was the idea of Captain George Thomas Montgomerie of the Great Trigonometric Survey of India, who recognized the relative ease with which Indian natives were able to get across the border. The British were politically unwelcome in Tibet and China, and the lower reaches of the Tsangpo, in the Arunachal Pradesh region of India, were inhabited by hostile, aggressive tribes. Fearing a cycle of ambushes and reprisals, the Indian government wisely halted all British exploration through the territory. Thus the dirty work was left to the mostly Indian "pundits" who were trained in Calcutta and cleverly outfitted with boxes and baskets with false bottoms (to conceal a compass and sextant); prayer wheels with a lid that could be opened (for notes, written in verse form and in hieroglyphics, recording the heights of passes or swings in the river); and strings of one hundred rosary beads, rather than the customary 108, to conveniently pace off distances. Tucked-away thermometers allowed them to record the boiling point of their tea water, from which elevations could be determined.

Their mission was ludicrously daunting: One million square miles in Tibet were veritable blank spots on Western maps. The British government, fearing encroachment on their valued Indian holdings by expansion-minded Imperialist Russia, moved to survey the high Tibetan plateau from west to east, hoping to suss out potential invasion routes.

The Tsangpo itself was less of a military worry, but gained mounting prominence as the one part of the globe that seemed resistant to the exploratory will of Victorian England. In an age when the world's other great rivers had been triumphantly sourced and mapped, when Everest (then known as Peak XV) had been identified as the world's tallest mountain, the character and course of the Tsangpo remained a stubborn and much-debated mystery. What became of the Tsangpo as it plunged down off the high Tibetan plateau? Was it a tributary of one of the great Asian rivers to the east—the Yangtze, the Mekong, the Salween, the Irrawaddy—or did it flow to sea by way of India and the Brahmaputra? The latter was the most probable answer, but if that were the case, it meant the river fell 10,000 feet in only a hundred-plus miles. Proof meant tracking the river through its uncharted and seemingly impenetrable gorge.

Beginning in the 1860s, and continuing for two decades, the pundits' dozen-plus overlapping odysseys began to fill in the blank spots, each picking up where the last left off. In 1875 the pundit and native policeman Lala was turned back short of the gorge, but reported back to the Survey of India that he'd been told the river flowed to a "country governed by the British." In 1878 the Sikkimese lama Nen Singh and Kintup penetrated the gorge to Gyala, a small village at the foot of the massive snow peak Gyala Peri. A year later another pundit returned from a three-year journey with observations ruling out the possibility that the Tsangpo was a tributary of the Yangtze, Salween, Mekong, or Irrawaddy. For all intents and purposes—and though one hundred miles of the gorge had yet to be set foot in—the outstanding geographical question of its day had been answered. The Tsangpo was the Brahmaputra.

In 1880, Kintup, who was then thirty-two, and a Mongolian lama were sent out to put the exclamation point on the Survey's work. In a scheme dreamt up by Captain Henry Harman, the officer in charge of the Survey of India, the "pilgrims" were ambitiously directed to penetrate through the entire gorge, past Gyala, and all the way to Assam and the Indian border. If the gorge stopped them, however, they were to send a note to Harman, then prepare five hundred specially marked logs and throw them into the river. (Each was to be bored with a hole and outfitted with a tin tube enclosing an identification paper.) On the prearranged date, Harman would have men posted on the Dihang in India, the Brahmaputra River's largest tributary, where they'd watch for the logs. If one floated past, it would prove conclusively that the Tsangpo and the Brahmaputra were one and the same river.

The plan failed famously. Kintup's traveling companion proved not only less than conscientious in his duties, but the rogue of all rogues. Well short of the gorge, he lost the expeditionary funds in a gambling session; later he took up with a host's wife; and finally he went AWOL, but not before selling the luckless Kintup into slavery. Escaping from his initial owner and binding himself to another, more lenient master, the plucky Kintup didn't give up. Why he would feel honor-bound to complete a reconnaissance for Her Majesty's Service is hard to comprehend, but he soldiered on. He asked for, and was granted, permission to make a pilgrimage to Lhasa, where he managed to get off a note to the chief of the Survey of India:

> *Sir, — The lama who was sent with me sold me to a Dzongpen as a slave and himself fled away with the Govt. things that were in his charge. On account of which the journey proved a bad one; however I, Kintup, have prepared the 500 logs according to the order of . . . Captain Harman and am prepared to throw 50 logs per day into the Tsang-po from Bipung in Pemako, from the 5th to the 15th of the 10th Tibetan month of the year called Chhuluk of the Tibetan calculation.*

Passing up the chance to escape in Lhasa, Kintup returned to serve his slave master—an abbot from a gorge monastery—and carry out the plan. Nine months later the abbot granted Kintup not only another pilgrimage, but also his freedom. In November 1883, on the prearranged date, Kintup repaired to a cave where he had cut, shaped, and stored the footlong logs, and began dumping them in the river. Some four years after he started, Kintup had completed his task. Unfortunately his labor went for naught. The note never reached Captain Harman (whose failing health forced him to leave India) or apparently anyone else in the Survey. The logs were never seen, because nobody was there to see them.

When Survey officials finally got around to taking down Kintup's story—a full two years after his return—not much was made of it, with one notable exception. In his debriefing, Kintup described a point on the Tsangpo near Pemakochung, where the river "falls over a cliff . . . from a height of 150 feet. There is a big lake at the foot of the falls where rainbows are always observable."

Survey officials, armed with specific numbers of how dramatically the river dropped, seized on the vague description as evidence that a great waterfall, maybe the world's largest, lay in the Tsangpo's tortured, most remote stretches.

By the time Colonel Frederick M. Bailey of the Political Department of the Indian government took it upon himself to launch a self-styled, not entirely endorsed expedition in search of the waterfall, the year was 1913. In the meantime the fanciful legend had grown exponentially. Bailey was well educated, a savvy traveler who spoke several languages, including Tibetan. His plan was to trace the footsteps of Kintup. He also traveled extremely light and with only one companion, Captain Henry Morshead, believing that a small lightweight expedition would prove far more nimble and be better received locally than the usual siege-style British campaign. In a remarkable six-month campaign, Bailey and Morshead mapped some four hundred miles of the Tsangpo (including the previously undocumented snow peaks, Gyala Peri and Namche Barwa), eventually grinding their way some ten miles farther downstream than Kintup. In leaving just fifty miles unexplored, Bailey and Morshead told a decidedly hostile press corps in Darjeeling the glum news: There was no falls. So ingrained was the myth, and so intense was the disappointment, that Bailey and Morshead were initially chastised by old Tibetan hands like Holdrich, who felt they'd jumped the gun.

At a lively June 1914 meeting at the Royal Geographic Society in London, Bailey silenced his critics with a full accounting, including the news that he'd tracked down Kintup himself—the source of the waterfall story. Apparently Kintup had never claimed a falls lay on the main river. Instead, the story had been garbled in translation (unable to write, he'd had to dictate his observations). Kintup had found, just as Bailey and Morshead had found in Gyala, a small side stream that fell 150 feet over a cliff. The stream joined the Tsangpo at a placid portion of the river (the translator's "lake"). Farther downstream, where the river constricted to fifty yards in width, he'd also observed a rapid estimated to be thirty feet high. As Bailey told reporters, and as Kintup confirmed, "There are no falls. Just miles of rapids, and in one place a big jump."

That was it. The Royal Geographic Society's president, impressed with the pair's diligent research, nonetheless expressed the stunned mood of the moment:

> So I am afraid we must give up any idea of magnificent falls in the Brahmaputra; but knowing and expecting that such falls might exist, that idea was doubtless partly due to our own imagination. We are, I think . . . disappointed that we have not found them. However that may be, to my mind the vision of that important river sliding from plateau to plain through a series of tremendous rapids enclosed by gigantic cliffs, now and again extending into an open and placid river of a breadth which enables it to be accepted by Tibetans as a lake; still enclosed by mountains of extraordinary steepness, clothed from the river up to the sky with rhododendrons and firs—this seems to me to be a prospect quite as alluring as any that we might have met with had those falls existed.

Bailey almost certainly would have found his way back to the Tsangpo to account for the last unmapped miles, but six weeks after his appearance in London, World War I broke out. Instead, the final major expedition came in 1924, led by another Englishman, Francis Kingdon-Ward, a well-known naturalist and author/explorer. Coincidentally, it launched at the same time as— and actually crossed paths with—the ill-fated Mount Everest

Expedition featuring George Mallory. (Of course, the disappearance of Mallory and his companion, Andrew Irvine, high on the peak—perhaps after summiting—led to another long-running mystery. Mountaineers discovered Mallory's corpse in 1999, but Irvine's body was not found, thus leaving the question of the team's ultimate progress still unsolved.)

Kingdon-Ward, like a lot of England, remained hopeful that somewhere in the last unexplored stretch of the Tsangpo, beyond the steps of Kintup and Bailey, lay the fabled falls. "There remained a gap of fifty miles more or less, about which absolutely nothing was known," wrote Kingdon-Ward in his classic adventure narrative, *The Riddle of the Tsangpo Gorges*.

> *Indeed, for half that distance there was said to be no track of any sort near the river, which was hemmed in by bare rock walls several thousand feet high. Was it possible that hidden away in the depths of this unknown gorge there was a great waterfall? Such a thing was quite possible, and it was this question we were resolved to answer. We would, if possible, go right through the gorge, and tear this last secret from its heart.*

Approaching through the head of the gorge at Pe, Kingdon-Ward and his companion, the Earl of Cawdor (along with numerous Tibetan porters and a guru nicknamed Walrus), traversed the landscape up and down, from riverbed to ridgetop, taking painstaking survey readings and seed samples of alpine and subtropical flora, the diversity of which elicited a reverie bordering on ecstasy: "We were approaching another stratum of vegetation, for there now appeared for the first time a large deciduous Magnolia with leaves twenty inches long by ten inches wide. . . . It must be a magnificent sight in leaf and flower!"

Cutting track and scaling cliffs to progress ever deeper—past Kintup's and Bailey's stopping points—Kingdon-Ward's keen eyes turned increasingly to the river, which "continued to advance by jerks in a general north-east direction, with fierce rapids which ate hungrily into the core of the mountains," he wrote as they marched on.

Already we seemed to be far below the level of the ground, going down, down, into the interior of the earth; and as though to emphasize the fact, the temperature grew steadily warmer. And the Gorge was growing even narrower, the gradient steeper, till the power behind the maddened river was terrific. Its blows fell on rock and cliff with frightful force; and at every turn a huge cavernous mouth seemed to open, and gulp it down faster and faster.

On November 29, Kingdon-Ward's party came up against a cliff they couldn't advance past—but before the "nightmare" vertical climb out of the gorge, they were able to catch sight of a great cloud of spray a half-mile away. "'The falls at last,' I thought! But it wasn't—not the falls. A fall, certainly, perhaps forty feet high, and a fine sight with rainbows coming and going in the spray cloud. But a thirty or forty foot fall, even on the Tsangpo, cannot be called the falls, meaning the falls of romance, those 'Falls of the Brahmaputra . . .'" Still, doing his part to please the fluvial topography fans in London, he famously dubbed the juncture Rainbow Falls.

The expedition, now some nine months along, wasn't done yet. Having survived the soggy vertical ascent out of the gorge, Kingdon-Ward took a few days' respite in Payu, then charged on, crossing the river by way of rope bridge about four miles downstream of the confluence of the Tsangpo and its major northern tributary, the Po Tsangpo. Kingdon-Ward was the first westerner to see the much-anticipated confluence and peer upstream into the inner gorge. Describing the point where spurs from Gyala Peri and Namche Barwa drove down to the riverbed from opposite sides of the river, he wrote: "Then when you think the gap must be sealed up, and the door bolted and barred, out of the very heart of this tomb, swinging round the spurs, leaping the rocks, comes the Tsangpo just as hard as it can go, a roaming, bouncing, bellowing flood."

The sight left Kingdon-Ward more hopeful than ever that the Falls of the Brahmaputra lay within the part of the gorge he'd been unable to access—the fourteen-mile section between Rainbow Falls and the confluence. "Our excitement may be imagined; and the fact that the river between the Rainbow Fall and the confluence dropped 1,851 feet was favourable to the theory of a 100 foot waterfall somewhere." Reluctantly guided by native hunters to a ridge high above the unexplored gorge, the party forged a way down to the riverbed. Kingdon-Ward, scrambling up cliffs and over boulders, spied two impressive but hardly gargantuan falls. The bigger of the two, located in the "narrowest and most profound depths of the gorge," was an estimated forty feet. Figuring that he had either traveled through or seen all but five miles of the gorge, Kingdon-Ward concluded dispiritedly that the falls was myth after all:

"There is a legend current among Tibetans, and said to be recorded in certain sacred books kept in the monastery at Pemakochung, that between the Rainbow Fall and the confluence there are no less than seventy-five of these falls, each presided over by a spirit—whether benevolent or malicious is not stated." In other words, the Tsangpo wasn't characterized by one behemoth falls, but rather by a glut of rapids, the total of which accounted for the river's great drop.

Back in London, news of Kingdon-Ward's findings effectively ended speculation about the falls. True, he had left a small opening—the five-mile "gap" remained—but in the popular imagination the issue was dead. Shortly after Kingdon-Ward's return, the region was essentially closed to westerners for nearly fifty years. Not surprisingly, the Tsangpo mystery fell into almost complete and utter obscurity.

THE GREAT SAGA, ITS UNREQUITED EXPLORERS, AND THE MYTHIC pot of riverine gold (just ever so slightly beyond the range of human eyes) made deep claims on a select few. Those who chanced upon the narratives in remote special collections, or on a friendly tip here or there, felt as if they were privy to something special, as if they'd been led to the entombed story for the express purpose of writing the last chapter. If Wick saw a little of Colonel Bailey in himself, who could blame him? He was a geology major at Dartmouth and an Army officer trained in map making. In the eighties he'd surface from time to time on the Potomac, usually preceded by rumors of having just returned from some seething global hot spot. "What was the boating like in Afghanistan?" asked the whitewater pups who got a chance to paddle with him. "Can't talk about that," Wick said with a grin.

Tom used to cart around a copy of Kingdon-Ward, and when people asked him why, he'd point to the page where the author mentions the seventy-five falls, each presided over by a spirit. "The image of those waterfalls one after the other...," Tom would drift off. "Some of them gotta be runnable!" Unlike Wick, Tom was more of a pilgrim than an explorer, the sort of person who doesn't come calling for the sake of the motherland or for scientific fame, but because his life is intertwined with all rivers, and this is the last one.

Unfortunately, the modern age of exploration in the Tsangpo Gorge dawned inauspiciously. The permit price tag for a gorge expedition circa 1985 (and there were several people asking) verged on extortion: a million dollars. As the Chinese were well aware, two marketable "firsts" were at stake in the Tsangpo: a first descent of the river through the gorge, and a first ascent of 25,436-foot Namche Barwa, then the highest unclimbed peak in the world. Sneaking into the region, à la Bailey and Morshead, was a particularly bad idea. The extreme lower end of the gorge near Medog was only a few miles from the border with India. With China and India in a volatile border war—and outbreaks of fighting as recent as 1986—the area remained under acute surveillance, girded with military installations.

In 1990 the first breakthrough, and one that would presage the opening of the region, came with the announcement that a joint Chinese and Japanese climbing team would attempt Namche Barwa. (In the interim China and India signed a formal cease-fire treaty, and the cash-needy Beijing government began taking the first steps in promoting tightly controlled adventure travel trips in Tibet.) In the fall the Sino-Japanese team scouted Namche Barwa. Naturally basing its strategy on specific conditions seen during its 1990 scout (just as the Walker team would, years later, with the river), the team returned in the fall of 1991 to see a peak that looked nothing like what they'd previously seen. Huge winds, unrelenting snowstorms, and far more technical climbing than expected not only forced the exhausted team to retire, but also claimed the life of a Japanese climber, Hiroshi Onishi.

In 1992 the Japan/China Joint Expedition returned and got its historic summit. Around the same time, another milestone occurred: The first American was granted official permission to take a peek at the illustrious gorge. Rick Fisher, a Tucson-based outfitter, might seem a curious choice. A longtime canyon explorer, Fisher, then forty, championed a hybrid sport he called "canyoneering." The sport used a hodgepodge of outdoor techniques—whitewater boating, rock climbing, and backpacking— to probe previously unexplored canyons. He photographed, wrote about, and guided trips to canyons in the American Southwest, Mexico's Sierra Madre, and elsewhere. Fisher's boyish enthusiasm and campfire charm amused most, but some were uncomfortable with the hype surrounding his discoveries and his me-first marketing of canyoneering, an exploratory method that seemed to be around for generations. Wrote an entertained but skeptical Jon Krakauer in *Outside* magazine after a chasm-hopping week in Arizona with Fisher:

"How then, in the name of John Wesley Powell, can anyone conclude that one, or two, or 20 canyons are somehow better than the rest? To understand why Fisher insists the Mogollon canyons could be considered more worthy canyoneering objectives than the most celebrated defiles of Zion, the Escalante, Canyonlands, or the almighty Grand Canyon it is first necessary to understand what is properly termed canyoneering in the eyes of Fisher, who is something of a zealot when it comes to this newly christened phylum of backcountry play."

In later years Fisher became knotted in a controversy regarding the Tarahumara, a tribe living in the remote canyons of the Sierra Madre. Fisher got to know the Tarahumara—renowned for their long-distance runners—during his frequent treks in the region, and eventually persuaded several of the best to showcase their talents on the U.S. trail-running race circuit. Nobody doubted Fisher meant to do the right thing, but by anybody's accounting the project was a disaster. He seemed to make a mockery of their cultural traditions by rounding them up into a "team" and then acting like a deranged Little League coach at their races. Rather than bridging the cultural gap, the short-fused Fisher seemed to tear it asunder, antagonizing local race promoters and runners, who felt he was bent on embarrassing them. Though he claimed some notable victories—a fifty-five-year-old Tarahumaran named Victor Churro won the prestigious hundred-mile Leadville 100 trail race wearing huaraches, for example—the discredited Fisher found himself unwelcome at several races. Eventually the Tarahumara runners sought to put distance between themselves and Fisher.

Yet at his best, Fisher was good, defying convention, questioning authority, and always up for a wild-ass trip. On September 15, 1992—after years of hapless attempts to gain entry to the Tsangpo—his latest Chinese contact called, saying, "Show up in nine days with $8,000 in your pocket and you can go." On that solo recon trip he not only saw a canyon unlike any he'd ever seen, but, more important, he gained permission to come back. Offering himself as a westerner who could help promote the region for tourism and who wouldn't do anything to embarrass the Chinese, he used his canyon savvyness to advance both his agenda and that of the Chinese. His order of business was to retrace Kingdon-Ward's route and explore the hidden gap, document the gorge as the deepest in the world, and maybe make a first whitewater descent.

In the spring of 1993, Fisher's attempt to make history got off to an inglorious start. Guiding a team of ten (including six ecotourist clients paying up to $10,000 apiece), Fisher unexpectedly ran into another American explorer near the entrance to the gorge. David Breashears, a filmmaker and Everest mountaineer, was everything Fisher was not: well-known, well connected, and well subsidized. He was in the gorge, retracing the steps of Kintup and Kingdon-Ward just as Fisher was doing. Only he was being paid a lot of money and getting to write a story about his travels for *National Geographic*. Breashears, along with the whitewater rafting pioneer Richard Bangs, had actually first queried Geographic with a Tsangpo proposal in 1981. Undoubtedly Fisher, who'd tried to interest *National Geographic* himself, felt betrayed. He received Breashears badly, and the two got into a heated shouting match. Though Breashears and photographer Gordon Wiltsie had failed to get to Rainbow Falls (their mutinous porters having ditched food along the way in order to force them to exit prematurely), they figured they'd salvage the trip by detouring around the gap (as Kingdon-Ward did) and reentering the gorge at the confluence of the Tsangpo and Po Tsangpo.

Fisher figured to beat them. In a surreal episode Fisher dispatched part of the team on the same route Breashears had tried. He also enlisted his two strongest client trekkers—a forty-year-old American woman and a twelve-year-old boy—to race around the gap and beat Breashears to the confluence. Who beat whom remains a point of conjecture, but Breashears calls the affair "regrettable," and isn't much interested in revisiting it beyond that. Clearly the race brought out the worst in everyone. In many ways the clash didn't make much sense. Breashears was an established name with two Everest summits to his credit. Fisher was a relative nobody. But there was something about the Tsangpo that bit everybody hard. Whether it was the growing "last great undone" hype, or the burden of sponsor and client expectations, or simply the weight of the region's fantastic history, the gorge seemed to make the big personalities drawn to it a little crazy. "I'll tell you one thing," said Breashears shortly after he returned. "That place is real adventure travel."

Breashears's trip never did produce a story. The constant cloud cover and incessant rain—Breashears was daily stripping dozens of leeches off his body—didn't exactly produce the kind of Shangri-la photographs that the *Geographic* editors yearned for. Among the unpublished photographs, however, was one keeper. Breashears snapped the shot after climbing a high ridge near the confluence. It revealed a wildly exotic hydraulic event, a jet spray of water pulsing over a huge drop within the inner gorge. Breashears was jazzed by the photograph, but owing to the distance from which he took the shot, it was impossible to say for certain what it was. "I knew it was big," says Breashears, who paid tribute to his hero Kintup by placing a Nalgene bottle into the current with the explorer's name, a promised finder's fee, and the number 501 written on a slip of paper within. "I think I estimated in my notes it was about sixty to ninety feet. I certainly didn't consider it the fabled Lost Falls. I called it Kintup Falls."

In the fall of 1993, a still-rattled Fisher returned to the gorge with a group of scientists from the University of Arizona. The team, which joined forces with scientists from the Chinese Academy of Sciences, was successful in verifying the lowest point in the gorge. At 16,500-plus feet (and later revised to almost 18,000 feet), it was indeed the deepest gorge in the world (a finding essentially confirmed two years later by the *Guinness Book of*

Records, though they preferred to characterize the region as a valley). Six months later a triumphant Fisher returned to the gorge with the idea of boating it, his final objective.

Back in Phoenix, Gil and Troy Gillenwater, wealthy real-estate developers and intrepid outdoorsmen, responded to a Fisher newspaper ad looking for river runners. The two brothers had boated on most of the major rivers in the West, though they'd hardly describe themselves as cutting-edge paddlers. Eric Manthey, a buddy of Fisher's, joined them. Fisher describes the trip as a well-calculated probe, a sample test to determine the viability of the project. The Gillenwaters describe the escapade as a classic misadventure in which they were fortunate to come away unharmed. With no support, dubious scouting (the muddled Manthey reported only flat water downstream), and a twelve-foot paddle raft, the water portion of the trip lasted all of three or four miles. "We came up to a Class V rapid, this huge pour-over," recalls Troy Gillenwater. "Rick and Eric wanted to do it and Gil and I were saying, 'This is suicide! We have no support. If we don't make it we don't have any fallback.' They finally agreed to walk out, but it became an epic. Eric said it would be a couple of hours. Actually it was four days and we completely ran out of food."

Shortly thereafter, Fisher declared the gorge unboatable. For those who thought it possible (and thereby questioned the competency of Fisher's own effort), Fisher offered a bizarre wager: a thousand dollars to anyone (but especially to David Breashears, who'd suggested that some combination of big-wall rock climbing and boating might be a solution) who boated the gorge in its entirety. "Put up or shut up!" he challenged.

Confused as Fisher's method for discouraging future attempts was (fortunately for him, the wager, faxed to a few magazines, never became public), he wasn't really bluffing. He did believe the gorge was unrunnable, and he based the conclusion on a tragic episode that took place a few months prior to his own aborted trip. In September a pair of Japanese kayakers put in near the confluence—well downstream of Fisher's trials. Both kayakers were woefully inexperienced, though one was a well-known survivalist who'd paddled the Indian Ocean. Both capsized immediately and Takei Yositaka died within minutes. Months later the deceased kayaker's father returned with a massive rescue team, convinced that his son had dodged another bullet and was living with Monpa natives farther downstream. The effort turned up nothing. With the help of villagers, the father somberly erected a gravestone with family mementos and planted cosmos seeds and a peach sapling near the accident site. Describing a patch of white sand where a tower of boulders muffled the thudding roar of the river, the father wrote: "After being there awhile I could feel the peace filling my heart somehow, but I wondered if it happened by the silence or not."

At about the same time as the Japanese tragedy a well-read article in *Outside* magazine appeared, addressing for the first time in the mainstream media the growing fascination with the Tsangpo. Titled "What's Left Out There," the story ranked the Tsangpo run at the top of its list of epic undone expeditionary feats. The piece didn't immediately result in a stampede to the Tsangpo's banks—the place was too far away and too expensive for anything as impetuous as that—but it removed the river from the realm of obscurity and began a distinct buzz. The Tsangpo came up in conversation wherever river runners hobnobbed, from car shuttles to campsites.

Meanwhile, the trekking expeditions mounted. Fisher returned multiple times, as did a former tripmate of his, an American named Ian Baker. Baker, trained in Tibetan studies, was part of Fisher's spring 1993 team, though he'd peeled off with three others and pushed remarkably close to Rainbow Falls, the terminus of Kingdon-Ward's attempt. In addition, the Chinese dispatched several teams of botanists, geologists, and wildlife experts to survey the gorge.

Clearly the dozens of expeditions were chipping away at the edges, but nobody had progressed at or near river level into what Breashears aptly called the "gorgiest part of the gorge"—the unseen place where the waterfall might lie.

Despite the Japanese tragedy and Fisher's pronouncement, several prominent boaters began seriously planning for the gorge in 1997. There was an international team led by Doug Ammons (a Montanan with vast big-water experience) and Lukas Blücher of Germany's Alpine Kayak Club, the best-known extreme boating club in the world. The wealthy Blücher's occupation of late was to travel the globe paddling five-star wilderness rivers. Ammons, a Ph.D. in psychology who was the only person ever to solo British Columbia's Grand Canyon of the Stikine (the closest thing to the Tsangpo in North America), had been quietly amassing data on the Tsangpo for fifteen years. Steve Currey, the commercial rafting first-descent specialist out of Salt Lake City who'd run a stretch of the Brahmaputra in India, was advertising a once-in-a-lifetime trip to clients. Also organizing a run was Scott Lindgren, a young hotshot from Northern California, who made and starred in slick, action-laced, extreme whitewater videos. Lindgren called the schizo waters of the Tsangpo the "most powerful shit on the planet." Many considered Lindgren and his videographer companion, Charlie Munsey, the prototype Tsangpo boaters: young, fearless, and absolutely willing to "hang it out there."

Unlike the early nineties, when the consensus was that the Tsangpo was unrunnable, more and more boaters seemed to view the river "within the realm of craziness," as one boater put it. Whether the subtle shift coincided with the sport's rebellious no-limits ethos, advances in boat materials and design, or simply had to do with deflated permit fees and keen sponsor and media interest, is hard to say. Whatever the case, the Tsangpo was suddenly the focus of relatively widespread interest. Worldwide, easily a half-dozen expeditions were in some stages of planning. At a major outdoor trade show in the United States, no less than four parties were shopping proposals, hoping to get sponsors to bite. In many cases the alliances weren't set, each paddler jockeying for the best possible deal, each trying to figure out who was going when and with whom. The fairly well-publicized Fisher/Breashears rift—and their incomplete but tantalizing reports—had sparked sponsor and boater interest alike. The secret was out, and the race was on. As with Everest in 1953, there was an intuitive sense among many of the Tsangpo suitors that the time was at hand, that the Tsangpo, like Everest before it, was ripe "to go."

Trying to unravel who was the most qualified wasn't easy. Those who were most seriously entertaining runs all had some substantial, time-invested connection with the gorge; they weren't Johnny-come-latelies looking for publicity. For most of them, just like Wick and Tom, the place had occupied their imaginations for years. For most of them, too, the idea of a race to get there first was anathema. But for one reason or another each group felt that its stake in the place had a little more credibility and import than the others.

Because of their scouting, their experience, and their contacts, Wick and Tom probably always had the leg up in terms of recruiting a big-deal sponsor. Selling themselves and their trip was a foregone conclusion. In an ideal world it would be nice to do things as they'd always done: quietly, modestly, à la Great Falls. But the Tsangpo was on another fiscal scale: Wick's first budget was $157,000. He'd whittled it down since then, but it was still over $100,000, and $100,000-plus trips didn't get done unless sponsors came on board. At heart, Tom and Wick seemed to possess the same sort of idealistic, vigorously anticommercial ethic as your average old-school Yosemite climber or whitewater pioneer: Doing any adventure for anything other than personal reasons (read fame or wealth or media) corrupted purpose and hobbled judgment. After all, you did what you did in many cases to get away from consumerist culture. But in the late 1990s—the era of Expedition Inc., as one magazine put it—the climate had shifted. There was no stigma attached to getting sponsored to do things. Nobody wanted to be involved in full-on marketing gim- mickry, and nobody wanted some evil-empire sponsor like a tobacco company, but the partnership between ambitious, highly skilled adventurers and corporate America was sort of inevitable: The hardest climbs—the hardest anything—were increasingly in obscure, logistically expensive places to get to, such as Baffin Island, Antarctica, and the Tsangpo.

Other than the Bhutan trip almost twenty years earlier (and in that case only in a modest way), Tom and Wick hadn't really attempted to play the sponsor game. They'd always prided them- selves on conjuring up first-class whitewater trips to places like Mexico and Canada, where they wouldn't have to spend a lot, or ask for a lot of money. They'd gotten by on gear donations for the most part. But Wick recognized that to get money—far harder to come by for expeditions than in-kind gear donations—they needed to do what the pros did and offer a first-rate package of deliverables. Hence their proposal offered not only a line-by-line budget, but also a concise and well-written history of the gorge, writing samples of some of the members, Wick's photo credits, and an attractive theme that emphasized applying technological innovations to the "century-old problem." In order to link themselves to the colorful explorations of the past, they called the project the "Riddle of the Tsangpo Gorges" expedition (a nod to Kingdon-Ward's 1926 book of the same name).

A curmudgeonly few worried that Wick was slipping to the dark side, with all the fussing with sponsors (he efficiently lined up a longer-than-average roster of gear and apparel sponsors and assorted grants). But there were plenty of other people who were impressed by the unusual maturity and value he brought to the table. One of them was Peter Miller, head of the National Geographic Society's newly formed Expeditions Council (whose purpose was to parcel out money to projects showing promising potential for any media—film, TV, or print). The Society's $60,000 grant to "complete Captain Ward's interrupted traverse" clinched the trip and was one of the largest amounts ever awarded to a kayaking expedition.

Working for Geographic, the nation's most prestigious exploration institution, was a dream for Tom and Wick. They'd applied for a major grant from Rolex, the watchmakers, but Geographic was always the emotional first choice. Wick was not only a lifelong reader and explorer, but also an avid amateur photographer with hopes of getting in Old Yellow. An assignment from the Geographic Society is considered by most, but especially by men of Wick's generation, the pinnacle moment in an adventurer's career. The late Ned Gillette, a maverick American adventurer in the 1970s, once recalled that his desire for producing a crack "Silk Road" story for Geographic pushed him to travel into war-torn Central Asian countries he had no business being in. Geographic didn't ask him to risk his life, he said, but he felt a kind of soldierly obligation to go the extra yard. And Gillette wasn't alone. The same lofty institution that sent Peary to the Arctic and Ballard to the *Titanic* had that kind of effect on people. A stroll through the Society's Explorers Hall museum, in downtown D.C., was enough to send a chill down the spine of even the most low-key guy. "Why do people risk their lives to explore?" asks the entrance placard. "Whether it be climbing the highest peaks or descending the deepest trenches, those who explore share the same exhilaration of meeting nature's ultimate challenges. . . ."

Peter Miller had also made the Breashears assignment, and, according to industry insiders, felt the heat when it didn't work out. (At the time the Society was in the throes of a rather acute financial crisis, and a five-figure outlay without anything coming of it hardly made people happy.) Miller badly wanted a home run this time around. In addition to the cash grant, Geographic also outfitted the team with SLRs and remote-control cameras. They had a staff photographer give them a picture-taking tutorial at Great Falls. Everybody on the team was flattered by the VIP treatment. There would be an Explorer TV film, and there was excited talk of an entire issue devoted to the Tsangpo's final, millennium-ending exploration. Clearly Geographic, attempting a makeover into a younger, more mediagenic outfit, was counting on them.

After the Tsangpo trip, some wondered if getting backed by such a prestigious organization had affected the team's judgment, making them get on the plane and push forward when otherwise they might not have. It probably wasn't a question anybody on the team could answer, but perhaps in more subtle ways the high-profile sponsorship and the competitive buzz did add a layer of confusion that Wick and Tom's undertaking at Great Falls never had. That project had been done in a figurative vacuum, known to no one, cared about by no one. It was purely personal. The Tsangpo, for reasons not entirely in their control, was anything but.

"I remember when Doug told me the big money had come through from National Geographic," says E. J. McCarthy, an old Connecticut friend with whom Gordon regularly corresponded. "He said, 'Eej, I don't know whether it's good news or bad, but we've got our big sponsor.' I loved Doug. He was my idol. He taught me everything I know about running wilderness rivers, and a whole hell of a lot more, but the whole sponsorship thing and all that crap that comes along with it seemed to run contrary to everything he was about."

≋ [We] accept no responsibility for diminished career opportunities, and the inevitable chronic relationship problems which accompany the slow but undeviating downward spiral into the dark underworld of professional whitewater trash—you wouldn't be the first one to have whatever contribution you could have made to society stymied by whitewater addiction.

—FROM THE INFORMATION SHEET OF A
NEPALESE WHITEWATER OUTFITTER

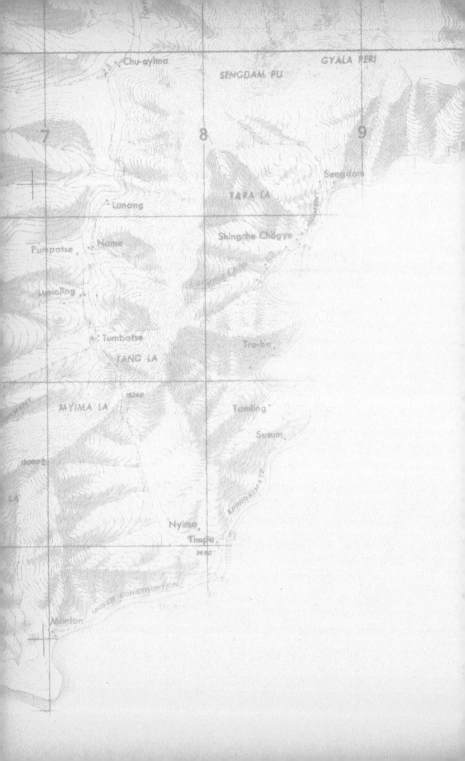

Kathmandu, Nepal, late September 1998

IF THERE IS ANY QUESTION WHY DOUG GORDON HAS CHOSEN to fly halfway around the world, through umpteen time zones and four different airports—putting life and limb on the line, job and family on hold—it's clear now. In the final airborne minutes of the team's two-day Washington-London-Delhi-Kathmandu marathon flight, the twilit Himalaya rumbles into view for the first time. Gordon, unlike the McEwans and Walker, has never seen these mountains. Maybe not so oddly, the distant flurry of conical, snow-capped, eight-thousand-meter peaks distracts him only momentarily. They appear far off; a combination of the dusky light and lowlands approach. On the return flight from Lhasa to Kathmandu, which they'll make at trip's end in six weeks, they'll scrape right over the top of the peaks, he's told, a prospect Doug and everyone else is eager to witness. But for now the mountains loom on the horizon a bit elusively and Doug's eyes almost immediately search the wide valleys breaching the east-west massif for lithe, mocha-colored torrents. Nepal's fabled whitewater jewels, long since immortalized in the tales of Western boaters, run from one corner of the country to the other, dropping from the proverbial heavens. The giant summits of Annapurna, Dhaulagiri, and Everest—great lodestones for mountaineers and mountaineering fans alike—pass by with barely a second look. Gordon begins to see the topography with the peculiar perspective of a whitewater veteran: His focus is down deep in the dark, shadowy crevices of rippling landscape, not up.

The Nepalese Himalaya is a river runner's paradise. The stats speak volumes: a hundred-mile-wide kingdom in which the land tilts from near sea level to 29,000-plus feet. Stuffed into the topography is every type of river imaginable, from the large-volume, snowmelt behemoths like the Tibetan-born Karnali to the white-sand jungle tributaries of the Far East lowlands. The Dudh Kosi, the Arun Gorges, the Tamur—obscure names to all but a few dozen river runners around the world—occupy Doug Gordon's and his teammates' thoughts. Gordon is particularly well versed in the tales and tribulations—the glory, deaths, and near deaths—to emerge from these exotic rivers. He has raced boats around the world and traveled all over North America in search of wild rivers that might match the intensity of focus he had to offer, but the vastness of what he hasn't seen and hasn't done is coming into picture-perfect view right now. Everything he has seen seems puny by comparison. Everything he has done, a little minor-league. In precisely eleven days, the occasion when he and his teammates will first feel the driving surge of the river beneath them, they will know even more intimately how different the landscape is from what they knew before. In the measures that matter to a river runner—a river's volume, velocity, pitch, and remoteness—there are two distinct worlds: the Himalaya and everything else.

The date is September 24, the eve of the popular, post-monsoon fall trekking and commercial rafting season in Nepal. There are only a handful of climbing expeditions on Mount Everest (the vast majority occur in the spring), but one, by a local climber named Kaji Sherpa, will put a cap on one of the mountain's most accommodating seasons in history by sprinting to the top in a mere twenty hours. His speed record marks the 123rd summit of Everest this year—just six summits short of the 1993 record. That year, however, there were eight deaths; in this year a mere three have perished on Everest. In the wake of the disastrous 1996 year chronicled in Jon Krakauer's *Into Thin Air,* the 1998 El Niño season (and its companion phenomenon, La Niña) is showing just how mercurial and occasionally vulnerable even the Himalaya can be. Experts offer no startling reasons for the banner year other than the obvious: The weather lightened mercifully at the right time. Put another way, everybody lucked out in 1998.

Unfortunately the monsoon, whose delayed onset this summer accounted for the rash of late-spring Everest summits, has made up for lost time. A record rainfall, which has swollen some Himalayan rivers to more than a hundred times their low-season level, is just now letting up. The rivers are running fast and brown. Expert boaters who like to spice things up by coming at the tail end of the monsoon season, when the rivers run amok, have seen things they've never seen before. A few weeks earlier a trio of rafts on the Dudh Kosi, which drains the southern slopes of Everest, got caught in a huge, near-deadly flood. In a wrath-of-God phenomenon peculiar to the high Himalaya, a pent-up glacial lake exploded its banks and swept down the valley. Termed Glacial Lake Outburst Floods, or GLOFs, such catastrophic surges are neither predictable nor defensible. In 1985, according to Nepal guidebook author and famed British river runner Peter Knowles, a GLOF sent a thirty-foot-high wave of mud racing down a tributary of the Dudh Kosi. The 1998 GLOF produced similarly apocalyptic conditions. The freight-training river was the consistency of "liquid mud," and chocolate brown in color. Massive exploding waves and sucking whirlpools churned with big trees and the remains of houses. Hundreds of dead fish floated on the surface of eddies. The rafters and their kayaking companions survived the mayhem, but just barely. "It was a huge relief and I cried when I heard the noise of the helicopter on the third day," said one of the swept-downstream boaters, fearing all his companions were dead. In an even more publicized incident that occurred a few days after the team's arrival, one of Nepal's rapid-braving cargo boats—rafts that shuttle passengers and goods on the Sun Kosi river in eastern Nepal—overturned in the high water. Several died.

In spite of the mounting tales of out-of-control rivers, the team's mood isn't gloomy. Conditions at the other end of the Himalaya where they're headed might be utterly different. With no eyewitness reports having surfaced to say otherwise, everybody is hoping for the best. "We know there is a lot of rain in China, but we don't know what that means," says McEwan. "The scenario we have in mind is similar to when we get hurricanes on the East Coast. They drench the coast, but a few hundred miles away, in the West Virginia highlands, they might not see anything."

The gnawing should-we-or-shouldn't-we deliberations of the past few weeks are replaced by both the thrill of the hunt and the lovely reality of what any expedition craves: forward momentum. Tom McEwan, who initially wanted Wick to delay the trip a month and was as unsure as anyone about getting on the plane, finds himself in a familiar mode: He wants to see this thing for himself. Like everybody else on the team, he's been warned of dire conditions at dozens of other rivers, only to arrive and find that what had been described to him was not at all the case. Making decisions based on anything but see-it, feel-it, hear-it sensory experience isn't his way. He heard good reasons to postpone the trip and good reasons to go. Now that he is here—and this pretty much sums up the whole team's view—he is sure as hell gonna see what the river looks like. It is just a river after all, he reminds himself—rocks and water.

Doug Gordon is jacked to be in the Himalaya. Finally. Like everyone else, he scurried around in the final days before departure, getting things in order at home and work. At forty-one, Gordon is the team's youngest, and unquestionably the team's best. Lantern-jawed, he's strikingly handsome in a sun-weathered, wind-flushed *Outside* magazine sort of way. He has a warm, youthful smile, keen blue eyes, and plenty enough wavy brown hair so that unlike others his age he needn't be forced to wear a ball cap twenty-four hours a day. His face bears out the baby-boomer ideal: seasoned but searching.

Gordon has a hot desire to run big rivers, something he has been doing at a high level for almost twenty years. Unknown to a lot of racing friends, he actually cut his teeth doing extreme multi-day descents in Northern California back in the late 1970s. In the 1980s he set his sights on racing, channeling his talents into something a little more explainable—wins and losses. He was a good racer, but not the country's best. On the other hand, in the big, chaotic water of a wilderness river, he was special.

In 1989, Gordon paired up with Tom McEwan for the first time, for a ten-day, self-contained trip on the Class V Aguanus River in Quebec. In a story McEwan is fond of telling, he recalls the image of Gordon bronco-busting a portion of the swollen river where it seemed to cliff out. Gordon saw a way through. Not hesitating at all, he disappeared into the watery tumult, then banked up several stories high where the boil met the cliff. Watching him niftily roll up after the free fall, a mesmerized McEwan shook his head, then walked the juncture. Clearly the episode established Gordon as the type of teammate any serious expedition might covet. (Some of the boaters who declined to go on the Tsangpo trip, familiar with the story, were scared off by the tale, thinking that if Gordon was gung-ho to run stuff that even McEwan wouldn't, then the two of them together could be a handful.)

On another occasion, Gordon joined a few comrades to run the Middle Feather, an expert, multi-day wilderness river in Northern California. On the rebound from knee surgery a year earlier, Gordon sprained the same knee on the first day. Hiking out of the deep gorge was a virtual impossibility. Gordon's teammates rallied around him, saying they'd carry him (and his trusty old river-running boat) at the worst rapids, since everyone expected to make portages. "Instead, he ran everything," says Ethan Greene, a Colorado graduate student who'd never met Gordon before. "It was really pretty funny. Here we were thinking we'd have to take care of the guy—I mean he could barely walk— and three days later he'd nailed the whole thing. Never missed a move. It was intense."

At five foot ten and 150 pounds, he wasn't physically imposing, and sporting rivals almost constantly underestimated him. "It's funny, he never looked very good in practice," says one competitor, "so when he beat us in competition, and in particular at the U.S. team trials (for whitewater slalom racers), we'd always comfort each other by saying it was a fluke—you know, the guy had one lucky day. After he beat us year after year, we realized it was no fluke. Doug was just one of the most mentally tough athletes I'd ever seen. When it counted most, he never missed a move he had to make." To the astonishment of even his coaches, Gordon made the U.S. national whitewater slalom team every year between 1981 and 1987, earning a silver medal at the national championships in 1982 and a bronze in 1985. In 1984 he won his one and only World Cup medal at Merano, Italy, then considered the premier race course in the sport.

Everybody on the team knows exactly how good Gordon is. He's old-school: tough, smart, and attractively understated. Like Tom McEwan, he downplays his big-water battles—as if they are between him and the river and no one else. His few articles on his trips are dry, giving no inkling whatsoever that he—as a friend said—has "a burning desire to have that one run in the zone." Many racers and former training partners were astonished at this apparent transformation, remembering Doug as uninterested in the side dares and whitewater romps that routinely took place at competition sites. "He never wanted to mess around like everyone else," says a fellow racer. "If it didn't have to do with race training, he didn't do it." Only those who'd more recently been on a river with Gordon or were closest to him knew how deep the draw was. "On the trips Doug liked to do, you brought only what you needed to survive and left everything else behind," says

E. J. McCarthy, who accompanied Gordon on lean, self-supported river exploratories from Costa Rica to British Columbia. "Every decision you make has importance. Not a lot of people like to live out of their boat, but for Doug the payoff was simple: You went to sleep next to the river and you woke up next to the river. Doug's whole point, the thing that was so cool about kayaking, was the purity of it." Not that anybody who didn't do it would understand, but there was a huge intellectual draw to something so seemingly crazy. Running hard whitewater, like ascending big, risky mountains, demanded a here-and-now intensity that was virtually impossible to duplicate in any other civilian medium. First descents, where the river's makeup is unknown and untested, raised the ante even higher. His purpose, as counter (and as intrusive) as it might seem to everything else in his life, was to go to the wildest places on Earth.

≋

DOUG GORDON DIDN'T GROW UP IN ANY ONE PLACE. THE SON OF Cornell-trained economics professor Donald Gordon, Doug and his brother, David, and sister, Denise, lived in university communities from Germany to New York. His parents divorced when he was twelve, and Gordon moved cross-country with his mother, Diana, to Seattle, where, in 1969, he attended Lakeside, the premier private school in the Northwest. The new kid made an immediate impression by showing up the first day in seventies-chic attire: dress zip boots that came just above the ankle, well-tailored bell-bottoms, shirts with long cuffs and longer collars. He'd also acquired, during his dad's most recent teaching assignment in Rochester, New York, the trace of a street accent. "In a class of self-proclaimed iconoclasts," recalls classmate Brian Kinkel, "he fit right in."

Years later, Doug credited Lakeside—not Harvard, where he was admitted as a sixteen-year-old into a sophomore class—as the place that had influenced him most. A wealth of programs challenged students to get involved, to get vocal, and to get outdoors. Gordon thrived in the environment. Like most everyone else there, he was tirelessly active, physically, mentally, and socially. Especially slight of build then (having skipped two grades, he was only twelve when he entered Lakeside), he even gave freshman football a go. During a fumble-recovery drill in which Doug was paired with a much larger teammate, Gordon's rep grew. "Doug and Bill grabbed [the football] at the same time," says Kinkel. "Bill twisted and turned and yanked, but Doug held on for dear life, getting tossed around like a feisty fish being reeled in. The whole team was hollering as this spectacle went on at least a minute. Bill's evident frustration was as funny as Doug's tenacity."

By the time he was an upperclassman, Gordon was firmly established at the core of the school's charged intellectual circle. Many young Lakeside students, Gordon included, had found their voice in the antiwar protests, but as Vietnam waned, he was one of a handful of students who ramped up the debate to include every social, academic, and moral topic under the sun. The shift was radical: You were no longer so much defined by what you were against (e.g., Vietnam) as by what you were for. The family-style lunch hours, in which teachers dined at large tables with a random mix of students, became joyous, blazing free-for-alls of Socratic fireworks. Doug took particular glee in these sessions, and was especially good at staking his beliefs against any and all comers. He wasn't "just hot air, he knew his stuff," recalls a classmate, and he seemed to live to put his opinion to the public test.

But Gordon was most impressive in the classroom. He was one of two standouts in the school's advanced-placement calculus course—the other was future Microsoft founder Bill Gates. (Gates's own career track—Harvard dropout turned software genius turned world's richest man—would be vastly different from Gordon's, but in some ways equally enigmatic.) Gates and Gordon were good friends; the two of them were fixtures in a basement student lounge, where they spent their senior years skirmishing against each other in chess, wonkishly battling over algebraic theory, and tinkering together on one of Gates's pet projects—an early personal computer.

"There were five or six guys in the advanced calculus class," says Lakeside alum David Halpern. "Fred Goodman, a young guy just out of Harvard and extremely bright, taught the class. I remember the first test: We all got there early, had our pencils sharpened and the whole bit. I think Bill sauntered in about halfway through and scratched a few things. The next day Fred said we'd all done well, got our A's and B's and stuff, but he said, 'Bill posed a question a little more interesting than the question I posed and here it is. . . .' From that point on, Doug, Bill, and Fred were the only ones who followed. I mean, you have to understand we were all bright—my father was a physicist, my mother a mathematician—but I just didn't know what the hell they were talking about most of the time and neither did anybody else. Their intellect was staggering."

Gates didn't share Doug's outdoor interests—a part of Doug's life that was already beginning to compete for his time. A stellar young history teacher named Dwight Gibb had introduced kayaking to Gordon his junior year. The program at Lakeside was unusually advanced for the time: Students made their own boats (pouring fiberglass into ready-made boat forms) and raced one another on a whitewater course with gates strung above it. Upperclassmen were expected to mentor the younger students. Gibbs wasn't hellbent on creating Olympic paddlers—though he did—but he believed the precision required of weaving in and out of gates improved one's skills much faster than blitzing down rivers.

By the fall of 1972, the start of Doug's senior year, he was in love with the sport. Through the school's club, he'd surveyed everything whitewater had to offer—slalom racing, weekend trips in the Cascades. And that summer, like the rest of the small but ardent U.S. paddling community, he'd watched on TV as a miracle unfolded. An obscure nineteen-year-old American paddler by the name of Jamie McEwan had gone to the Munich Olympics and overcome the heavily favored Europeans to capture a bronze medal. He was the first American ever to win a medal in whitewater, a new sport added to the Olympic roster. Inspired, Doug was one of several would-be slalom racers who now were asking themselves, *If he could do it, why not me?*

At the same time, Doug's orientation was decidedly Western—he adored competition, but he also felt the pull of big, bombing rivers. In the summer of 1972, around the same time Jamie won his medal, *Sports Illustrated* brought the maniacal edge of the sport into the national limelight by publishing a riveting diary account of a big-water descent on the Alsek in Canada and Alaska. Walt Blackadar, a forty-nine-year-old Idaho doctor who'd been paddling only a few years, "looked in the mirror and realized I wasn't getting younger," took out a two-week accident policy for $50,000, and solo kayaked the most savage stretch of rapids anyone had ever heard of. Blackadar's survival of sheer-walled Turnback Canyon, the crux of the run, would later be likened to a psychological barrier–busting, Everest-like achievement. He'd done what people said couldn't be done: He'd run a big, high-volume river, lived to tell about it, and given a glimpse of what might be possible in the future. He also wrote in a way that jolted upright any river runner who'd ever felt fast water beneath him. "So I paddled furiously through the easiest spot to crash the roller, which was well to the right of center, accepting the risk of plummeting into a terrible hole some distance below should I fail to roll up in time," he wrote. (Moments earlier he'd narrowly avoided huge icebergs that were calving off a glacier.) "Got my paddle and body through the wave and hung on upside down, feeling my boat tear apart above me. Missed my roll and in fact found I was outside the kayak. My first instinct was to swim to the surface, but instead I snuggled back into the overturned boat. Before I could roll up, the kayak washed into the feared hole. I got scrubbed, tumbled and shaken; rolled and missed—rolled and missed. Finally I caught a breath, calmed my nerves, jammed my knees solidly into the side of the boat and on my sixth try made a perfect roll and popped up. . . ."

Before Blackadar, and especially after him, Gordon and a whole generation of young Western paddlers believed that the real fun—the ultimate goal, even—was to apply the skills they'd honed on gated racecourses and put them to the test on great wilderness rapids in far-flung, do-or-die gorges. Doug and his classmate Halpern, who trained and raced together and ran rivers every weekend their senior year, hatched plans to tackle all the Northwest's epics: the Skykomish, the Nooksack, the Stillie, and Tumwater Canyon.

But by the next fall, Gordon was at Harvard—not exactly the place for unrequited big-water river runners. Cambridge's languorous Charles River was about as interesting as bathtub water.

Still, he posted notices looking for a training companion, taking advantage of a few downstream stretches where the river coughed up a rapid or two. With gates on the river prohibited, Gordon found a painstaking solution by burying sixteen-foot-long dowels in the river mud. "We called it the River Chuck," says Lamar Sims, a Harvard buddy. "We would paddle up-Chuck and down-Chuck." Almost every weekend they drove somewhere and raced.

Gordon motored through Harvard, completing his chemistry major in three years and graduating in 1977 magna cum laude. Though his athletic career wasn't at all certain—Olympics or no Olympics, whitewater was still an immensely obscure sport—his academic one was: He was a star in the making. He accepted a job in Palo Alto as a research chemist but left after two years, disenchanted with pesticide-making work and eager to get back to racing. Thus began the true challenge of challenges: balancing life, sport, and genius-level promise. In 1979 he relocated to Connecticut, took a job teaching chemistry at a small private school, and fell in with a spirited band of paddlers. The so-called HACKS (Housatonic Area Canoe Kayak Squad) were neither cutting-edge nor nationally known, but they were fun. Doug Gordon and Jamie McEwan, who lived in Connecticut too, quickly became their champions. To Gordon's immense embarrassment, they dubbed him the Kayak God of New England. "Doug's frankness could rub people the wrong way," says E. J. McCarthy, a wisecracking construction worker who became Gordon's unlikely protégé. "Some people thought he was aloof—even though he was anything but once you got to know him." The HACKS, better known for winning the post-race parties than the races themselves, lightened up the cerebral Gordon. "We always said that Doug brought us up a couple notches and we brought him down a couple," says McCarthy. "It was good for everyone."

McEwan and Gordon became particularly close. Their friendship dated back to the 1981 U.S. Whitewater Slalom Trials in South Bend, Indiana. McEwan happened to be watching as Gordon began losing gas in a long flatwater stretch—his first-ever berth on the national team slipping away. An animated McEwan swung into action, racing along the riverbank and imploring him to dig deep. Gordon did, getting the time he had to get to make the team by a second and a half (in fact, the guy he beat out for the last spot, and one he'd never beaten previously, was his Lakeside rival, David Halpern). Getting cheered by America's best-known paddler had certainly given him a boost. Afterward, an uncharacteristically giddy Gordon tracked down McEwan to thank him.

Jamie, an unpublished novelist, and Doug, a lapsed academic, found they had more than boating in common. The two became instant friends, and in the mid-1980s Gordon and McEwan started training together on the Housatonic in northwest Connecticut. By 1985 the two trained hours a day, year round, and had an almost Bunyanesque reputation. In winter, when other racers were headed to sunny southern climes, Gordon and McEwan were cracking ice off their paddles, their decks, and their faces and paddling up-stream and upwind in subzero windchill. What possessed them is hard to fathom. There was no Olympics (whitewater had been dumped as an Olympic sport after Munich), no money to be made, no prestige to be earned. "We weren't thinking the 'O' word," says Cathy Hearn, a world-champion D.C. racer who moved to Connecticut in the eighties to train with Jamie, Doug, Bruce Lessels, and others. "We were thinking, 'How can I kick Bruce's ass this afternoon—gee, I hope it's really snowing and blowing, because he's gonna be a wimp.'"

Jamie and Doug set the virile tone, pushing each other on the river and teasing each other off it. "It was good-natured, but there was a lot of Harvard this and Yale that or kayak this and canoe that," says Hearn. "We pretty much reveled in this kind of *uhrr* attitude." What seemed to distinguish them most, as U.S. team coach Bill Endicott said, was a willingness to put much more into it than it was worth. Of course, in the competitive arena it didn't hurt to have a psychological edge. They were the all-weather crazies from New England. Who could compete with guys who'd go through what they went through? When asked about it, Gordon simply joked that he couldn't stand the heat in D.C., where most elite paddlers trained. "I'm a shade guy," he said.

In the late eighties, Doug began to feel he had reached his potential. He didn't want to hang on if he wasn't getting better and beating guys who were beating him. If he had any doubt about exiting racing and moving on, he didn't after meeting Connie. A beautiful, green-eyed architectural engineering student at University of Colorado, Connie met Doug on the Housatonic River the summer after graduation. She was just dubbing around, an energetic though surprisingly adept beginner, who was living at home in upstate New York for the summer and had taken up paddling to avert terminal boredom. She'd managed to hook up with some of the HACKs faithful, and soon became a regular on the Housatonic. Over the course of the summer the two bumped into each other both on the river and at Clarke Outdoors, the boating shop where Doug worked. Everyone knew he liked Connie, but she was seeing someone else. Shortly before he left for Mexico that September and his first expedition paddling trip with Wick Walker, Doug was still waiting on

Connie. "If Connie breaks up with that guy, I'll ask her out when I get back," he promised friends. Then he added jokingly, "If she doesn't break up with him, then she's gotta be too dumb for me anyway."

The two-week trip to Mexico ended well for Doug; he and the others explored several remote limestone gorges, and Wick snapped a memorable picture of him (it would later be a sponsor's poster) playing in a rainbow-shaded hole near the misty base of three-hundred-foot Tamul Falls. The photo seemed to capture everything that needed to be said about paddling wild rivers: Doug's boat seemingly defying physical laws, with its bow half stuck, javelin-like, into the frothy depths and its bright red stern rising vertically against the cascade behind him. Doug's head is inches above the boil, his mouth gaping wide for a gulp of air.

And there was welcome news at home, too: Connie had broken up with the guy after all. There were a fair number of women (and men) who weren't exactly sure what made Doug tick—he could be aloof—but Connie figured she had a fair idea. He was a lot like her: rational, smart, and definitely driven. He was also fun and extremely handsome. Doug lived at the River House, a rambling structure turned whitewater training compound. Jamie and his wife owned it. There weren't many amenities in the old farmhouse, but there didn't need to be; it was located a few feet downstream of the Falls Village hydroelectric dam. Releases literally surged past their backyard. What else did a boater need? There were always paddlers coming and going, and barbecues on the weekends.

The group's passion for whitewater was contagious, and Connie got swept along. River dates with Doug turned into biking dates, then turned into skiing outings. In the winter she and Doug would pile into a car, stop somewhere in the Green Mountains, strap on skis, and go. They didn't exactly know where they were going, and didn't care. Rarely did they find themselves on actual trails. Instead they'd bull their way through heaps of ungroomed snow and low-slung pine boughs. They called it jungle skiing, their specialty. Both seemed to find something in the mountains they needed. Connie, an expert-level Nordic skier who used to train with the ski team at CU, said that when she went fast, she felt the stuff that nagged her just race away. There was an immediate understanding that amid the whirl of unknowns—career, racing, and their relationship, to name three—one thing was certain: Their future, if they could swing it, lay in the mountains.

In 1987, Doug retired from slalom racing and a year later took a "real job" at Advanced Technology Materials (ATM), a chemical company in Danbury that produced coating solutions for silicon chips. In 1989, Doug and Connie were married on a piece of land the pair had bought on the Housatonic. The reception was at Jamie's house. Using blueprints Connie made up, and after a year's worth of backbreaking weekends, they hammered in the last nail and finished what Connie modestly called a barn-style "New Englandy thing." They planned to stay in the East indefinitely, but Doug's meteoris rise through the ranks at ATM (they'd promoted him to department manager, a job title usually reserved for a Ph.D) had an unintended effect. Doug got bored, losing interest in the mundane work of what he described as "ordering stuff." What captivated him, in the same way that whitewater did, was the edge-of-the-world stuff. Start with an unsolvable problem—a death-defying rapid or a chemical riddle—and find a line through it. In 1993 their first child, Tyler, was born. A year later they relocated to Salt Lake City, leaving behind the home they'd built for another new start: Doug would finally get busy on his Ph.D. while Connie took on her first corporated job, a well-paying, family-supporting post at a major downtown architectural firm. Connie isn't sure why Doug chose the University of Utah; he could have gone anywhere. "I guess we needed to find a city that was booming a little economically since I needed to support us," she says. "And I think Doug knew that I needed to have snow or else I'd go crazy."

Even with a couple of thousand miles between them, Jamie and Doug stayed tight. In the summers they did river trips, and in the winter Jamie traveled out to Salt Lake to ski powder in the Wasatch. Jamie was amazed at how cleanly Doug had cut the cord from competitive paddling. (He did make a casual comeback attempt in time for the 1992 Olympics in Barcelona, but that was more an excuse to train with, and spur on, Jamie, a medal favorite.) If he wasn't getting any better, he moved on. End of discussion. When he scouted rapids, he didn't hem and haw. He looked at it, figured out the string of moves, and acted. They were both aggressive, but Doug was just a little bit more at ease in the big-water environment. He was happy and challenged, Jamie reported back to his wife, Sandy, after a winter 1997 visit. He said Doug and Connie's newborn son, Bryce, was beautiful. Doug and he were no longer roomies, but nothing had changed. The river was always a powerful touchstone, easily making up for time and distance away. The promise of the Tsangpo challenge offered the kind of extreme athletic focus their relationship thrived on.

≋

THE TSANGPO OPPORTUNITY DIDN'T ACTUALLY COME UP AT THE most convenient of times. Having completed his research, with only the write-up left, Doug had job prospects hinging on his finding the time to get it done. Dr. Joel Miller, the chair of

Doug's Ph.D. committee, wondered briefly if he should even grant his ace student a sabbatical. It wasn't exactly according to protocol, and a few of his colleagues raised their eyebrows. But Miller figured Gordon had earned his time off. He had worked hard, punching out important research and winning himself a prestigious National Science Foundation fellowship in the process. He was one of the few NSF fellows in the university's history. Miller made a deal with Gordon. He'd give him the time off, but Gordon had to do something for him—get his research in order and present it at a major conference in France. Gordon wasn't exactly thrilled. The conference was days before the team's planned departure for Tibet. The scientists in attendance wouldn't be breezing through on holiday; they were the elite in Doug's field of research, an esoteric branch of chemistry investigating molecular magnets. Ten years earlier, Miller and his associates had serendipitously stumbled upon a discovery with revolutionary possibilities: They had combined molecules to form a nonmetallic material with magnetic properties. Unlike countless other molecular magnets synthesized in subsequent years, Miller's compound was one of the few that were magnetic at room temperature (most molecular magnets became magnetic at far less practical minus-100-degree Fahrenheit temperatures). Yet the precise reason the reaction occurred, or the active chemical root that produced Miller's mystery material, had never been explained. This was the essence of Doug's work, and while he was drawing near a persuasive theoretical answer, he didn't have the final lab evidence nailed yet.

Nonetheless, Doug did as he'd promised, flying transatlantic to present his work on the baffling creation of the compounds, known as V-TCNE, then leaving before the end of the program so he could get back home with his family.

The kids were at an even better age than when Jamie had been out to see them. The brown-haired, blue-eyed Bryce was barely one and already walking. He had a cheerful go-anywhere, do-anything demeanor that charmed everybody who met him. Tyler, months away from kindergarten, was already doing math problems. When Doug went to train or hike, the boys usually went with him—Bryce in the toddler backpack, and Tyler by his side or, when he tired, straddling his dad's shoulders. Leaving the kids and leaving Connie, who was working full-time, didn't please either Doug or Connie. Like Nancy and Roger Zbel and Jamie McEwan and Sandy, they debated the trip long and hard.

Doug's career had been derailed more than once by paddling—hell, he'd left chemistry and impoverished himself for much of the 1980s to pursue amateur whitewater racing full-time—so Connie wasn't exactly panicked about a hiatus of a couple of months. She did have her share of practical worries, though—the kids, her sanity, her work—but she steered clear of examining the flurry of pre-trip E-mails exchanged between Doug and the other team members as the trip got closer (one of Doug's roles, and probably the only one he wasn't particularly well suited for, was hoofing it around the Salt Lake City Outdoor Retailer trade show, looking for sponsors). Her bottom line was that of any young parent: She wasn't thrilled to be without her husband for two months. But she'd survive. Denying Doug the trip of a lifetime hardly seemed fair. She knew Doug on the river. She'd met and fallen in love with him on a river ten years earlier, in Connecticut. He wasn't going to do anything stupid. Moreover, the people with him—lifelong friends and paddling compadres—weren't whitewater cowboys who'd ask him to do anything stupid.

When Doug left for D.C. on September 22, Connie wasn't scared, but she wasn't naïve, either. Doug went to dangerous places, or at least what others might perceive as dangerous places. Every year or so, she knew, he had to "scratch the itch." The remote rivers he'd run in the past three years—most notably the Homathko and the Dean in British Columbia—each had seen fatalities. He clearly loved the charge of being on a big river, loved the challenge of managing the risk, making critical decisions, and, above all, executing. The question of whether he was being responsible as the father of two young children wasn't an issue in their household (which, as some people would later argue, was the only place it mattered).

Neither Doug nor Connie viewed what he did as daredevilry. Besides, he possessed the trait that defines extreme wilderness paddlers, the ability not to "lose it." On rivers in Canada, Mexico, and the western United States, he had demonstrated that he could shine when the plan went haywire—"turn lemons into lemonade," as he liked to put it to his protégé McCarthy. In the dark, oxygenless moments when a violent river was burying him, he was, somehow, poised. Thinking. Of course, a big-volume, ultra-remote Himalayan river was a more prepossessing crucible. Like the others, he'd never been on a river of the size and character of the Tsangpo. Like the others, he'd never been in a full-on "Himalayan" situation, where the thunder of the river never abates, where rapids run into rapids with no relief, where everything comes upon you so *fast.* But nobody doubted Doug was up to it. In fact, it seemed he'd been preparing for this all his life. As a purely precautionary move, Connie asked Doug to take out a life-insurance policy before he left. It wasn't a big, emotional thing, just sensible. Connie bade him farewell, pleased that she'd found it within herself to let him do what he needed to do and confident that when he returned he was going to owe her big-time.

≋

THE TEAM HAS ONLY BUDGETED A COUPLE OF PREPARATION-HEAVY days in Nepal before piling into vehicles for the long trans-Himalayan overland journey to Lhasa. Their route along the Friendship Highway, a 920-kilometer stretch of road that gains 12,000 nausea-inducing feet in elevation in the first hundred or so miles, is sure to be a taxing if scenic journey. After a brief stopover in Lhasa, they've got another several days' shuttle over even more treacherous, landslide-prone roads to reach the river put-in, two hundred miles to the southeast. Everybody on the team is accustomed to long shuttles on sketchy rural roads, but this is of a different order. Using Kathmandu, some six hundred miles away, as their gateway city, is unconventional, but Walker has his reasons. In organizing the trip, he could have avoided the caravaning marathon by flying through China instead of Nepal— the more normal route for travelers into Tibet—but he figured they were safer and less susceptible to bureaucratic mischief if they connected through Kathmandu, a well-established hub for foreigners bent on all sorts of crazy alpine escapades. Four kayaks and an arsenal of esoteric paddling equipment wouldn't necessarily get anybody's attention at the airport or at the border crossing into Zhangmu, Tibet, forty miles north of Kathmandu. Kayaking and rafting expeditions in Nepal were routine. In Chengdu, on the other hand (the gateway city in western China), they were anything but.

At least initially, Walker's plan works well. The rigmarole of customs, visas, trekking permits, and repacking their gear for transport to the border goes quickly. The team hunkers down in a small, modest inn on the outskirts of the city, away from the congestion and confusion of the bustling Thamel district, the usual site for budget travelers. On forays to the central immigration office and stores in Thamel, a few of them get a look at what they're missing. Gritty bazaars and ornate Hindu temples share sidewalk turf with outdoor shops hawking logo'd expedition hand-me-downs; with Mexican restaurants; and with cybercafés where you could browse the English-language newspaper and link up with the guy from Tahoe who was currently trying to ski off the summit of Everest. There are Sherpas from the famed Khumbu region lurking about, looking for portering jobs, and expats on every street corner eager to exchange info. At the Rum Doodle the signatures of famous Everest summitters grace a display behind the bar, an honor of no small import since they are forever more entitled to free drinks when in town. Though culturally exotic (and at times even rhapsodic), there is nothing terribly puzzling or paranoia-inducing about how to get along in Kathmandu. Walker has chosen well. Everybody knows the difference between here—a veritable info highway for globe-trotting adventurers—and Chinese Tibet is like night and day. Even Kathmandu's famous wilderness attraction, Everest, is wired in a way that familiarizes it to everyone. Everest is among the most hostile places on Earth, but it is known—almost every inch of it, seemingly. Indeed, at the other end of the Himalaya—the easternmost end of the range, where the bookend peaks of Gyala Peri and Namche Barwa ominously shield the entrance to the Tsangpo Gorge—utter mystery prevails.

Nepal, not Tibet, was the original whitewater grail. By the late sixties it was already a fixture on the hippy trekking circuit—an obvious destination for an emerging school of shaggy bohemian paddlers. Coming from Great Britain, France, Germany, Czechoslovakia, and occasionally America, they were driven by various aims, from pure wanderlust to spiritual enlightenment to sporting thrill. The free-spirited Brits (some of whom, like the Walker team, were ex–whitewater racers) dominated the earliest river-running exploits in Nepal, but other vaguely organized and underfinanced national teams soon spun out to South America, Africa, and Alaska. They applied the mind-set of cutting-edge mountaineers—move fast, move light, move boldly—with a skill set that was part explorer, part waterman, part engineer. Part of the high was the fellowship itself, part the awe-inspiring country, and part the ability to plumb a place nobody else could. Neither trekkers nor mountaineers had the tool—the then-fiberglass, load-carrying whitewater kayak—to traverse the deep primordial gorges of Nepal. At the very top of the game, there was another appeal: Nowhere on the planet were the river gorges deeper, steeper, or more challenging. In these places risk was intensely personal, intensely consequential.

The difference between Nepalese climbing and river running could be summed up in a single word: safety. Mountaineers roped up in dangerous situations; they had direct team backup. At least theoretically, if they fell they'd be caught. Boaters had no tether. The inability to breathe was only 180 degrees away. If they got into trouble in a bad place, they'd likely have to find their own way out. Help could be minutes, hours, even days away. Surviving days on end in big, pulsing whitewater, at the bottom of a bottomless canyon, was analogous to life at altitude, some said— each its own Death Zone. Whitewater was, however, far less subtle in the end. Life didn't slip from one's body, as it so hauntingly did on big Himalayan slopes, where the compounding effects of high altitude sapped energy, breath, and brain function.

On a big river, life was snatched away with incomprehensible violence. On a big river, for example, a swim—euphemistically known as a "wet exit" and a rather common method of escape—wasn't an option. If you swam, you were done for. The current of a big whitewater river dragged a human body the way it dragged an inert log, and drove it over the river's fall line. On a big mountain, success was predicated on staving off the degenerative effects of living above 25,000 feet. On a big river, success was a matter of trusting your body to boat and nature, no matter what. The Nepal river-running fraternity felt that no sport so dynamically, or so purely merged performance, risk, and self-reliance. As some put it, a big river changed you from the inside out. Often it had as much to do with sheer trauma as with anything else.

In a way, Tom McEwan finds Doug's trip role enviable: He will be free to run the river as he pleases. McEwan's role, however, as trip leader and "tone setter," is far more complicated. As leader, McEwan is well aware that if he takes on tough rapids, the implication to others is that they should do so, too. Building a supportive, noncompetitive team dynamic is critical. Things might turn disastrous if anybody on the team feels pressured—intentionally or not—to go beyond his comfort zone. It is a very fine line, however. All four boaters are by nature extremely competitive and goal-oriented, accomplished as racers.

What worries a trip leader most on extreme rivers like those in the Himalaya is a teammate getting unduly "tigerish," as the Brits like to call it—a moment when normal good sense doesn't prevail, when a rogue adrenaline override wipes out all the usual impulses *not* to do something. A decision is made not because of how you're feeling, but in spite of it. Often the result is harrowing. Almost every leading expedition paddler who takes on big-volume, deep-gorge rivers—the sport's most extreme challenge and an epicenter of which is the Himalaya—can recount a story of a moment gone horribly bad. In hindsight the death brush almost always seemed prompted by something external: by teammates laboring to raise the level of their personal game, by personal troubles, or by extensive obligations (like to sponsors). There are a thousand things that can mess with a man's judgment, that can turn an honest appraisal into a dishonest one. A day of expert whitewater paddling calls for a level of conscious and continuous risk analysis that few sports require (and on the Tsangpo there'd be an estimated forty-five days on the river, not just one). In fact, it's not unusual to hear paddlers assess a dangerous rapid with a numerical model: Is there a one-in-a-hundred chance of missing a line and getting worked in the hole? Is there another one-in-a-hundred shot that the hole might not only work you but also kill you?

The line represents the top-to-bottom, move-to-move route you intend to follow to boat through the rapid. A bad hole is the penalty you pay for either missing the line or misreading the river. Also known as a hydraulic or reversal, and often deviously hard to gauge, a hole is easily discernible from the bottom where the plunging water erupts (though holes occur anywhere on a river where falling water pours over ledge and rock). The pile-driving current causes a depression there, and water headed downstream is violently sucked back in to fill it. The result is vortexlike currents that are given robust nicknames like Jaws or Meat Cleaver or Mixmaster. Although modern-day freestylers, or "rodeo" boaters, play in benign holes intentionally, others are avoided at all costs. Generally, the bigger the water and the steeper the drop, the more powerful the hole (other factors, such as shape and width of the hole, also determine severity).

Not all holes are man-eaters. But in the worst hydraulics, also called "keepers," the currents rip to the deepest, darkest point in the riverbed, then cycle back up to the surface and back down again endlessly. Bodies and boats go along for the tormented ride. Bruised swimmers often have sandals and clothing ripped off their bodies, and because of the dramatic pressure drop, blackouts and bloody eardrums are common. In most cases the best escape is to stay in the boat, since its mass is greater than a swimmer's and it is better able to punch through the hole's imprisoning currents. In terminal holes, where the perfectly formed, wrenchingly powerful vortex won't let go, the only option is to crawl out of the boat and scrape on all fours along the riverbed, hoping that a tiny slipstream of current might leak away from the washing-machine chaos above.

"The way I used to look at bad rapids was very simple," says Norm Bellingham, who was once the youngest paddler to descend Great Falls. "I'd say, 'If a hundred Norms ran the rapid, how many would miss?' If it was one or two, I'd probably do it. More, I wouldn't." Of course, the odds-making is based on absolute honesty and a great deal of subjectivity. If external or internal distractions intrude into the assessment process, then the whole game is poisoned. It's for this reason that expedition kayakers, who rely on the adrenaline surges to sharpen their senses, also fear them. "This burst inside happens, I've seen it happen, felt it happen," says Lukas Blücher, one of the world's top expedition paddlers. "On big exposed rivers the adrenaline rush kicks in and changes your perception. For a split second you feel sort of invincible and decide to do something you never intended. You see people in car races do this, too. Suddenly and inexplicably they take this bizarre and obviously suicidal line. These are sensible, cool, calculating professionals. But if you're exposed to your own adrenaline for too long, it seems inevitable that it does you in. It's the one thing I have always feared on a Himalayan river trip more than anything."

The Himalaya accentuated everything: the dangers, the friendships, the spiritual heft of being on a magnificent stretch of wild river for days on end. Maps were either nonexistent or primitive. More important, river gorges were never part of the usable landscape in places like Nepal and Peru the way mountains were. Villages in Nepal exist up to elevations of 15,000 feet. Conversely, the habitation of gorges in Nepal and throughout the Himalaya is, for obvious reasons, rare. Local knowledge is often spotty. Wilderness rivers and their pounding rapids are the work of angry gods. The fixation of westerners with getting to the top of the tallest Himalayan mountains wasn't exactly understood in the hill villages, but after seventy-five years of expeditionary coming and goings, the Nepalese had acclimated to the idea. On the other hand, caging oneself into a wall-pinched, wave-tossed gorge was without context. Those who did it, especially in the early days, would almost always be told by locals that what they planned to do was not only impossible but certainly deadly. It was as incomprehensible as a guy scaling the steps of the World Trade Center and telling passersby along the way that he planned to fly off the top.

In 1976 a British team led by Mike Jones and Mick Hopkinson made headlines in Nepal and around the globe by "canoeing down Everest" (a tributary of the Sun Kosi, the Dudh Kosi flows through the Khumbu region and is fed by Everest's meltwater). To the astonishment of villagers lining the banks, the kayakers survived the river. When a subsequent expedition ventured down the same river four years later, the kayaks the first team had left behind were still being exquisitely cared for by Nepalese, who were under the impression they possessed supernatural value. In

1986 another British team returned with some of the same members. According to Roger Huyton, "Our sirdar told me he was talking to the owner of a teahouse who said that ten years ago 'other people came down the river—they were like gods; they had big muscles and nothing could kill them.'" The film about the Dudh Kosi descent led to a spate of Himalayan first descents and eventually to a sprawling whitewater trade in Nepal, which soon supported not just the occasional BBC or *American Sportsman* made-for-TV novelty, but well-heeled clients paying thousands of dollars for guided runs on rivers in every region of Nepal. The Nepal buzz led to explorations throughout the world's most remote and formidable riverways, including the Amazon, the Blue Nile, and even the uppermost Brahmaputra, or, as it is known in Tibet, the Yarlung Tsangpo.

Officially the Tsangpo was closed to Western adventurers, but in 1986 Arlene Burns, a free-spirited twenty-six-year-old American outdoorswoman living in Kathmandu, caught sight of it on a winter trekking trip through Tibet and vowed to paddle it. She returned to Kathmandu, hastily recruited a willing accomplice, and proceeded on an unauthorized one-hundred-mile journey from the headwaters near Mount Kailash to Shigatse. It was a trip in the spirit of the times—spontaneous, romantic, and just a little dumb. Organizing the trip in a mere four days, Burns had sixty-five dollars in her pocket and a 1920 Buddhist pilgrim's map for guidance. To avoid detection by the Chinese, she and her companion, Dan Dixon, paddled at night and slept in caves. Burns quit abruptly (and as anonymously) as she started, deciding to ditch paddling in Tibet for beachgoing in Thailand. "I was crazy, of course," says Burns, who ironically was on an apparel company's panel that approved grant money for the Walker team. "It was a trip that really just kind of emerged from the lifestyle I was leading. I'd been living and guiding in Nepal for years. Tibet was my backyard. Why not go? When it was time to end it, I ended it." The expedition, probably the Tsangpo's first by Western hands, was as different from the Walker-led professional operation that pulled into Nepal in 1998 as one could possibly imagine.

≋

THERE ARE TWO MAJOR ITEMS ON THE WALKER TEAM'S TO-DO LIST IN Kathmandu. The first item—beefing up their support team—they accomplish quickly, using the help of Jonathan Meisler, a Colorado outfitter who specializes in Himalayan alpine adventures and who accompanied Wick and Tom on the scouting trip to the Tsangpo a year earlier. Having recently completed a western Tibet mountaineering trip, he'd contracted with the Sherpas on that trip, Pemba Sherpa and Ankame Sherpa, to join the Walker team. The Sherpa support is one of the biggest reasons for electing to come to Nepal first. World-renowned as high-altitude performers and accustomed to westerners, the Sherpa help would be the team's insurance against the less reliable aid they were sure to encounter in the tiny villages that dotted the banks of the Tsangpo. Veteran travelers like Ian Baker, and even Walker on his scout the year previously, had had bad experiences. The indigenous Monpa and Lopa tribes that lived in parts of the gorge and hunted other regions were notoriously skittish about probing its depths (at least with westerners in tow). Stories were rife of overland teams being abandoned or extorted for more money. Several years earlier the porters hitched to David Breashears's team had fled in the middle of the night with all the food, days from any trailhead. Fighting incessant torrential rains, Breashears and his photographer, Gordon Wiltsie, survived by eating a dead monkey freshly killed by a panther.

The Sherpas would be the team's sirdars, heading up a still larger team of porters and local help they'd hire when they got to the gorge. Theoretically they'd set up the night's camps, but more important, they'd dole out load-carrying duties, manage disputes, and negotiate fees. They'd also help interpret. The Sherpa hirings, expensive and inconvenient, seemed an ideal solution to a less-than-ideal possibility: rebellion and abandonment in the Tsangpo hinterlands. The "leapfrog" support strategy required bodies: There would be two independent support teams, one led by Harry Wetherbee and the other by Wick, each with distinct duties and itineraries. Harry and Wick needed to be at predesignated down-river spots in order to provide the river team with food, gear, and muscle (in the cases of extreme portages). If the support team lost its guides and trailbreakers and load carriers, it might not reach the agreed-upon rendezvous spots with the boating team. Without resupply, the boating team would be without food to proceed and without climbing gear to evacuate from the gorge. The more likely abandonment scenario would come at the end of the trip, when the entire team might be faced with scaling a high, snowbound pass in order to exit the gorge and reach the roadhead. The Monpa might still run out—they had no experience with, or tolerance for, navigating the high passes in harsh winter conditions—but at least the team would have Pemba and Ankame in support.

The second order of business before departure is a visit to Ian Baker, an American expatriate who has lived in Kathmandu for twenty years and is arguably the Tsangpo region's most knowledgeable westerner. Baker is a fascination to all who meet him. Just forty-one years old, he's carved out an Indiana Jones–like career. A 1980 Middlebury College graduate turned on to Tibetan Buddhism by the prominent and theatrical scholar/author Robert Thurman, Baker's own strange journey to what he called the "Hidden Lands" began in earnest with a one-month postgraduate turn in a cave in a remote valley of Tibet. Baker had been led to the cave by a lama whom he had approached for information about Pemako, a place the lama was said to have been. The lama suggested Baker begin his pilgrimage by meditating alone for a month. Energized by the experience, Baker returned to Kathmandu, where he led trekking tours, learned to read and speak Tibetan, and collected and dealt artwork and antiquities. In the early nineties he burrowed deeper into the Hidden Lands myth, following an assortment of leads and collecting ancient monastic texts that alluringly described the Pemako region (the Tibetan name for the Tsangpo gorges region) in southeastern Tibet as an "earthly paradise and the ultimate place of pilgrimage." It wasn't just a sacred place, but, in the view of Buddhist pilgrims, the holiest place on earth. To die in Pemako, a pilgrim later told Baker, ensured rebirth in the realm of the Buddhas—the Awakened Ones. "Even to take one single step toward Pemako," Baker wrote, quoting an eighth-century sage, "is to be liberated from mundane existence."

The source of legends of Shangri-la, a mysterious geographical riddle that had confounded Western explorers for more than a century, a transformational place of outrageous natural beauty, Pemako thoroughly engrossed the adventure-seeking Baker. In a 1993 expedition organized by Rick Fisher, Baker got a slot. Shortly after setting out, he separated from the main entourage, striking out into the heart of the gorge with three trekking mates. It was the start of a series of ground explorations that Baker framed not as typical Western fare, that is, as an "exploration of physical terrain," but rather as a path that followed "indigenous models of pilgrimage and focused on the cultural topography."

Whatever it was, Baker clearly paid his dues. The 1993 journey was a true wilderness epic. Following a route etched into the jungle by Francis Kingdon-Ward some seventy years earlier, the rain-drenched, leech-riddled Baker and his companions lost their way for days, "feeding on wild animals snared with our climbing ropes until we were chanced upon by two native hunters and their dogs." On another occasion, an avalanche on one of the high passes stranded part of their party neck-deep in snow and spindrift. Local hunters told Baker that the protector spirits of the region were powerful. If a journey was taken purely for self-advancement—in other words, in contrast to Buddhist beliefs and tradition—they believed the spirits would go to extraordinary lengths, avalanches and rock-falls included, to deny them access to the land's innermost secrets. In subsequent journeys, Baker used the narratives of his ancient texts as guides and became more reliant on the local knowledge of hunters.

As a sometime anthropologist, Baker found himself intrigued by what he called "the sacred hunt." In apparent contradiction to Buddhist teachings, the local Tibetans of the gorge aggressively tracked and killed a rare animal called the takin, related to mountain goats. There was an ornate set of rituals associated with the kill, and according to Baker's reading of the ancient text, the Pemako takin had been deemed a sacramental species for the region's inhabitants. Year after year, Baker followed the hunt, and slowly but surely the hunters, who had at first refused to acknowledge any trails deep in the gorge's unexplored heart, began to take him into the farthest reaches. Baker explains his patient, years-in-the-making breakthrough as the result of local hunters finally persuaded that he was in the region for the right reasons, a true selfless pilgrim—albeit a bearded one with a DVD camera. Whether they confided in him for the reasons he believes, or simply because he wore them down, is impossible to know, but Baker's industriousness paid off in the fall of 1997. Three clients of his—a Minnesota bookseller named Ken Storm (who'd accompanied Baker on the 1993 epic) and a pair of Arizonans, Gil and Troy Gillenwater (who'd been with Fisher on his ill-conceived rafting run)—splintered off from a Baker-led trip to do a reconnaissance on the flanks of Namche Barwa.

In a series of fortuitous circumstances (not the least of which was not getting caught, since they didn't have the appropriate permits), the trio stumbled upon an apparent discovery. From a ridge overlooking the gorge, the perpetual cloud cover dramatically parted to reveal an enormous and uncharted waterfall thumping into the abyss. Storm, in particular, was ecstatic. He pronounced what was before them—though at some distance—was nothing less than the long-lost falls of the Brahmaputra, the gargantuan cascade that British explorers had prominently (and with complete futility) searched for in the late 1800s, but had written off by the early 1920s. The trio made a pact with Baker, agreeing to hold off an announcement to the media until they made a return trip in the fall to instrument-measure and photographically document the cascade.

In the spring of 1998, Baker returned to the region with colleague and friend Hamid Sardar and a leading adventure filmmaker, Ned Johnston. Sardar had persuaded his adviser at Harvard University, Bob Gardner, to help underwrite the expedition, pitching their upcoming journey as a documentary look at the Monpa's sacred hunt. The project appealed to Gardner, an anthropological filmmaker who directed the prestigious filmstudies center at the university. From the start, according to

Johnston, both Baker and Sardar were obviously distracted with the business of the waterfall. After an initial attempt to find the takin herd with a band of hunters, Sardar and Baker instructed the guides to take them into the area where Storm and the Gillenwaters had been. Unaware of the change in plan and feeling duped, Johnston was irate. When they reached the ridge, Sardar insisted the hunter guide get them closer. They traveled through dense jungle that finally dead-ended on a 1,000-foot bluff almost directly overlooking the falls. The view was magnificent, and both Baker and Sardar shot film. Obligated to get a film made of the hunt, the team left the perch soon thereafter in an attempt to catch up with the herd. A week later the guides announced that the herd had gone up to higher pastures and that the pursuit was futile.

The trio was invited to come back next year. As disappointed as Johnston was, Baker and Sardar knew they were on the brink of a huge announcement. With the new knowledge of both the falls and a vast network of trails throughout the unexplored inner part of the gorge—the five-mile gap previously unseen by Western eyes—they made plans to return in the fall to complete their historic survey. "I was duped in a way," says Johnston. "But I still liked Baker a lot. He's a great storyteller and I found him very sympathetic. What exactly his motives were or his agenda was I never really figured out. But like a lot of great storytellers, he doesn't always let the facts get in the way of a great story."

Weeks prior to the Walker team's arrival in Kathmandu, they and Baker had convened at Harry Wetherbee's house in McLean, Virginia. As it turns out, Baker had been recommended to the team as a gold mine of a resource by National Geographic. Geographic staff had met with him and Steve Currey in early August—Baker then agreeing to be part of Currey's massive proposed expedition in the lower Tsangpo region. (Later, critics of Baker's would say his willingness to be part of an aggressive, high-impact expedition revealed a less comely, more opportunistic trait.) Rebecca Martin of the NGS Expedition Council wasn't interested in Currey (or in his kayaking allies, Scott Lindgren and Charlie Munsey), but asked Baker when he planned to return. Baker told her of his forthcoming and as yet unfinanced expedition in October to explore the five-mile gap left by Kingdon-Ward after his 1924 expedition to the Tsangpo. Martin encouraged him to write a proposal for sponsorship. "I was told that this was the kind of expedition they wanted to promote," says Baker. Maryanne Culpepper of National Geographic television also expressed interest in wanting to send a cameraman on the expedition to make a film that would "contrast with Wick's kayaking expedition, which, as she expressed it, was approaching the region in a very . . . high tech [way]." Baker followed up with a proposal, but had heard nothing when he met with the Walker team.

Baker was an important resource for Walker. He was the only person at the time to whom they felt they could entrust their plans and maps. In McLean, and later in Kathmandu, the team shared their cache of topo maps and satellite photographs of the Tsangpo. In turn, Baker told them about his momentous eighteen-day, inner-gorge journey in 1993, which had extended from the team's proposed put-in point below Pe to a kilometer or so above Rainbow Falls. That trip, organized by Fisher had originally been drawn up as a rafting adventure, with Baker signing on despite never having rafted before. "I told them clearly that there was no way I would ever attempt to run such a river," says Baker, acknowledging that he was anything but a seasoned river-runner. Baker also told the team about a 1996 expedition in which he had attempted to "close the gap" from the Tsangpo's western bank as it flowed northward into the Great Bend. In river terms this was "river-left," the side of the Tsangpo that Walker and company thought offered the only opportunity for a successful descent. "We had not been able to follow the river upstream toward Rainbow Falls, but instead reached a small col or pass on a spur of Gyala Peri that looked down on the Pemakochung region of the gorge," says Baker. "There were clear animal tracks leading down into the gorge, and I told Harry that this pass could serve as an important 'escape route' if the kayaking team was not able to continue further downriver into the steepest sections of the gorge below Rainbow Falls."

Walker left the brief meeting in Kathmandu pleased and feeling that Baker had been both gracious in spirit and fairly generous with information. Yet it was a strange and more than slightly awkward situation. The world's most prestigious exploration society was potentially bankrolling two teams bound for the exact same place at the exact same time. Baker had objectives—namely, measuring the waterfalls and continuing downstream into the unexplored regions of the gorge—that might or might not coincide with the Walker team's exploratory probe. Baker elected not to tell Walker about either the new waterfall he'd spied a few months earlier or the network of trails and cave shelters on the Tsangpo's right bank, deep in the inner gorge. Well after both teams' trips, Baker would argue that the information he withheld had no relevance to the Walker team. Yet, at the time, he told friends he felt morally conflicted in not telling his fellow explorers all he knew.

Clearly, Baker's interest in the region was far different from that of Walker and company. Baker saw himself as someone who had both literally and figuratively put in the legwork. His was a journey in sync with the surroundings, not in opposition to them.

In truth, he thought assailing the Tsangpo with high-tech plastic boats was the height of nonsense, that reducing a region teeming with spirituality and wonderment to a freakish sporting challenge was a farce. He cooperated with them to the extent that he did because he liked them—and, one assumes, because he hoped to stay in the good graces of Geographic. Different as the two team's agendas were—at least in Baker's view—their objectives for their October trips were actually remarkably similar: to see the parts of the river that hadn't been seen, as close to the waterline as possible. To penetrate the inner gap. According to Paulo Castillo, the team's videographer, Walker was keen about trekking into the small pass Baker had told him about and cutting a trail to river level. He didn't need Baker to tell him there were huge waterfalls in there; he had the maps. "Wick talked about it all the time," says Castillo. "That was his goal. To get in there and take a look." Walker, of course, was familiar with the literature, with Kingdon-Ward, with Bailey and Morshead, with Kintup. For him the expedition was never a one-dimensional whitewater trip. It was an exploration, by land, by water, however.

≈

ON THE EVE OF THE OVERLAND DEPARTURE, SEPTEMBER 25, THE team is set. Permits are in hand, trucks packed to the gills. Back in the States, word is out among the interested big-water boating rivals that the Walker-McEwan team is moving forward. A mere handful of people have boated on Himalayan big-volume rivers at high water. In almost every case it was not intentional; they got caught on a river that rose suddenly, and they rode it out until they could escape overland. The idea of running the Everest of rivers, the biggest of the big-volume, deep-gorge rivers, at high water is hard to fathom—especially to those who have a stake in the action themselves. In a phone call to the well-known white-water expeditionist Richard Bangs, an agitated Steve Currey is beside himself. "Those guys are headed out there!" he growls. "They're gonna kill themselves."

The team is gathered in the courtyard of their Nepalese-style guest house when Walker decides it's time to confront the same topic. "If the worst happens and somebody dies on the river," he asks, "what's our plan?" Quit, carry on, what? Would they extract the remains, or limit their risk-taking to a rescue only? It's not the sort of thing river runners, or anybody else for that matter, much like to talk about, but bringing the subject up is completely consistent with Wick's hard-boiled philosophy. As trip leader with Tom he needs to know now, he says, before the emotions and fatigue of the trip take over, how far they're going to take this. Still, the creepiness of the subject, coupled with the formality with which it's raised (and the fact that it's all of a sudden being filmed for posterity), throws off some of the team members. Nobody says a thing initially—except Doug. "I don't think any of us will forget the moment," says Roger Zbel, who'd been silently brooding about the death question, wondering and worrying whether they had a back-down point. "Doug was just so straight on about it. He said if it happened to him he was gone and it didn't matter. He wouldn't want us to quit just because of him. He'd want the rest of us to go on. But as soon as we get off the river, the obligation was first and foremost to the family. He also said if somebody else on the team was lost, he probably wouldn't have the heart to keep going."

≋ As we parted, the easygoing Tibetan said
≋ something that was to serve me in good stead.
The haste of Europeans has no place in Tibet. We must
learn patience if we wished to arrive at the goal.

—HEINRICH HARRER, AUTHOR OF *SEVEN YEARS IN TIBET,*
WRITING ABOUT ONE OF HIS DETAINMENTS
DURING HIS EPIC TRANS-HIMALAYA ODYSSEY TO REACH
THE FORBIDDEN CITY OF LHASA

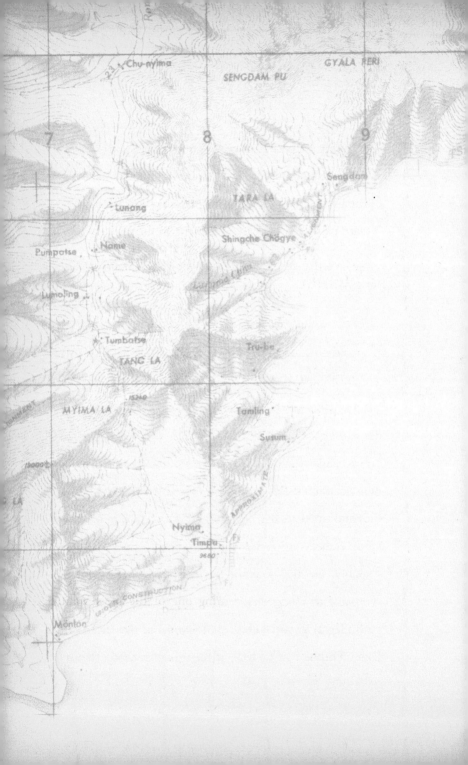

Lhasa, Tibet,
September 29, 1998

LATE MORNING IN THE BARKHOR, THE CITY'S OLD QUARTER. The bustling market square is heating up, the sellers' ramshackle, cloth-covered stalls offering dried fruit and grains, devotional textiles, kitschy yak skulls, and the ever-popular orange paperback, *Say It in Tibetan.* At Lhasa's 9,000-foot-plus elevation the sun is intense, scorching the square's pale tiles and the bare, dry hills in the distance. Chinese surveillance cameras ring the gilded roofs of the square, presumably on the lookout for suspicious gatherings or sympathetic westerners bearing one of the most wanted (and illegal) import items: photographs of the exiled Dalai Lama. On the eastern edge of the square a steady stream of murmuring, shuffling Tibetans pass by, walking the popular half-mile pilgrimage circuit around the Jokhang, the ornate seventh-century temple that is the city's religious heart.

Roger Zbel, Jamie McEwan, and Doug Gordon, having pulled in late yesterday after a grueling day and a half on the road, wade into the clockwise-flowing current of prostrating monks, child beggars, harvest-celebrating farmers, and plains nomads. The monks' famous mantra—*Om Mani Padme Hum* ("Hail to the Jewel in the Lotus")—hums in the background while pilgrims beckon in the here and now for more tangible blessings. *"Guchi, guchi,"* they sweetly beg the Americans. "Please, please."

This touristing, the earlier calls to home, and the opportunity to dash off a few postcards, provide welcome relief from the overland grind. They've been away a week and still are nowhere near the river. A little self-consciously, Doug, then Roger and Jamie, spin one of the large golden prayer wheels on the *khora* circuit. Each cylindrical wheel is filled with upwards of a mile of prayers, which are "repeated" with the revolutions of the wheel. To the pilgrims a spin earns devotional merit and focuses the mind on the mantras and prayers they are reciting. The ceremonial twirl of the prayer wheel is a clichéd staple of films chronicling Western adventurers bound for the Forbidden Himalaya, but in this case the gesture actually has meaning. To the visitors from America, this invocation of Higher Powers—given what they've seen already—seems like a pretty good idea.

On yesterday's drive they saw the upper river for the first time. Near Lhatse, about three hundred miles upstream of Lhasa, and about five hundred miles from the gorge, the water was running big and wide. Later in the day, closer to Lhasa, they took several bankside inspections at a point where the river funneled slightly into a small canyon: The current looked stunningly powerful. Zbel piled out from one of the three Land Cruisers they'd hired and shook his head in disbelief. "This is huge!" he blurted out. The volume of water pushing through a dusty desert landscape was hard to comprehend. All around was this seemingly infinite stretch of arid, empty territory, and yet through it coursed the widest, deepest river he'd ever seen. As they paralleled the Tsangpo for dozens more miles, Zbel became increasingly troubled. All the river's gradient and "gorginess" (not to mention two major tributaries) lay downstream, yet flood damage was everywhere: roads eaten away by the recent flows or covered with rockpiles. Bridges washed out. Local after local said the same thing: These were the highest waters in years. Though unreported in the West, the 1997–98 winter had been one of the worst in recent memory. Abnormally large amounts of snow and an extended and especially brutal cold spell gripped the same west-central high plateau region the Tsangpo drained. The deep freeze wiped out 20 percent of the livestock herd. Months later the resulting melt-off, then the late-occurring monsoon, compounded the damage. How did the monsoon season stack up to others? Zbel asked Pemba Sherpa to query villagers and road workers en route. "Don't know," one replied. "I have never seen it rain this much."

In banging around Lhasa, everybody got their minds off the river, but once they sat down, they were abruptly refocused. Sitting next to them at the just-off-the-square Snowlands restaurant was Lukas Blücher, the German paddler who was rumored to be considering a run himself. Blücher, having breakfast with his sister, had overheard the trio talking in detail about the gorge's profile and something that sounded like "bungy jumping" and couldn't help himself.

"Are you from Currey's team or something?" said the heavily accented Blücher, mistaking them for the American rafting contingent led by Steve Currey. A little stunned to be in the company of a rival Western boater, and echoing ever so slightly the what-are-you-doing-here awkwardness that occurred when Rick Fisher and David Breashears clashed four years earlier, the tea-drinking Americans swallowed hard and cautiously offered that they were not. "So you must be the Walker-McEwan team, yes?"

The tension broke almost immediately. The German was friendly, charming even. They were not adversaries, he suggested, the river was the adversary. Blücher went on to introduce himself fully. He had been on the go for months, trying to put his trip together. He had taken a much different tack from the Americans in dealing with the Chinese: He had gone "front channel," cultivating Beijing contacts, and going so far as traveling to the capital city a few weeks earlier to nail down his permits. He had paid a price, but not the exorbitant one feared by Walker. He had, in fact, gained permission to run the entire gorge right down to the Indian border, an achievement the table marveled over.

Blücher said he had tried to correspond with the Americans months ago, but had received a rather brusque E-mail from Wick or Tom. The team apologized, explaining that they wanted to keep a low profile as the trip drew near. Blücher nodded vigorously, understanding their desire to steer clear of the ruthlessness that seemed to be overtaking everyone. In early 1998 he'd been invited to be part of the same program with Steve Currey, then he'd found out Currey was going around his back and making plans without him. "That was my brief contact with Currey," Blücher confessed. "I don't need any more."

Blücher and Gordon, each in their early forties, hit it off particularly well. Blücher said he'd once been, and hoped again to be, an academic. A former physics student, he simply had been distracted in recent years by a profitable business and lots of rivers. In some ways, he said, his best years might be behind him—he was married now and the father of a young son—but the passion to run hard whitewater seemed to grow if anything, not abate. In comparing river lists, it turned out Blücher's team made the first descent of the Homathko in Canada, a run that Gordon, Jamie, and E. J. McCarthy were among the few to duplicate. River people are quick to size each other up. In the brief exchange, both Blücher and Gordon knew they were not only eminently compatible to share a cup of *cha* in a tourist restaurant, but to run rivers together. Before they said good-bye, they made plans to do so someday.

Blücher's big news was that he'd already scouted near the put-in just upstream of Pe. Pulling out his DVD camera, he asked the others if they wanted to see some of the video he'd taken a week before. Gordon was the first to take a look. The river he saw was out of its banks, 2.5 kilometers wide.

"It's a fuckin' lake," said Gordon, handing the DVD player to Jamie, who in turn passed it to Roger. If they were stunned by their first glimpse of the river yesterday, they were mortified now. According to Blücher, heavy rains in the east days earlier had aggravated the situation, causing the major tributary that flows into the Tsangpo upstream of Pe to overflow. "I don't know if we'll be able to do anything," lamented Gordon. Blücher nodded again. He said he planned to do some more scouting, but he wouldn't be running the gorge. Not this season, at least.

The trio invited Blücher back to the team's hotel to meet Tom McEwan and Wick Walker. In the spirit of cooperation, Walker shared maps with Blücher, showing him their "sky shots" of the gorge. Blücher provided some data on seasonal water levels on the Tsangpo. They were all perfectly simpatico except for one thing, thought Blücher. The team wasn't going to back off. Blücher left with the impression that the team's organizers weren't inclined even to delay. By his reckoning the team was planning to launch far earlier than he would, even in an average year (in the right conditions, Blücher was hoping to do so in late fall or early winter). Of course, this was no average year. Because of the record monsoon, the river was anywhere from four to seven weeks behind schedule in coming down. "The people who had done all the organization obviously were in a hurry to get to the gorge," recalls Blücher, noting that their plans called for reboarding the Land Cruisers later that afternoon for the final push to Pe. "They basically said, 'Thank you but we must go now.' They were kind of like, you know, when you drive horses? They were really chasing them out of that hotel. The kayakers were, I wouldn't say put off, but having seen the pictures I showed them, they appeared quite cautious."

Hours later, Blücher dashed off an E-mail to Doug Ammons, his would-be paddling partner from the States, about his run-in with the Walker-McEwan team. "If I could," he wrote, "I'd want to advise them to put their gear in the barn and come back next year and tell their sponsors that they'd called it off before they spent too much. In retrospect I don't know whether I should have said something directly or not. Sometimes I feel it was right not to say, because they got the message anyway."

Roger Zbel in particular heard the message. The rush to stay on schedule seemed to miss the point. The river was plainly unrunnable. Why not scrap the itinerary, suggested Zbel, and map out another first descent in one of the upstream canyons near the India border (a plan Blücher was also interested in). "He certainly seemed to be telling us not to go," says Zbel. "I can't speak for anyone else, but after what Lukas had to say and having seen the river upstream of Lhasa, I just felt really nervous and really reluctant to even want to put on."

≋

ALMOST FALSTAFFIAN IN APPEARANCE, ROGER ZBEL WASN'T CUT from the same cloth as the others. Big-boned, rosy-cheeked, his face awash in a flowing orange-blond beard, the forty-two-year-old looked more like the merrymaking protagonist of the children's book *King Bidgood's in the Bathtub* than an Olympic-class athlete (which he was). He could be a little unruly and very outspoken, but he could also be extremely sweet. Often his voice—which had operatic-sized heft in a river canyon—registered no louder than a whisper with a newly met stranger. His three teammates, and Walker, too, were more emotionally restrained, not eager to show their hands. But Roger didn't hold much back. When his beloved Lab had died a few years back, he'd wept like a baby—and he didn't mind people knowing that. His background was different from the others', too. He'd never gone to college, much less an Ivy League one like the rest of the team. He'd been on only one expedition, and that had been twelve years earlier, with different partners. For the latter reason he wasn't the Tsangpo team's first choice.

Wick had initially contacted him about the trip in May. They'd been out of touch for years, but back in the late seventies and early eighties, when Wick was stationed nearby, they'd regularly paddled the local rivers. Back then Roger was well on his way to becoming a local legend in West Virginia paddling circles, both for his ballsy runs in high-water conditions and for his dominance of almost any downriver race he chose to enter.

In early summer Zbel got another call, this one letting him know they'd awarded the last spot to John Weld. Tom McEwan explained that the decade-younger Weld, a student of his from the Valley Mill days, was simply somebody they'd paddled with more and who possessed the kind of expeditionary experience they were looking for. A disappointed Zbel couldn't really argue. He'd never organized, nor been a part of, a high-profile expedition. He'd wanted to, but he'd always seemed tied up with something or other. Besides, the Allegheny and Appalachian Rivers in his own corner of the world—choice Eastern whitewater runs like the Gauley, Cheat, and Youghiogheny—rarely left him wanting for something better. Zbel thanked McEwan for the consideration, and told him he'd keep training in case somebody on the team canceled at the last minute. At the time he had no doubt he'd take the slot if they offered it.

From the time he was a kid, growing up in suburban D.C., he'd fantasized about going to the Himalaya and climbing Mount Everest. Everest wasn't going to happen at his age and income, he knew, but he saw the Tsangpo as an irresistible substitute. He wasn't a student of Tsangpo literature and lore (unlike his teammates, he had only vaguely heard of it), nor was he really intent on "pushing the boundaries" of the sport (the way Wick and Tom sometimes explained their motivation), but he felt ripe for a big challenge. The Tsangpo offered a parallel version of Everest—only they'd be heading to the bottom of the world, of course, not the top.

When the trip finally became a go with the funding from National Geographic, the entire team confirmed, with the surprising exception of Weld. Over the summer he'd had a bunch of second thoughts. He and his wife, Kara, a national team paddler herself, were in the throes of starting a river apparel business. The high-performance, fashion-friendly duds were proving a hit with the skateboard-aged crowd. He was looking at the prospects for earning a decent future living. He also felt the trip was a little more ponderous than he was comfortable with. His specialty—multiday, self-contained trips to places like Baffin Island, Newfoundland, and later Borneo—were true bare-bones, alpine-style expeditions. The only money he'd ever received was a Shipton-Tilman Grant, a prestigious if limited cash award recognizing an expedition's cutting-edgeness. (Eric Shipton and Bill Tilman, daring turn-of-the-century British explorers, are universally viewed as the forefathers of the stripped-down, purist approach; the former is famous for having quipped that the back of a napkin ought to be sufficient for planning any expedition.) In his heart Weld didn't really feel the Tsangpo was a Shipton-Tilman-style trip. Nor, for that matter, did the people awarding the grants. The Tsangpo team applied for a grant, but was refused. "They thought we were too big and fancy," huffed Walker. The team took the decision—rather meaningless in funding terms—as a bit of a snub. A determined Gordon went so far as an appeal. He calculated (with the help of his brother David, an economist) the costs of Shipton's Everest attempt in 1927—an expedition analogous in terms of ambition to a descent of the Tsangpo, he thought—and showed that the trip, in current U.S. dollars, was actually more costly than theirs. They still didn't get the grant.

The trip's widespread trophy appeal also made Weld pause. He'd always gone to places nobody else knew about or was much interested in. The Tsangpo was the last great thing, and Wick was treating the "mission" with the gravity of the Manhattan Project. When he arrived at Weld's tiny clothes-making business in Confluence, Pennsylvania, population 875, to show him maps and other confidential details of the forthcoming trip, he insisted

Weld shut all doors and close the blinds. The satellite topo maps no longer bore the name of the Asian country that had produced them. The stealth protocol, enacted in this case for a half-dozen middle-aged seamstresses, bordered on the absurd. "He's asking everyone to leave the room and I'm thinking, 'Currey and twenty guys from Boise, Idaho, are probably looking right now at the exact same map,'" recalled Weld.

Zbel and Weld knew each other well. They lived within a half hour's drive of one another—Weld on the lower Youghiogheny and Zbel on the upper part of the river, in Friendsville, Maryland. Both ran river businesses. Zbel's Precision Rafting was one of the original companies to set up a commercial operation in the region. Weld's father-in-law (whom John helped out) was a friendly competitor. Zbel and Weld had raced each other for years. For seventeen out of eighteen years, Zbel beat Weld and everyone else in western Maryland's Upper Youghiogheny River race, one of the oldest and most remote extreme-whitewater events in the country. Zbel's dominance sort of baffled Weld. He was obviously a great paddler, but he didn't appear to train or approach the sport anything like any racer Weld knew. Actually he didn't appear to train at all. "He's gotta be doing something," moaned Weld after another defeat.

Weld was straight up with Zbel about his reasons for bowing out. While Zbel listened to Weld, he didn't understand him—he couldn't really imagine not going. It wasn't the best time to leave his business, which was weathering a couple of tough years with low flows on the Youghiogheny, known familiarly as the Yough (pronounced "Yock"). A good chunk of the year's revenue would come on the fully booked, fall-release trips to the Gauley River in West Virginia. Of course, he wouldn't be around to oversee the hectic campaign of transporting (a three-hour, one-way shuttle), guiding, and caretaking for dozens of clients over six consecutive "Gauley" weekends. That responsibility would be left to Roger's highly capable business partner, his wife, Nancy.

A blonde-haired Baltimore-area native who moved to Friendsville in the early nineties after graduating from nearby Frostburg State, Nancy found herself in a very similar position to Sandy Boynton (Jamie's wife) and Connie Gordon. She was supportive—Roger had taught her to kayak shortly after they'd met—but reluctantly so for many reasons: There was Roger's time away from the business during its crucial, make-or-break part of the season; there was time away from their three-year-old daughter; and there was time in a part of the world they knew nothing about. Moreover, Roger, unlike the others, wouldn't be paddling with guys he regularly boated with. He knew Tom McEwan casually, and was aware of Jamie. Doug he'd never formally met. For the other team members, a chance to reunite with old, dear friends was a major reason to run the river. Roger didn't have that motivation. Meshing with an established crew would be a challenge. They weren't sure what to expect from him—nor he from them.

But Roger assured Nancy none of it would be a problem. Wick and Tom had been very clear that nobody would pressure anybody else. He might be the quasi-outsider, but they wouldn't treat him that way. Appearances to the contrary, he added, the rest of the team was a lot more like him than not; they were mature, and had jobs and families to get back to. There wasn't a cowboy among them. Nancy looked hopeful but not entirely convinced. Roger sensed this was a scenario where your loved one tells you what you want to hear, but hopes you'll know enough to realize she doesn't really mean it. Roger slept on the decision several nights, but then decided to follow his gut. He promised

Nancy that if he didn't train like hell—if she didn't feel that he was truly getting himself prepared—she could pull the plug on the whole thing. Moreover, he promised he'd run only sure-bet rapids. If there was a possibility of a flip, he swore he'd walk it. Nothing tougher than Class III, he said. Nancy, who cofounded and ran with Roger, the Friendsville Paddling School, could do Class III. And Roger could run Class III in his sleep.

Zbel had never been a super-disciplined racerhead like the gate runners down at the Brookmont Feeder Canal in D.C. He'd always been a free spirit. Even his Precision Rafting business in Friendsville, which he cofounded with boating pal Phil Coleman, was a maverick operation. When he'd set up shop in the early eighties, nobody rafted the rugged upper Yough. Most considered the river's hundred-feet-per-mile drop too steep and dangerous, and the locals depressingly hostile. Creating a successful, safe enterprise on the Yough, in the middle of the boonies, wasn't anything like a given. "Things were a lot different then," says Zbel, who grew up in D.C. and later in the golfing mecca of Pinehurst, North Carolina, the son of a construction inspector with the U.S. Post Office. "People didn't really like outsiders. I got shot at a few times." Things were so intense that Zbel and his customers would launch commando-style, using stealth and quickness to avoid harassment. "We'd pull up to the put-in all set to go," he says. "The boats were hitched to the roof with quick-release knots and we'd get the people all suited up and ready to go. We'd throw the rafts off the bridge, race down to the riverbank, jump in, and be gone before anyone knew better. We had it down to three minutes."

Using equal parts wit, skill, and stubbornness, Zbel improbably survived the Wild West era. Each of his rafting trips featured a "safety" kayaker—an innovation that did provide more rescue options as well as allow Roger to boat to his heart's content. Eventually his business attracted other outfitters to the area. Some of the same guys who'd lobbed bottles at him in the early days were boating a few years later, attracted by Zbel's realness and passion—and the friendly beer keg stationed in his riverside cottage headquarters.

Throughout all that time, Zbel made only one real foray into organized, U.S.-sanctioned racing. With the 1989 World Championships conveniently held at the Savage River, only twenty minutes away, Zbel tried out and made the U.S. national wildwater team. He was proud of the accomplishment, but chose not to jeopardize his fledgling business by winging all over the country to compete.

Besides, the hassles of racing, especially judged slalom racing, with gate-touching penalties and man-made course designs, didn't really call to him the way paddling the Youghiogheny or some other Class V West Virginian classic did. Nothing compared with high-water runs, those rare times when torrential rains would drive everybody off the river except him and a few friends who'd chase the rains from river to river, from Maryland to West Virginia. The appeal of high water was simple: You had to start from scratch. Lines you'd run the day before disappeared. Minor holes became keepers. Massive house-sized boulders vanished beneath the rising waters. In essence, it was always a first descent. The most memorable of Zbel's super-high-water runs came in 1983 when he and a few others tried to run the upper Yough, a brutally steep, boulder-clogged, ten-mile run, at six and a half feet. At the time water levels half that were considered lethal.

"It would take like forty-five minutes to scout a drop and ten seconds to run it," says Zbel, who raced out the door so fast to catch the swollen rapids at Bastard and Triple Drop that he forgot his shoes. "The funny thing was I woke up the next morning and my feet were all cut up, swollen, and bleeding. I was in a good deal of pain, but I had no idea what happened. Of course, I'd been walking around the woods barefoot for hours. I was so keyed up on the river and focused I hadn't felt a thing."

The rush from flood runs was addictive—like his dad who had to do all the crazy roller-coaster rides when the family went to amusement parks, Zbel liked the heart thump of a wild ride—but Zbel also recognized how dangerous his game was. Risk probably never truly diminished the more you put yourself in such extreme situations. Sure, experience increased safety at most levels of river running, but at the utmost extreme level, everybody knew it was a game of diminishing returns. Like a marathoner, who has only so many personal-best races in his legs, a boater, no matter how good, tempts fate with flood run after flood run or repeated forays to big-volume rivers. Like a lot of people of his caliber, he'd lost his share of close friends (though he'd been fortunate enough never to be in the situation paddlers feared most: being a helpless eyewitness when the river claimed someone). Accordingly, Zbel began to back off. When his daughter was born in 1995, he backed off some more.

But the Tsangpo deal was different. It wasn't a nostalgic step backward to a crazy part of his life he missed and wanted to reclaim. Yet he'd invested a lot of time in the sport, his business, his community. It felt as if it were time to stretch, to invest in himself. To get out and see what he'd been keeping himself from all these years. Expeditionary paddling—a part of the sport peopled by a dying breed, by the paddlers he respected best—had somehow passed him by. He hadn't been stuck in Friendsville—he'd chosen to be here—but he couldn't help feeling a little restless.

In 1995 Roger bought out his longtime partner Phil Coleman, who sold his share in the company to start up a new river-running business in Costa Rica. For a brief moment Roger contemplated some sort of extended partnership, but he decided it was a risky business venture. Around the same time several other longtime friends and guides, part of what gave the extended family feel of the place, left to pursue other jobs and places to live. "It was something I guess I didn't really see coming," says Roger, "I just thought, 'Hey, I'll be working with these guys forever.' We'd all moved to the area together and wanted to make the business work just because we all loved to kayak the river so much." With all its manic turbulence, big drops, and treacherous boulders, it was a guide's river and those in Roger's group who ran it when nobody else did had a special attachment. But increasingly the people who worked for him were those he'd recruited and trained. Precision had begun to feel more like a cash-starved enterprise and less like a great scam where best buddies got to make money for doing what they loved anyway. Given this chance, with this team, to this place, he was taken with a strangely urgent feeling for a guy who wasn't by nature goal-oriented. He really wanted this trip to happen.

So Zbel went to work, training with a sort of discipline that amazed Nancy. Forewarned that the portages were likely to be extreme, Zbel focused on leg conditioning. He mountain-biked, ran, and went for lengthy, loaded-down hikes in the nearby West Virginian highlands. Once a commercial trip got safely through the upper Yough's gorge, he'd paddle ahead on the long flatwater stretch, then bike the several mountainous miles back to the river's start and retrieve the company shuttle bus. Just prior to leaving, he paddled day after day on the Gauley, loading his boat with fifty pounds of river rocks to feel how it handled. On the

Tsangpo they'd be carrying as much as one hundred pounds of gear. The rock-paddling was a humbling experience. Each peel-out or quick change in direction was an adventure. As the rocks tumbled from one side of the hull, Zbel would scramble to brace in order to keep from pitching over.

By the time the team was scheduled to depart, Zbel felt that he was in the best shape of his life. Part of his readiness had to do with another vow he made. He was going to do his damnedest to fit in. Running his own business had made him a control freak, he knew, but Zbel told Nancy he'd leave that crap in the States. As he explained, if he pissed somebody off on a West Virginia river, he could paddle away for a few hours until it all blew over. There'd be no such luxury on the Tsangpo. "I'm the last one asked on this trip," he told himself. "I'm gonna do whatever they say. I'm not gonna create any waves."

≋

ZBEL ALSO INTENDED TO KEEP HIS WORD TO NANCY. MUCH AS HE might have wished to be the silent partner, once he finally got to the river and saw how it was, he knew he couldn't just say nothing. Zbel wasn't militant, but he voiced deep reservations about staying the course. Distressingly, the closer he got to the river, the more he seemed to lose his enthusiasm. His confidence had begun to slip back in the States, weeks before departure, with all the news about flooding. He also read an article in the Explorers Club journal in which Ian Baker chronicled the myriad non-whitewater ways to perish in the gorge (falls from crumbling cliffside walking tracks, starvation, and poisoning at the hands of an indigenous cult who believed the practice gave them possession of the victim's luck). Though he didn't share it much with anyone, he felt increasingly mortal. "I guess it began to fully dawn on me," says Zbel, "that I was leaving my family behind and that a trip of this magnitude had potential for someone not to come back."

Tom McEwan always felt that the most critical unknown factor, from a team-dynamics standpoint, was how Roger might blend in with the rest of the team. Here they were, two hundred miles from the put-in, and already they had a smoldering crisis. In basic terms, Doug and Jamie wanted to get to the put-in and, if at all possible, work their way methodically downstream, hiking, paddling, doing whatever it took to keep the soul of the trip together. In their minds the Tsangpo was still viable as a white-water trip, even if it was to be a truncated one. Tom continued to want to see the river, then make a decision. He was open to tweaking the trip, making it less a classic whitewater descent and more a hybrid exploratory.

But part of the strain wasn't just about how adaptable every-one was, or how willing some might be to downsize their goals, but about a certain mind-set. At present Roger was considerably more apprehensive than his teammates. Whether that was just Roger, or had to do with the family promises he'd made, was hard to say. Guaranteeing you won't run anything harder than Class III on an extreme river like the Tsangpo put pressure on everyone. The rest of the team weren't do-it-at-all-costs risk freaks, but they seemed to accept that there'd be times when they'd have to do things they didn't really want to do. Drawing a preemptive this-is-what-I-will-and-won't-do line, as boldly as Roger had done, was something that was going to take some getting used to.

Roger looked at danger differently from the rest of the team, thought Tom. He, Doug, and Jamie really felt they could get very close to danger but not be dangerous—that they could be in extreme conditions, crashing whitewater and such, but be in control. Expeditioning at this level required, as others put it, an almost radical acceptance. You accepted your surroundings (remote, with no chance of rescue) and your condition (lethal whitewater, lots of discomfort), and moved on, keeping a kind of Right Stuff, super-composed mind-set that eluded 99 percent of the world. Roger had the Right Stuff, but he chose to hold back, a little less committed to the Tsangpo investment the rest had made. As Tom put it, "He really preferred to stay well away from any danger. He seemed to be saying he either wanted to have control or be off the water."

During the next few days spent driving, the plans seemed to change daily. There was no mutiny, not even close to one, but the closer they got to the river, the farther away they seemed from having a plan. One of the things that troubled Zbel, though he kept it to himself, was that there seemed to be no specific event, or combination of events, that would result in their scrapping the trip. On Everest, summit climbers routinely commit themselves to turnaround times. If they're not on the summit by, say, 2:00 P.M., then they're committed to turn around and head back down. The turnaround times eliminate decision making when you are least likely to make a good one. It's commonly known that most big-mountain deaths come on the descents (when ambition-fed adrenaline can no longer sustain, and exhaustion overwhelms). In the case of the Tsangpo, there was nothing equivalent to a "turnaround" time, mused Zbel. Of course, part of the reason was that they were missing a key piece of information. As high as the Tsangpo appeared to be, they had no idea how anomalous a situation it was. Water-level information wasn't available. At least to them. Had they chosen to organize directly through the official Chinese agencies, they might've had a chance at getting what the government considered classified information. But by "sneaking in" (they intentionally applied for a recreational-class "floating and trekking" permit, not an expeditionary one, in order to keep a low profile), they had fewer avenues to gather the data. Blücher showed them some numbers on water levels for the year 1964, but that was it. If they had known water levels for a range of years, and how quickly levels dropped from month to month, they could have made a comparison to the river's current condition and made a "go" or "no go" call. But absent water-level data, the put-in decision became more subjective.

The indecisive mood wasn't helped by the punishing overland trip itself. With the Friendship Highway in complete disrepair east of Lhasa, they ground along slowly and sometimes not at all. Road crews were blasting their way through landslides in several locations, causing half-day delays and backing up traffic for miles. Frustrated by the inactivity and desperate for progress, the team offered to take up shovels and aid the crews. Castillo, who'd traveled extensively in rural Asia and Africa, told the others he'd never seen worse roads.

The farther away from Lhasa they drove, however, the more alluringly remote they got. They saw no westerners and once camped by their trucks in the company of nomads in four-sided, yak-hair tents. The poor herdsmen warmly greeted the foreigners, even inviting them inside their homes for *tsampa* and tea. Tom McEwan, who had kept himself busy in the rumbling truck by scribbling translations of Tibetan phrases, offered a rudimentary greeting or two, then as a bridge to the language barrier (and as was his wont), he began to sing. *"Tseng, tseng, gons."* Sing a song, beckoned the delighted hosts. The song swaps entertained both parties. Clearly, Tom had picked up a thing or two from his dad, a community-theater stalwart back in Bethesda. On the scout trip the year before, Tom had even managed to leave his Monpa guides humming "Bad to the Bone" and "Barbara Ann."

One day out of Lhasa, Zbel woke up and decided he needed to go for a hike. Looking out into the vast wilderness expanse, he picked out a small hill and challenged Tom and the Sherpas to summit it with him. "I feel like I am wasting away in the trucks," he explained. Zbel also figured the act of choosing a target in the distance and tagging it in a proscribed period of time would be good practice for the portages to come. Accurately judging distances, in the face of an epic and utterly foreign landscape, was bound to be no small feat. In short order the wake-up hikes became part of everyone's routine. Initially, Pemba Sherpa and Akame Sherpa, well acclimated to life at 12,000 feet, bounded past the gasping Americans like springy deer. After a few days everybody got their wind, but, more important, the team began to coalesce with the activity. On all but one occasion they got their peak.

By the time they got to Bayi, a less-than-charming eastern Tibet frontier town known for hassling travelers (and summarily sending most back to Lhasa), everyone seemed a little less uneasy. Despite an onerous inspection (with permit wrangling resulting in a sizable bribe), they got out of Bayi and progressed onward. Wick and trip medic Dave Phillips split off, taking the road up over the northern flank of Gyala Peri en route to the confluence. Near the confluence they'd begin their trek into the heart of the gorge and Rainbow Falls. With precisely what the river team would do still in doubt, Wick was unsure whether he should be driving away, but told Tom he figured the decision to put on wasn't much his business. "Even if I go to Pe, I'm gonna keep my mouth shut," said Wick. "I'm the expedition leader and I plan to make the big decisions, but what you guys do is absolutely not my decision to make."

On October 4, a day after waving good-bye to Wick and Dave, the rest of the team crossed the Yarlung Tsangpo at a bridge just upstream of Pe. Moments later the snow-capped, sun-polished pinnacle of Namche Barwa was before them, the river galloping directly toward it. Four more peaks, all higher than 20,000 feet and spanning the Namche Barwa massif, blotted out the horizon, so big and so close they mocked any sense of real scale. Any distance short of the peak looked insignificant, if only because the peak itself loomed almost next-dimensionally large. Like those pulsing fireworks that cascade down once, then press-ingly reappear in faster, tighter, and brighter concentric rings, so it seemed with the peaks. Every time you looked up, it was as if the mountain crash-boomed into your field of vision. The four paddlers sat and stared, dumbfounded. The barren, gale-chilled plateau scenery of only a few days ago was now replaced by soar-ing alpine peaks, a soft river breeze, and the welcome beginnings of a fast-greening riverscape.

Downstream, on the left-hand side of the river, they could see a major tributary, the Nyingchi, flowing muddily into the Tsangpo. At the put-in, the medium-brown river was one-third of a mile wide but inside its banks. The river gauge consisted of eight one-meter stakes below the floodplain. Tom McEwan wrote in his log that the level showed about 0.1 meter on the eighth and final stake. He estimated a drop of about fifteen feet from the high-water mark of ten days earlier. The plan was to spend the next two days scouting on foot, scoping out as much whitewater as possible. They'd also measure how fast the water was receding. Then they'd make the call about whether they'd boat or scrap the river trip and hike. Late in the afternoon the four ascended a high ridge and got a good look at the first four rapids. The mood sud-denly brightened. They all looked doable. Even Roger had to agree. It didn't look nearly as bad as he'd feared. In fact, the first major rapid looked "scrapey," meaning a relatively low-volume flow plunged over the drop. Deciding to cut short their scouting venture, they returned to the put-in area, set up camp, and radioed Wick that they were going to run the first rapid tomorrow morning. It wasn't a commitment to the entire river, but at least they'd get a taste. And since there was a trail adjacent to the rapid, Paulo could easily shoot some video.

Zbel didn't dissent. Even the center of the river featured a friendly-looking wave train, a series of classically humped, grin-producing rollers stacking up one after the other. A nicely sculpted, roller-coaster-like wave train is uniform, predictable, and simple—one of the few types of rapids that offer all exhilaration and almost no risk. It's the reward that river runners get for all the other squirrelly whitewater harassment they put up with. The eighteen-mile stretch beginning here in Pe and ending in Gyala was always supposed to be a comparatively casual paddle where the team could get some strokes in and play their way into shape (physically and mentally) before the heavy-water sections downstream. The high-water warnings seemed to throw this part of the plan in doubt. Maybe there'd be no gimmes. But now the scout appeared to show that their fears were unfounded. Even if Zbel decided not to run one of the rapids, he had options. The boulder-strewn banks of the riverbed were walkable, and the trail paralleling the river extended for miles downstream. Because of the trail, the Wetherbee-led support team was right at river level. It all seemed surprisingly, well, controllable. "I didn't fly halfway across the world just to look at it, to back off right away—even though I sound like I want to," said Zbel. "I want to. I really want to be part of the team."

Tom didn't say much, but Doug and Jamie were obviously excited. They'd agreed to the cautious extended scout plan, but it was no secret they wanted to pursue downstream. Though they'd all conceded that the trip might be greatly abbreviated, they'd been talking for days of a best-case scenario in which they were able to hike and boat downstream to the deepest part of the gorge, a spot about thirty miles downstream of the put-in, near the storied Pemakochung monastery. They might not get through the 140-mile gorge, or even to Rainbow Falls, but paddling past the point where the gorge measured deeper than any other gorge on the planet would be a hell of a thing. A thing to make the trip.

Contrary to the vibe they'd been getting for weeks, there were no swarms of teams amassed at the put-in, either. Hundreds of miles upstream, a Chinese rafting team of eight was floundering. They'd started back in August at the river's headwaters, near Mount Kailash, and had quickly run into problems. Led by Yang Yong, who had famously made a first descent of the Tiger Leaping Gorge a decade earlier, the team wasn't expected anywhere near Pe for at least a month.

Nobody else was on the river. The gorge was all theirs.

By the seventh day of our ten-day trip, the river had grown to twenty times its original volume. The power of 15,000 cubic feet per second falling over twenty-foot drops was both inspiring and intimidating. In seven days we had run hundreds of rapids, but we had reluctantly walked around about a dozen major falls after long study failed to reveal dependable, clean routes. I had teased Tom that he would surely have run most of them if they had been on the Potomac. But this was different, a long way from home, a long walk from anywhere at all. Still, I knew I would be disappointed if by the end we had not run any of the big ones. This was the one! Marked on the map as a twenty-five-foot falls, it was a hundred-yard arc of falling water broken two-thirds of the way down by a smooth, green, angled ramp. The falls ended in the inevitable explosion of white foam. There was a hint of recirculation on the left side, but the main flow went to the right of it. And no mistake about it, where the water went was where I would end up. For all my years of racing, for all the hundreds of hours I had spent putting my boat within inches of slalom poles in difficult rapids, in water like this I would relinquish control to the river as soon as I crossed the lip of the falls. The key, therefore, was to come over the lip in the right spot . . . Within minutes, Wick was in position, and Mike was in his boat below the falls, ready to pick up the pieces if necessary. I was disconcerted to see how small Mike looked, bobbing in the waves below, and I was dismayed to realize that my tiny landmark curler on the lip towered at least five feet over my head. It was too late to worry. I felt my boat accelerate suddenly and braced for the impact in the cauldron below. It never came. With a shower of white, like falling while skiing in three feet of fresh powder, I emerged unscathed. Even if we had walked everything from here to the Gulf of St. Lawrence, the trip would have been a success.

—DOUG GORDON, IN A 1990 *CANOE* MAGAZINE WRITE-UP OF
HIS RUN ON THE CLASS V AGUANUS RIVER IN QUEBEC

south are the rhododendron-jungled slopes of the Doshong La, a 13,500-foot pass used by villagers to bypass the bending river and reach Medog, the southern terminus of the Tsangpo Gorge. Far below the camp are the first rapids, the narrowing river churning as it begins a sweeping turn.

The relative anonymity of their arrival is contrasted against the crashing hubbub that greets them back at the river-level put-in this morning. Every man, woman, and child has seemingly shown up—so alert to their muted plans of departure it's as if somebody wrote the time, place, and date in the deep blue sky above. "There must be forty people here!" says a stunned Zbel, scanning the crowd that is milling about their roadside truck and the yard-sale-like sprawl of gear and boats. Apparently, Harry Wetherbee and his wife, Doris, had dropped word yesterday that their support team was looking for porter help for the trek to Gyala, thus unleashing a deluge of job-seeking applicants. Pemba Sherpa is trying to keep the order, valiantly attempting to keep track of loads that are supposed to be packed in a prearranged, highly meticulous fashion, but that are instead simply being shouldered at random or slapped onto donkeys and carted away. Other porters are rummaging through the loads either for curiosity's sake or simply to lighten their burden. The team looks on, practically helpless.

For understandable reasons, Harry is displeased. He'd been on the scouting trip last year. Usually the business of hiring porter help within the gorge is a tidy matter involving a village headman who arranges the desired labor force in exchange for an agreed-upon price. Loads are carried within an area to which the village has territorial claims. At the end of the territory, a new porter delegation is hired from the next village, and so on. But here in the upper gorge, where there is more foot traffic and a

Pe, Tibet,
October 5, 1998

PE IS THE GATEWAY TO THE GORGE REGION—THE BEGINNIN
of the sanctuary-like territory the Tibetans call Pemako. It
the obvious place to put in, since shortly after Pe the jee
track begins to curl away from the river and head for th
hills. Having quietly slipped through the less-than-romanti
army and civilian Chinese-style compound—Pe is also th
district hub—the river team had kept driving a few mor
choppy miles, eager to put some space between them and th
town, where their presence might lead to additional scrutin
from local officials. They stopped and set up camp on a high
terrace almost a thousand feet above the river and only a
short distance from Kyikar, a sweet, end-of-the-road outpos
ringed by flapping multicolor prayer flags. Viewable to the

cluster of villages within a few downstream miles of Pe, there is evidently a free-market system. There's regular exposure to trekking expeditions and an increasing entrepreneurial awareness of the money to be made. Compared with the small Western teams that had passed through previously, this expedition was big. Ultimately, and if only to get the river team under way, Harry digs deep into the trip coffers and signs on a whopping twenty porters.

Part of the confusion involving the baggage is because this isn't a simple trekking trip. The river team needs resupplies of food and gear periodically, but it also needs to travel self-sufficiently for days, even weeks, at a time. Despite everyone's best efforts, their boat-borne freight is daunting: The food-per-day rations weigh out to two and a half pounds; the white-water gear, about twenty pounds; the camping stuff, another fifteen pounds. Miscellaneous team items such as cameras, navigational and communication necessities (for example, a handheld GPS receiver and a cumbersome satellite telephone), and rock-climbing equipment (rope and protection hardware for cliff climbing) add more bulk. There's no way around it. With six days of food in the boat, the team is probably carting around an extra fifty pounds each.

On any extreme self-supported whitewater trip, weight is the x factor. The more you carry, the longer you can stay out. But the more you carry, the worse a boat performs. *Alpine-style* originated as a mountaineering term to describe daring, light-load-carrying mountain-climbing adventures. Often they included only a pair of climbers without porters and sometimes without supplemental oxygen. The idea was that being relatively unencumbered by loads and people, these climbers could move more quickly and climb more technically demanding routes. In that sense their expedition was utterly different. It certainly wasn't the prototypical Tom

McEwan outing with a space blanket and a bag of rice. Given the extraordinary demands of the Tsangpo, they were traveling relatively economically—but they weren't alpine-style lean, not nearly. Loaded, slower boats such as theirs aren't just less nimble, but more susceptible to the push and pull of a river's currents, and can more easily get held in a crushing hole or be stopped by a breaking wave. The adverse weight-to-performance relationship is so pronounced, especially on challenging whitewater rivers, that Tom and the others agree that each rapid will be designated a grade higher in difficulty than it actually is. In other words, a rapid they'd ordinarily categorize as an intermediate Class III in an "empty" boat is a hard Class IV with their luggage. Getting used to the technical handicap—physically and psychologically— is no mystery, but it is a challenge.

The trick to mitigating the weight penalty is obvious: get by on less. But on a cold river like the Tsangpo (at least in its upper part), where the water temperature can dip into the thirties, they can't cheat much. They have to have a full complement of technical winter gear, from water-barring dry suits and winter-grade, waterphobic insulating layers to expedition-grade parkas and special mitts to ensure they can keep paddling. Because of the complex land-and-river team logistics and the need to communicate with one another, they have to pack the satellite phone. The thing weighs, much to Tom's distress, an infuriating twelve pounds. (Before they left, the team had lobbied hard to get an Iridium phone, the world's first handheld global satellite phone. The one-pound setup was ideal for their situation—fitting in nicely with the team's expressed theme of using next-generation communication and navigational technology to solve the Tsangpo "riddle." However, Motorola, the makers of the phone, hadn't wrapped up a licensing agreement with China, so they couldn't have it.)

Carrying what they have to carry requires a big boat. The essence of a kayak is as it was millennia ago: a small, closed-deck craft with deft handling ability. Design and innovation has revolutionized the sport in recent years. Most modern river-running kayaks or playboats are about eight feet long, weighing only thirty or so pounds, with carving-friendly ends that look more like surfboards than boat hulls. Built of cutting-board-like plastic, they feature the nifty handling ability of a Ferrari and the bombproofness of a Humvee. The best-performing, most technically adept boats feel like an extension of the body. So snug is the hand-in-glove fit that subtle flexing movements of hips, butt, toes, knees—all contact points within the sealed hull—produce quick, precise corrections and countermeasures. The boat seems to respond to the merest whisper of movement.

Expedition-class kayaks, however, are a decidedly different creature. Termed high-volume boats (meaning they have relatively roomy belowdeck areas in the bow and stern for gear), they are two or three feet longer and up to ten pounds heavier than their sexy, radically shaped cousins. High-volume boats tend to be fairly well suited to larger-than-average paddlers but harder to handle for smallish boaters. An expeditionary kayak, especially a loaded one, requires a bigger engine. The comparison between an ocean liner and a wave runner is a gross exaggeration, but the point is, a high-volume boat feels far less like some aquatic appendage and more like, well, a boat.

For a small-framed paddler like Doug Gordon, the smallest member on the team at five feet ten and 155 pounds, the fit wasn't ideal. From the waist down—the part in contact with the boat—he was particularly slight, his short, twiggy legs looking like pins in the comparatively cavernous hold of a twelve-foot-long boat. During his spring-training trip to Northern California, Gordon got a chance to try out the boat, and both Jamie and E. J. McCarthy recall that he wasn't wild about it. The unusually large three-foot-long "keyhole" cockpit (designed for bigger paddlers to slip easily out of their boats during tricky eddy-to-riverbank transitions) made him feel as if he were swimming inside it. On the other hand, it had a lot of volume for gear and punching through hydraulics (and the manufacturer, as part of a sponsorship deal, provided it free). He could pad out the cockpit using adhesive-backed foam and other outfitting materials. Buying a custom-made kayak was hardly feasible for a grad student on stipend.

Jamie, however, thought seriously about it. Jamie's boat wasn't a kayak but a canoe. To the uneducated eye, the two don't look terribly different: Modern-day whitewater canoes aren't the voyageur-looking models of a New Hampshire summer camp. Instead, they share the sleek size, fast paint jobs, and closed-deck design of a kayak. What's different is that the paddler kneels on a saddle or pedestal glued to the hull floor. He strokes a single-bladed, T-grip canoe paddle. For anybody but perhaps an ex-Olympian, a whitewater canoe would be considered a gross handicap in big water. They are extremely rare on expeditions, and almost unheard of for pioneering Himalayan teams. Because of the seemingly gleeful way that elite whitewater canoeists embrace their disadvantage, kayakers tend to typecast all "c-boaters" as misguided and impossibly macho. Jamie didn't fit the description, but he didn't conceal the fact that he liked the idea of defying conventional wisdom. He'd originally hoped to lure a former teammate to make the expedition a two-kayakers-and-two-canoeists partnership, thus making the point that they weren't the second-class citizens on a big wild river that people thought they were.

On most expedition trips, Jamie wouldn't have thought twice about his chosen craft, but the big-volume Tsangpo had begun to worry him. "About the only advantage I have is I can see more," he said, his kneeling position elevating him another half foot above the waterline than Roger, Tom, and Doug. But a kayak actually had two major pluses: an inherently higher top speed and no "off side." Competition canoeists, and he was no exception, had a stronger paddle stroke on one side or the other. The potential drawback on a bulleting river like the Tsangpo was that a "righty" like Jamie might be called upon to crank a big stroke on his off side. Given the speed and power of the river, his canoe's slight speed disadvantage made him more vulnerable to getting stopped in a hole (where you need top velocity to punch through) or holding an upstream line as he ferried across.

The weight issue nagged Jamie enough that he investigated the idea of bringing a fiberglass-Kevlar composite boat instead. A good 10 percent lighter, the boats handled better, too. The downside was that they might not be as durable. Weeks prior to the trip, Jamie dragged his boat across miles of gravelly lane near his Connecticut house, attempting to gauge its resilience to what everyone expected would be a punishing level of rock-scraping, portaging abuse. Unconvinced that it would stand up, Jamie, like Doug and the rest of the team, elected to take a plastic boat.

The champion attribute of a heat-molded thermoplastic boat is simple: It is virtually indestructible. The manufacturer the kayakers chose, Prijon, was particularly well known for its HTP plastic. According to the lab data (something a molecular expert like Gordon actually appreciated), an HTP molecule was about ten times longer, with up to 30 percent higher longitudinal and torsional stiffness than the industry standard. The length of the HTP molecule, combined with the pressure of the extrusion and blow-molding process, produced very dense plastic with long and tenacious bonds between individual molecules. Translation: a boat made of HTP plastic could fly off your roof rack at sixty miles an hour and still be none the worse for wear.

In the early days of Himalayan river running, the hardest runs were almost always torpedoed for one reason: the boats broke. Fiberglass could be patched, but ultimately the power of a thumping whitewater river or, more succinctly, the rocks and "strainers" in its midst, was too much. Boats would crunch, bend, and ultimately break. End of trip. Teams would spend thousands of dollars and endless hours preparing for some grand Himalayan trip, only to find themselves walking out after two days with a boat that looked like debris from a plane crash. Plastic changed everything. No longer were big-water trips at the mercy of their materials. Audacious first descents began not only to proliferate but to succeed. Given the fact that a plastic boat with $3/16$-inch wall thickness could endure almost anything, the greater self-limiting factor became the judgment of the river runner himself. Most recently, some have wondered if that is such a good thing. A near-sinkproof craft might allow boaters an unnaturally large margin of error, adding to false levels of confidence and danger-ously long stays on perilous rivers. Evidence of the imbalance, some theorized, was the record number of fatalities among expert-level boaters. The 1998 season, to everyone's dismay, had already been marred by several deaths and was shaping up to be more disastrous than the year before it. Accomplished boaters had drowned on the Rocky Broad River in North Carolina, the Bruneau in southern Idaho, and the Upper Blackwater in West Virginia—hard runs everyone on the Walker-McEwan team knew well. In July, a leading expedition boater, John Foss, perished on a Class V first descent in Peru. Planning for a two-week expedition and paddling a ninety-pound boat, Foss vanished in a pounding rapid enclosed by sheer one-thousand-foot walls.

Of course, the Tsangpo team had decades' experience running loaded boats. One of Tom and Wick's goals had always been to see how much they could stretch a self-supported trip. Five days? Eight? On the Aguanus in Quebec they raised the bar higher still, paddling the river with no support for ten days. The Tsangpo would be another quantum leap, with boat-only stretches as long as fifteen days, but in advance of the expedition they'd all trained with weight in their boats. They understood its performance limitations: how you couldn't turn on a dime, or rip off a technical Z-turn, or accelerate the way you were used to. Frankly it was sort of depressing at times, the sporting equivalent of being handed a zippy twenty-four-speed mountain bike and told to ride swervy single-track trails with one gear, poorly inflated tires, and forty pounds on your back. As they stared at the river the morning of October 6, medium brown and flowing a little more crisply than they'd anticipated, the weight issue was never far from consciousness. Would they be able to run anything on this river?

To everyone's relief, Tom suggests they wait to fully pack the boats, that for the first time out why don't they simply paddle into the current, get a feel for it, and have some fun? With the first rapid so conveniently close to the road and the river-level footpath, they've designated this first day a "film" day, anyway. They won't move camp until tomorrow. As Paulo scrambles to get his gear in place, the highly eager river team shoves off.

Tom, who, on the long drive, sometimes secluded himself into a kind of self-inflicted snooze state to conserve energy and mentally focus, is the first to slip into the river, ferrying across the current almost perpendicularly to get to the other shore. There is an alertness and charge for sure—twenty-five years in the making, a team of three highly accomplished boaters under his command, the pulse-quickening sensation of life at almost 10,000 feet—but mostly he looks like he might be on the Yough or the Potomac. There is the contentedness of feeling the current's first tug underneath him, of seeing things from a perspective where he's more part of the river than not. Surprisingly the water isn't numbingly cold, its glacial edge softened somewhat by the fact that the river has had a good seven hundred miles to sun itself between here and its alpine source. He, like the others who have followed him into the water, quickly notices something less pleasant: the bullying force of the current. It's got to be almost fifteen miles per hour. "You know what this feels like?" asks the helmeted Zbel, who looks like a Norse warrior even if he doesn't exactly feel that way. "An Eastern river in flood. This stuff is pushy."

As they progress a half-mile downstream, they see that the "scrapey" rapid they saw from a thousand feet up isn't scrapey at all. The waves they'd estimated at three feet on their scout are more like ten feet. In dissecting the rapid, they'd asked the same question they always asked: Where does the main current go, and is that where *we* want to go? Yesterday they'd figured the "action line" looked pretty good—the waves were okay-sized and curling back upon themselves in a frothy green, meaning most of the water, or enough of the water, flushed downstream. In the inexact world of whitewater rapids scouting, where the object is to decipher what's happening on and below the river surface, there were all kinds of variables to consider: the color of the water, the degree of aeration in the pile at the bottom of the drop (fizzy-foamy pure white bubbles said one thing; hard percolating water meant another). Often the best observations came from the cockpit, the paddlers biting off small pieces of a rapid in order to best determine the line for the final crux move.

Giving a set of rapids a class rating—the difficulty scale ranged from easy Class I to extreme and exploratory Class VI—was generally a straightforward matter. From yesterday's scout the stretch appeared in the Class III and IV vicinity, meaning the rapids were moderate sized and of moderate risk. Now they looked to be high Class IV, maybe Class V, an expert-only category where "swims are dangerous, and rescue is often difficult." That having been said, and pushy as the water was, nobody on the team figures the bigger-than-anticipated waves are pushing the envelope. The river is wide and they have plenty of room to maneuver. They'll simply ferry high above the rapid, pick an off-center route, and punch it.

Jamie and Doug peel out first, Jamie looking initially at a centerline, then suddenly changing his mind when he realizes that the standing waves are even bigger than they looked a few hundred yards away. He traverses smartly above a large hole and pops through a series of big waves near the left shore. Pulling into calmer water, he gets his new SLR camera from a stowed dry bag and waits for the others. Immediately he sees Doug ferrying across the river, bound for a similar river-left route. But Doug is too far downstream to duplicate Jamie's line, and instead begins to forward-paddle hard, aiming dead center for the meat of the rapid. As he is sweeping into a big but seemingly friendly wave, the face suddenly topples over and explodes. He is stopped cold. Instead of punching through, Doug and his twelve-foot boat are tossed upside down, the swirl of aerated water "cartwheeling" him for several seconds. Doug's boat washes free but stays overturned for five, ten, fifteen seconds—Jamie can see he's trying to roll, but for some reason he's missing them. Now it's twenty seconds and Jamie is anxious. The next, much bigger set of rapids is only a few hundred yards downstream—he's got to get some air. Finally—miraculously, Jamie thinks—Doug rolls up in the nick of time, his yellow, cage-faced helmet shedding foamy water, his warm blue eyes as big as saucers. He instantly veers right, stroking deep to exit the conveyor belt he's on and to slice through the eddy line—a strip zone of rattling turbulence where the heavy main current gnashes against the opposing soft upstream flow near shore. Doug gets across safely, out of the current and into the eddy above the next drop. His chest heaving, his face stinging from the fifty-degree water, he slumps at the waist and voraciously sucks the cool thin air.

Tom and then Roger make the same eddy moments later. Both he and Roger had intended to follow Doug into the river's center, Tom says, but they'd veered off at the last moment, taking a more moderate and parallel line along the right-hand shore. Before Tom says anything, Doug points to his spray skirt which is ripped half off. No wonder it was hard to roll, he thinks. He was almost out of his boat. Doug tells Tom he's not sure what happened. "Man, this thing is just real powerful," he says. He should have been able to roll up, but when he tried, he found he was dislodged. Tom shakes his head. He's missed rolls before, but never because he got walloped out of his housing. As Tom well knows, even the most bombproof roll, which Doug has always had, is going to be sabotaged if you're not firmly seated in your boat. A roll, the most technical and essential maneuver in the river-running sport, depends on a crisp hip-snap motion. When your knees and hips are firmly wedged into the boat, the pivoting force of the hip-snap arcs the boat through the water to the surface. If you're not attached, the hip-snap does nothing, because you have nothing to lever against.

Crossing Tom's mind are the hundreds of occasions when he'd overseen boaters back at Valley Mill, back on weekend trips to the Yough, who—as is the common phrase—had seen God after a particularly violent whitewater encounter. Most times, Tom was in a position to save the day. The fear his students felt was real—and it was important to feel fear—but the danger, well, the danger was more illusory. No matter what everybody thought—and mind you, Tom would get some dirty looks marching toward the upper Yough with his army of go-anywhere, do-anything commando teens—he had control. Maybe one time he felt different was a day he and his son were on the Ottawa River in Canada. Andrew, then eight, jumped into a sucking whirlpool some of the bigger kids were playing in. Only Andrew didn't pop out like the heavier, more buoyant kids. Time passed and Tom began to feel the keen desperation of not knowing how and why something was happening. "The first seconds you're thinking, 'He'll be *up*,' the next five you start looking, and the five after that you get frantic." Finally, Andrew was spit out—none the worse for wear, it seemed—but Tom was shaken. It wasn't merely that it was his son in the iron grip of the bottom-scraping current, but the fact that those fifteen seconds starkly demonstrated how quickly a river day could go from "sunny, blue sky, birds chirping" to catastrophe.

The fact that Doug, of all people, would miss his roll stuns everyone. The roll is what gives a whitewater boater a confidence that at times borders on a sense of invincibility. Those who are good hit their rolls most of the time. Those who are extraordinary never miss. The best might go years without a swim, rolling up time and again in the most raucous, deadly-looking whitewater you could imagine. Yet Doug's roll had failed him minutes into the trip. There is uneasy silence. "You know what I like to do?" offers Tom as he, Roger, and Doug are idling in their boats, awaiting Jamie's ferry back across to where they are on river-right. "The moment I feel myself loose, I don't try to roll. Instead I put my paddle in one hand and wrap both of my arms around the hull of the boat like I'm hugging the thing and pull myself hard back into position. When I feel like I'm back in, my hips and knees braced, then I go for the roll. You know what I mean?"

Doug nods. It might be a tall order for most boaters—pausing to fasten yourself *deeper* and *tighter* into a boat while getting unmercifully thrashed—but Doug has that kind of presence of mind. Yeah, maybe he was too eager, he agrees. Or maybe he thought he was snug enough—the boat always felt big for him—and wasn't. Maybe there was too big a gap between his folded-up knees and the thigh brace. Or maybe he wasn't flexing hard enough to bridge the gap, he added. He certainly didn't expect the "friendly" wave to pack the wallop it did. Whatever the case, lessons had been learned. "I got humbled," he tells Jamie, now pulling into the eddy.

Jamie, who had the only good look at the incident, is sobered but also impressed by his buddy's save-the-day move. It's amazing Doug held on to his paddle with the hits he took. Geez, he's mentally tough, Jamie thinks, not sure he would've had the guts to hang in there as long as Doug did. It takes a certain audacious presence of mind to focus calmly on performing when you're upside down in a boat, your sinuses suffocating with water, and the next rapid coming up fast. Not pulling the spray skirt loop and swimming free is an act of composed restraint you can't compare to many things. If Doug had swum, he might've drowned. When whitewater boaters asked whether somebody was good in big water, Doug knew what it meant: Could you get throttled within an inch of your life and still make the move? Doug could, Jamie knew, but just the same, the bank-to-bank hazards on the Tsangpo left you with hideously few options.

Even the eddies needed extreme care. On normal rivers, eddies are harbors of calmness, catch-a-breath pools that lie immediately downstream of boulders. But on the Tsangpo the floodlike pump of water coursing through the middle of the river was actually super-elevated, causing the eddies on its downward slope to thrash with surging crosscurrents and seashorelike lateral waves. Rather than being on one plane, the different zones of elevation meant the business of getting into an eddy was nothing like routine. In many cases they wouldn't be skimming across a sticky interface but lurching off the main current into a precipitous seam. Innocuous eddy lines became towering eddy "fences." In other instances, where rock outcroppings formed boundaries both upstream and downstream, the normally harmless deep-water pools became super-powerful whirlpools. Jets of water cannonaded from the rapids, feeding into the pool and creating an endlessly concentric swirl of fierce currents that could easily entrap a boat and drown a swimmer.

When Doug had first glimpsed the river's Mississippi-sized girth, he'd allowed how he'd never paddled a river so wide. But that long and static view hadn't nearly done the place justice: On the water it felt as though you were on the leading edge of some ghostly avalanche. The depth of the river had to be phenomenal. While parts of a river nearest shore and along the channel bed are slowed by friction, the surface water isn't. High water meant a greater percentage of the flow wasn't slowed down by anything. The speed morphed known river features into unknown ones.

The holes, the waves, the eddies would each be an experiment of one. The river wasn't just impossibly wide, it was a tabula rasa—and maybe Doug sensed it.

The whole thing was kind of tough to take. Here they were at the biggest whitewater river in the world—first day, first rapid—and they realized in the space of a half minute they couldn't run it. At least they couldn't run the heart of it. Tens of thousands of miles, two years, $100,000—and they couldn't run it. If they were going to get anywhere downstream, Doug knew that they'd have to run the sides of things—"sneak routes," in the river-running parlance, where less dynamic volumes of water braided between boulders near shore. The real river was simply unavailable to them. The good news was that Doug was Doug. He did not seem spooked by the tumble, Jamie thought. Humbled, yes. But daunted? No. "Next time I'll just be more careful," he promised.

The complexity of the water *was* entrancing, living up to its larger-than-life rep. To one extent or another, all career river runners claim a devotional connection with water that isn't merely sporting. Who wouldn't want to move with the grace and purposefulness of running water? If the questing soul needs nourishment in places where the human feels speck-sized, where they are absolutely bowed before the force and cataclysmic beauty of nature, then a deep whitewater gorge is one of life's obvious destinations. It is a place of such life-changing visceral *oompf* that those who get a taste of an epic whitewater run—or a volcano eruption, or an avalanche fracturing off—often spend the rest of their lives chasing the very thing they're most scared of. The draw that river runners feel for getting as near as possible to something that might kill them is perfectly impossible to explain to a lay audience. Most stop trying early on, and simply draw tighter to the people who've been there. What reason could any-

one have for offering himself up to a massively storm-strewn place where logs are thrown around like toothpicks? To a place where the name of the game isn't getting across the water but being a human submarine through it? To a place where a stiff breeze (much less a twenty-foot-high wave) looks sufficient to capsize such a chattering little craft? About the only notion that makes sense to anyone is that there is something highly redemptive in being the David, not the Goliath—something deeply energizing in a place where you so freely swing between powerlessness and possibility.

For Doug the connection certainly seemed spiritual—a fellow paddler once wrote that "flowing water has all the mystery, challenge and magic of the world hidden in it," and Doug didn't disagree with that—but he also felt a less conventional bond. As a gifted scientist whose talents were bound up in synthesizing new and exotic compounds, he was attracted to water on a vast other scale, too. Its sublime molecular framework—namely the intensely stable, chemically potent coupling created when two atoms of hydrogen combine with one of oxygen—makes water one of the most peculiar materials known to mankind. The Yarlung Tsangpo might seem to defy physical laws, but so did water, plain water. It had lab characteristics that made no scientific sense: It didn't freeze or boil where it should. As a solid it was lighter than in its liquid form. Water molecules were corrosive enough that, given time, they'd disintegrate the toughest metal. And yet water was so benign that life-forms of all types flourished in it; indeed, none could survive without it. Even the stroke of water that gushed between the Tsangpo's banks underscored an unlikely trait that Doug knew well: Water's own molecules, like magnets, draw to one another more tenaciously than those of certain metals. Anyone and anything that attempts to break the

bond has to be equally tenacious. In so many ways water was a fear and a fascination. It was no wonder that so many religions looked to water as a foundational metaphor, but Doug saw water for what it most truly was: a mystery, big and small.

"You know what this is coming to," said Doug that night at camp, seemingly almost resigned to the fact that what they'd come to do wasn't going to happen. "Boat-assisted hiking." Clearly, if the water was this bad in the river's flattest section, the situation downstream was bound to be deadly. If Doug's episode earlier in the day showed anything, it was that little mistakes resulted in big consequences. They couldn't ever commit to the main current—neither on purpose, as Doug had done, nor by accident. In this part of the canyon, the banks were far enough apart that the current could drag you downstream into rapids faster than you could paddle to the other side. None of them had ever been on a river where you couldn't paddle from one side to the other. You could paddle like a windmill and only get across a fraction of the river. The thought of that spooked everyone. "There is no chance for recovery of the boat, and difficult for a swimmer," wrote Tom in his log that night, assessing the center of the river. "[Doug's accident] is just a warning shot for us."

In the future they'd use their boats simply to cross the river where they could, then progress downstream on foot. In essence they were redefining the usual parameters of a first descent. The boats would be largely used to access the best terrain to hike. Unappealing as that was—after all, they'd come to run the river—Tom tried to look at the bright side. It wasn't like it was a waste of time bringing the boats, he said. The boats gave them access to both banks of the river. No Tsangpo explorers had ever had that advantage. They might not be able to run it, but they might be able to stick to the river level.

When the boaters arrive at camp that night, Lukas Blücher, the German from Lhasa, is there to greet them. After scouting some of the canyons near the India border, he is back to take a closer look at the same Pe-to-Gyala stretch. He didn't see Gordon's wipe-out, but he's heard about it. Gordon looks ghostly pale, Blücher thinks, then he smiles, realizing upon closer inspection that the pallor is sun-block residue. As it turns out, they'd stayed on the river, successfully and repeatedly running the easier lines for Paulo to record on film. "So you did all right, I guess," offers Blücher, who arrived earlier in the day aboard a neon colored Klein mountain bike. Gordon shakes his head. "No, no," he says. "I took sixteen seconds to roll up, and nearly got thrown out of the boat. Nothing about it was all right."

Blücher assures everyone he's not reconsidering—and he's not—but there's a part of him that feels the competitive pull, a part of him that questions why his own tolerance for risk isn't greater. These are all reasonable men, he thinks. Every one of them he can see joining him for a trip. Maybe he's been too quick to judge; maybe the river can be handled in the manner that they are going at it. If he were a member of the American team, would he quit? The funny thing—no, actually the scary thing, he thinks—is that he doesn't really have an answer.

The conversation that night is all over the place. They can't get in touch with Wick for some reason, but Tom does call back to the States. He makes no mention of Doug's near-disastrous tumble, just that they're under way. Odd, thinks Blücher, overhearing the trip update but not sure whom Tom is talking with. Everyone has been right on with him: respectful of the river, fearful even. But the phone conversation strikes a different tone. Maybe it's just human nature. But it seems, at least to the outside world, that they really want to put a happy face on things.

With a few small but significant changes, Tom thinks they can continue to work their way slowly downstream. Probably the most unnerving of the day's realities is the gap between what the river appears to be and what it is. Even on film the river doesn't look nearly as dramatic as it feels. Consequently they need to be extra judicious with their scouting, seeing the river both from a macro overview perspective (so they know what is around the corner) and from a micro viewpoint (so they can truly distinguish friendly from nonfriendly features). They won't be fooled into rushing through a scout again. Tomorrow morning, they decide, they'll load up with six days' worth of food and camp at river level rather than tie up with the support crew. That way they'll truly test their setup, including their phone and radio communications, and know how solid they are. Once they get to Gyala, a two-day walk by trail, they'll reconnect by phone with Wick and make a decision about how and whether to proceed.

As it turns out, Wick, whom they can't get ahold of, has run into his own problems thirty miles from the Po Tsangpo village of Pailung, the starting point for his long hike into the center of the gorge. A massive landslide has obliterated the Lhasa-Chengdu road, and he's going nowhere. A five-mile chunk of roadway, near the northern flank of Gyala Peri, is simply rock rubble. There's been no traffic on the stretch for months, Wick is told. His only option is to unload and abandon the vehicles, hire porters, and launch out across the landslide by foot. When he gets to the far side, Wick hires more vehicles, more porters. The whole painstaking operation puts him a day behind schedule. More delays, he worries—he can't help but look ahead to the severe bushwhacking and trail-cutting he's going to need to do to get upstream to Rainbow Falls—and there's a real chance he might not arrive in time to resupply the others. Key parts of the plan seem to be crumbling, and his continued efforts to get a permit for the lower part of the gorge have proved fruitless. Given all the hoopla about the wicked river conditions, Wick can't believe that the overland is shaping up to be an epic, too.

Danger is one thing, but danger plus extreme discomfort for long periods is quite another. Most people can put up with a bit of danger—it adds something to the challenge—but no one likes discomfort—or not for long, anyway.

—Sir Edmund Hillary

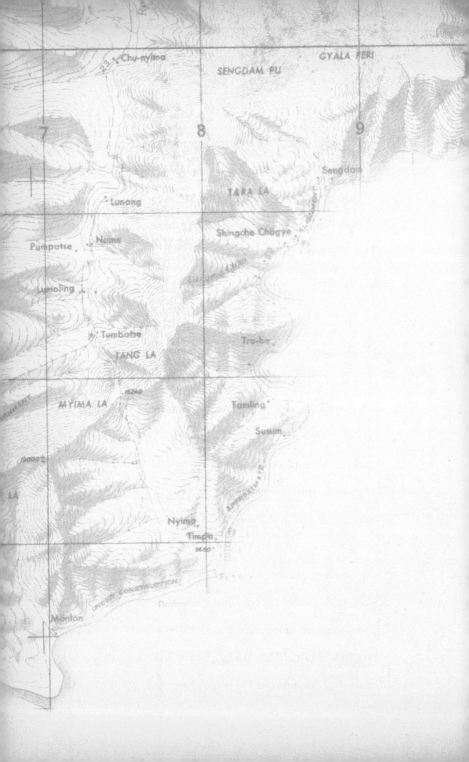

FJ GJ
FH GH
Gompano
Konung
Dokar (Approximate
19
Roge bridge

Pe, Tibet,
October 6

HAVING HUSTLED OUT OF THEIR BLUFF-TOP CAMP AND RE-
trieved their boats from the wooded shores where they
ditched them yesterday afternoon, the river team is consumed by the unending task of organizing, condensing, and
packing gear into waterproof dry bags for their journey.
They don't board their boats until 1:00 P.M., and after running the first rapid along the safe river-right line, the four
again regroup near the eddy they shared yesterday. They're
delayed once more. This time the pause isn't for a bracing
team-wide reality check, but because a well-wishing local
contingent is along the shore with a send-off basket of
peachlike fruit. *"Thoo jaychay,"* says Tom, beaming a bright
smile and chomping a big bite. Thank you.

None of them speaks Tibetan, but Tom is willing to wing it. The year before, on his and Wick's scouting trip, he'd taken copious if almost illegible notes, writing down phonetically the names of porters they'd hired, useful phrases, and even the lyrics (and an English translation) of a traditional hymn about the Yarlung Tsangpo. *Shoo Yarlung Tsangpo . . . O chay nay dintay ympam umpee ny yay samnang yongwee . . .* Tom sang, his voice rising and falling in imitation of the swirling melody. The rough, garbled translation didn't make much sense to anybody: "You like fast, don't go . . . in my heart or mind a great request . . . come back." Almost a sort of unrequited love sonnet, Tom imagined, the ode to the mythic river heroine said, "You have run away and I miss you."

Not surprisingly, the destination of the visitors and their peculiar mode of transport are the subjects of some curiosity. Using a flurry of hand-waving and other simple sign language, the delegation is keen to know where they wish to go and how they'll possibly live with the river. The appearance of a kayaker on the water—trunk visible, but lower half mysteriously disembodied—is a strange image to anyone unfamiliar with the sport. Visually, a paddler approximates some centaurlike creature—half man, half boat. Their already exotic form is even more puzzling given where they're headed. They plan to follow the course of the river through the gorges, Tom explains. Some shake their heads vigorously, as if to say, no, it's impossible. Others say nothing, wondering if theirs is some uniquely Western spiritual quest. Wick knew their intentions would be awfully hard to articulate, and as a result he'd asked Roger to clip images from magazines to show "what guys like us do." The "bragbooks," of which Harry's team and Wick's have copies, sport photographs of boaters portaging, running rapids, camping, and leaping off waterfalls. There are no albums with the boats, however, and besides they must get going. Tom politely winds things up and stows the fruit away. *Kaalay shoo-ah,* he says. Good-bye. The Tibetans nod, then stand and stare until they've paddled completely out of sight.

Clearly the upside to disappearing into the stony, shadow-filled gorge is also the downside: leaving civilization behind. Most of the Tibetans they've met are Monpa, the most numerous inhabitants of the gorge. (The original indigenes of Pemako were the Abhor, or Lopa, a hill tribe with scattered numbers mostly in the lower gorge.) The Monpa first migrated into the region five hundred years ago from the high mountains east of Bhutan, themselves following a Buddhist prophecy that depicted the lands as a "lost Eden." Another wave of exiles came to the gorge to flee the Chinese forces that invaded in 1951 and have occupied Tibet ever since. That, too, fulfilled a prophecy, since legend has it that the gorges would be a refuge if ever Buddhism were threatened. The Monpa call the gorges region Dechen Pemako, meaning "Lotus of Great Bliss."

Last year, during their scout, Tom hadn't had the best of luck with the porters he'd hired, but he'd found a few kindred spirits. Dima, a little older and more devout than the others, had impressed him most. Despite suffering from a nasty foot infection—something they'd easily cured with some antibiotic cream—he soldiered on uncomplainingly. Inquiring after him at his small village near the confluence, Wick finds out, and later relates to Tom, that Dima has died in an accident in the gorge in the interim, falling into the rushing Tsangpo waters from a high cliff. For the most devout Buddhists, many of whom regularly etched routes into the guardian slopes, a death is neither a tragedy nor particularly uncommon. As Dima had explained to Tom, the gorge was a rewarding but difficult place and laid claim to many.

Feeling that they are running behind, the four paddlers stay on the river late, paddling along the edges of big rapids, urged on by the looming presence of Namche Barwa in the near distance. They stop where the river takes a sharp right-hand bend, knowing they need to do a long scout before proceeding on. A solid half-day of paddling, unencumbered by video obligations of running the same rapid umpteen times, feels good. They're not running in place, but making progress. Not that the miles add up to much, but running a continuous stretch helps everyone. There are precious few spots where they'll be able to cruise for miles on end, and Tom, Doug, and Jamie are accustomed to running twenty-mile-long stretches where you can build into a rhythm. This is nothing like that. The fearsome power of the river means they need to be satisfied with boating gains in yards, not miles.

They need to create another method of *flow,* to find a routine that allows them to relax just a little but doesn't sacrifice focus. The link between flow and high performance isn't physical law, but it might as well be. Rhythm is essential to executing athletic movement. River runners aren't a well-studied model, but basketball players are. In that sport a shooter may stroke the ball flawlessly in the flow of the game—relaxed, instinctual—but fall apart at the foul line, where the flow stops and the consciousness of what he's doing becomes almost deafeningly loud. Missing free throws compound themselves. Bad free throwers are taught to search out a routine where they might replicate the game's natural rhythm. The Tsangpo team, to get the best out of itself and to relieve the tension that builds in the presence of a predatory river, is searching, too. Just coming to the understanding of needing a new systematic approach—and banking a day without any major scares—is a small victory. Their camp tonight is a good one: flat, riverside, and floodlit by a full moon so swollen that its buoyancy above them seems somehow in doubt. Amazing, thinks Tom, gazing at the glistening snow peaks of Namche Barwa.

The river's profile from here to Gyala is pool-and-drop, much like the classic western U.S. rivers such as the Colorado and the Salmon. Every mile or so a large rapid is followed by a flat but fast-moving stretch of water (the pool). Ordinarily they'd scout the big drops, deciding either to run them straight or along the sides, and make quick work of the flat portions. However, the high water negates much of the anticipated comfort zone. The volume, at an estimated 40,000 to 50,000 cubic feet per second, is some three times the flow Tom and Wick saw last year. The rapids aren't just bigger vertically, but more elongated, irregular, and bunched together, too. A month from now, when the waters have greatly receded, this will be an easy stretch. In fact, a Spanish paddler scouting several weeks later for a bid the following year will write in his logbook that half of this section is "completely calm." The Walker-McEwan team isn't so lucky. The water is coming down, but not appreciably—about two to four inches a day, they estimate. Given the river's far less predictable look—and the fact that they've never seen the river at anywhere near this level—the scouting becomes increasingly important and time-consuming.

If only to make it more palatable (as Tom has often explained to friends, a paddler hates portages, especially if he thinks the rapid is remotely runnable), they begin to make a game of it. Tom and Roger, as befitting their competitive glory years, are the wildwater team (wildwater is a no-gates, no-judges, point-to-point race down a steep stretch of river). Naturally, Jamie and Doug are the slalom team. The former go high along the right bank looking for a line, the latter eyeball the situation at river level. Neither route is particularly appetizing—Doug and Jamie return saying the right side is crazy. Tom and Roger aren't exactly wild about the left side, either, describing a cliffside route pocked with boiling eddies. Heretofore, there's been little debate about where to go—the scouts aren't long-dragged-out head-scratchers—in most cases the route is obvious: overland. But this one they hem and haw over. According to team protocol, they don't all have to do the same thing. River running is rarely a consensus-based operation. The team's approach is for everyone to evaluate each rapid independently—and collectively, if they wish the input—and make their own choice. "If any one individual wants to run the rapid even if the other three think it's nuts, so be it," Wick explained back in the States. "The duty of the other three is to be supportive, get in position, and post safety." Conversely, if three wanted to run a rapid and one didn't, the majority was responsible for supporting the portaging teammate first.

The method, to Wick's and Tom's minds, minimized peer pressure. Everyone knew how easy it was to be swayed into doing something you didn't really want to do. Internalizing the rush of information at a tough rapid took an almost superhuman degree of know-thyselfness. Sometimes adrenaline was good, sometimes bad. Sometimes fear was healthy; sometimes it got you killed. Sorting everything out—being right more often than wrong about yourself and what you were seeing—was the mark of a top-grade paddler. This was the heart of hard river-running: knowing your skills and emotions, but, more than anything, how you felt in that freeze-frame moment. Often it came down to that, being honest enough to recognize not how good you were on average, but whether you were "on" when the rapid needed to be run. The self-selected "green light" was both obvious and utterly impossible to articulate (since it often had to do with intuition and not guide-book statistics like the rapid's feet-per-mile drop). Tom, like a lot of top boaters, talked vaguely about the process, saying he rolled it around his head until something clicked and he saw and felt a path form. His process relied less on scientific certainty and more on what the Greeks called gnosis, or experiential knowledge, said Tom. At the highest level it was just a very fine line. And as much as boaters hated to admit it, sometimes running a rapid did have to do with what your teammates did. The first one down the rapids, usually called the probe, was the key person. What happened to him was the tell-all: Without the probe, they walked. With the probe, the assessment process might reopen. At the first rapid on the Tsangpo, the team's own pecking order, if ever in doubt, was firmly established. Doug's their undisputed probe.

Around midmorning the team, as one, opts for the worst of two evils—the left-hand side of the river. Though the water is much heavier than they anticipated and Roger nearly gets spun out into the middle of the river, they hop from eddy to eddy and make it around the pale granite cliff to where the river briefly widens. After clambering over boulders and making a little headway downstream, they run up against the final stretch of the same rapid. There is no discussion. It's plainly unrunnable. Roger begins to pick his way boulder to boulder, getting out far ahead of the others. Noticing that Doug has taken a high route, and assuming the others are with him, Roger realizes he's out of position and cuts back up the three-hundred-foot slope to meet them.

Suddenly, Roger sees somebody in the water. Jesus, he thinks, Tom's swimming. That morning the two of them had been talking, and Tom had said he might take a real swim in all his gear, just to see what it's like. Swimming helped demystify a river for Tom; he also thought it roughly approximated the paddling sensation, since it took place at river level. Not that Roger wanted to be the guinea pig, but he didn't object to Tom's idea—

at least they'd get some firsthand information. Then Roger looks again and realizes Tom's not swimming, Jamie is. He's out of his boat, getting surfed all over the place in the shoreline waves. He's going to make it to Tom, he sees now, but he also sees his boat and all his gear is getting drawn into the main current. In a matter of seconds it's around the bend and gone. Racing down to the bank to help, Roger's certain they'll never see the boat again. Jamie's trip is over. And if Jamie's trip is over, his is, too. Three paddlers aren't enough for what they're doing.

Jamie is okay, more infuriated than anything else. He and Tom explain they had decided to scramble along the bank instead of hiking up high, picking and choosing spots where they could paddle a bit. He was about to follow Tom down a couple of small drops when he and his boat inadvertently slid off a rock with his spray skirt unattached. The turned-over boat flooded instantly. "I wasn't upright when I landed. I had to grab my paddle and brace up, and there I was going downriver," he says. Paddling hard to get to the protected shore side of a house-sized rock, he missed the move, then plunged over another small drop. Flipped again, Jamie got spit out and tried to roll, but couldn't. Seconds later he felt the boat getting pushed beneath an undercut rock. Afraid that he'd get pinned beneath the surface, the boat sucking into the rock because of the pressing current, he dove out of the boat and swam for it. Finding himself momentarily out in the current to the right of the rock, Jamie felt the waves break over his head, then a ripping jolt submerged him—he was right on the eddy line, the frenetic spot where downstream current collides with the water racing in the reverse direction. Somehow Jamie swam into the next eddy where Tom's boat awaited him if he needed to grab hold. Tom had one shot at Jamie's boat, but rather than give chase and risk being drawn unprepared into the next rapid, he comforting to Tom or anyone. The most lurid predatory dangers of Pemako might be more myth than reality (such as the region's poisoning cult or the mysterious Yeti of common trans-Himalaya belief), but just the same, solo travel through hard, unknown wilderness is always a chancy proposition. Beyond the scree slopes rippling away from the river, the route-finding was certain to be difficult, with hazards ranging from ankle-snapping falls to unlucky encounters with snakes, swarms of stinging insects, bears, and the half-wild dogs patrolling the odd homestead. Tom knows he made the right decision by shepherding Jamie to safety and not playing hero, but just the same it's hard not to second-guess himself and wonder if he should've taken the gamble and chased down the boat. It might've saved Jamie's trip, maybe everyone's. About the only fortunate side of the accident is that it has happened early enough in the day so that both Jamie and the river team have some daylight to work with. They should be able to keep tabs on one another either visually or by walkie-talkie part of the way.

"Jamie, I no longer know where you are," radios Doug, scanning the steep river-left ridge a few hours after they leave him. The rest of the team, ready to stop for the day, is now on a sandy beach in a wide stretch a few kilometers downstream. Jamie relays his whereabouts, and Doug finally spots him: "I have a visual on you now and yes, you are pretty high up there." The two discuss the possibility of Jamie using a climbing rope to scramble down the steep cliff. The river is calm and they can probably ferry him across if he can make it down. With Doug's encouragement, Jamie is convinced he wants to give it a go, but Tom intervenes, urging his brother to stay where he is. "I don't like the look of the rappel," he says, scanning up the crumbling two-thousand-foot drop. "There are almost no trees, no good holds for the rope."

decided he had to let it go. "You're in, Jamie," Tom had said￼
two of them watching his boat disappear. "You're in."

As the shock of the scare wears off, the reality is even ￼
devastating. The trip is over for him. Three days on the river￼
he's done. With the way the current is moving (and the rapi￼
come downstream), the chances of his boat being anythin￼
debris are almost infinitesimal. Worse still, he is stranded o￼
left bank of the river. The trail to Gyala, where the support￼
is now set up and awaiting them, is on the opposite ￼
Nobody can take the risk of putting Jamie on his boat and ￼
ing him across. Jamie says he'll start hiking along the left￼
which, by the looks of it, starts with a several-thousand￼
bushwhacking climb. He wants to do something, he says,￼
action and blow off some steam. Two days ago he'd been ki￼
hamming it up for the camera, saying he wasn't planning to￼
lenge the river, but to coexist peacefully with it. He'd la￼
boyishly over how that sounded, but the sentiment seemed￼
on—and now this.

As Jamie marches away, he torments himself for puttir￼
trip in jeopardy. He's outfitted with a compass and a tw￼
radio, and Roger has lent him his own survival extras, a knif￼
lighter given to him prior to the trip by his former partne￼
Coleman. "Phil figured if anything happened, at least I ￼
start a fire and cut stuff up," says Roger. "I was hoping not ￼
it, but here you go." Always hard on himself, he thinks he ￼
ened out. He should've stayed with the boat. Roger thin￼
pulled off a hell of a self-rescue. It could just as easily have￼
him getting swept away downstream, not the boat. The att￼
at resuscitating morale, both for Jamie and one another,￼
easy to sustain. They know the expedition is in serious tr￼
Letting Jamie skulk off into the Pemako outback alone ￼

They're also losing light. "You're better off doing what you're doing and staying close to the river," he adds. "We'll meet you in Gyala, okay?" To Tom's mind the down climb could get Jamie killed. A night out—well, he wasn't going to freeze to death. Ultimately Jamie backs off the cliff descent and agrees to plod on alone.

Jamie: "My apologies for creating this situation for everyone."

Doug: "No apologies necessary. See ya tomorrow."

≋

HOURS LATER, AS JAMIE SCRATCHES HIS WAY ALONG GAME TRAILS, heading deeper into darkness and God knows what, he's still pissed. But he's also more than reflective enough to know he's been down this sorry road before.

There was a time in the early seventies when he and his older brother, Tom, never missed an opportunity to subject themselves to the what's-what of outdoor hardships. Each adventure was a little more out-there than the last. Though Tom was six and a half years older, Jamie was far more than the mere tagalong, as he sometimes remembers it. They were a lot alike in the way that mattered most then: They lived to be in the grip of rivers. They liked to race and were good at it, but the lifestyle was the addiction: the long car rides to nowhere, the bad maps and lousy food, the damp, near hypothermic nights spent on a riverbank, crashing through thorny briar looking for a road, any road. As racers, they thrived on the freewheeling amateurness of the era— there were few coaches and little structure. If you raced, you also probably set up the course, camped on the river, and wrote off a shower for days on end.

Both had sky-high aspirations, though Jamie had elected to paddle a canoe, not a kayak, in whitewater slalom competition, choosing in some small way to carve out his own reputation in what then was his brother's considerable shadow. They grew into the sport before science invaded every nook and cranny of athletics, before there were computerized training programs and peak-performance diets, and before there was an accepted way for the way things were done if you were serious. In their era there were two gold-standard tests for a boater: how many pull-ups you could do and how long you could hold your breath underwater. Jamie once did 40 pull-ups in a row; Tom swam underwater laps in a pool until he passed out. Wrestling, largely because of the agility and fierce intensity required, was also deemed an important cross-training sport. Both Tom and Jamie were state high school champions, and Tom finished his career at Yale never once having been pinned.

One of the pair's first big expeditions—and one that has some relevance to his wanderings right now—was the Linville Gorge. The Linville Gorge, in North Carolina, was simply the steepest, undone river of the era. It was remote, unknown, and had nearly killed Tom once on his first attempt with Wick. It was hardly surprising that the brothers set out for it, arriving in late fall, late in the day. Tom didn't make it far down the twenty-five-mile run before his fiberglass boat, rolls and rolls of gray patching tape notwithstanding, took a final ledgy hit and sank. Up ahead a mile or so, on the opposite bank, Jamie's boat met its maker on a boulder and sank also. Tom tried to hike out, figuring he'd run into Jamie either at the put-in or the take-out. Jamie clawed his way up a steep slope but got lost. The temperature plunged and snow began to swirl. While Tom made it to the road (hitching a ride to the put-in and spending what he describes as "a glorious night" burning a fire so hot he stripped down and simply sprawled out in the warm, insulating mud), Jamie found refuge in a foul outhouse, spending the night stuffing cold leaves under his paddle jacket to keep from freezing.

A day later, having taped the boats again, they returned to the gorge. Things went considerably better, the two of them running far more of the river than Tom and Wick had managed. Then, near dark, the boats broke again. Halfway up the mountain, night came and the pair lost their way. Bashing through thick woods and exhausted, they didn't emerge until 2:00 A.M.

Probably only a year ago Jamie returned, cruising by car along the ridge road when he ran into his nephew, of all people, beating back a retreat with a soggy, storm-ravaged gang of campers. "What are you doing here, Uncle Jamie?" Alex Markoff asked. "I dunno," Jamie said. "I wanted to come back and reflect on what the hell we were doing here."

Linville Gorge. At least in the Linville Gorge, he had his boat. Now out of walkie-talkie range, Jamie keeps expecting to find a village—at least there's one on his map—and after that a major trail to the Gyala ferry crossing. He could probably even jog the latter. But the trail never presents itself. To the east, barring the way to the blue poppy- and primula-filled Rong La, are a string of high passes. To his west is the river. He passes a village on a 3,000-meter plateau, then a handful of farmsteads. Here he has his choice of dozens of footpaths, none of which amounts to anything. For hours he's crashing around, the bamboo forest lusher and more dense as it plunges off the plateau. Finally he stumbles on the main trail. It's midnight. He's sure the support team got word he's out here, but there's still no sign of anyone.

Tom never tired of these kinds of experiences. He didn't see the mishaps as dreary luck so much as a tangy ingredient. Jamie recognized the value, but looked at things a bit more linearly. At the end of the day, he liked a cleaner, more conventional tally—wins and losses were easier to measure oneself against than the more general merit that came from scattershot bouts of suffering. His more pragmatic side—and, maybe not coincidentally, his big break—actually began to assert itself out of the ruins of another Tom-and-Jamie endeavor. The year was 1971. Tom was a senior at Yale, Jamie a freshman. It was summer and they were training together, both hoping to make the U.S. national team that was going to the Olympic Games in Munich. It was the first year whitewater slalom racing had been accepted as a sport in the Olympics. Shortly into their program, Tom crunched his knee on the upper Yough and was effectively done for. He and Jamie did, however, in their odd, self-styled approach, continue their training, migrating south that same winter to the Okefenokee Swamp.

The plan was to escape the cold and train on nearby rivers. Jamie disappeared for California after a few weeks, smartly abandoning their wacky effort for a semiformal training camp on the Kern River. Tom stayed, living in a mid-swamp tree hut that Jamie had helped him build. Living on scraps, reading Ayn Rand, and paddling ashore for a daily jog, he quickly came under local suspicion. Law-enforcement authorities stopped him on his jog one day and had the scraggly-bearded McEwan lead them to his hut, which they felt sure was a covert drug-smuggling den. After laboring to shinny up the pole to his twenty-foot-high platform, the team's narcotics specialist asked him to empty his pockets. A plastic bag revealed a suspicious chunky-hard substance. Tom winced. The specialist rolled a piece around his tongue. Mouse scat, Tom explained. In a continuing campaign to keep his digs clear of mice, he'd been catching them in plastic bags then disposing of them, eventually, ashore. The police left quickly. Ultimately, McEwan, too, left the swamp. Around the same time Jamie was beginning to attract notice as a real candidate for the Olympics, Tom embarked on a seven-hundred-mile, several-week-long Huck Finn journey, paddling from his swamp abode into Florida and Georgia and up the Intercoastal Waterway almost to Chesapeake Bay.

Tom made one last valorous bid at making the same U.S. team, showing up at the pre-Olympic races with special rigging in his boat that effectively strapped his still-gimpy knee into the boat to keep it immobile. "How are you going to get out of that if you flip?" a fellow racer asked. Tom shrugged dismissively. He wasn't worried about that. He competed anyway, but other than making several organizers nervous, he didn't get much done.

Jamie fared better, coming from nowhere not only to make the U.S. team, but to become the first American ever to win a medal in whitewater racing at the Olympics. His teammate at Munich was Wick, who finished eleventh in the same canoe class. Jamie's success, at nineteen years of age, was so improbable that Wick wouldn't have believed it if he hadn't seen it. Only a handful of Americans had even competed at the European-dominated international level, and none were considered medal-class caliber. For guys like him, Jamie's triumph was a miracle, a true-life, made-for-TV, cynicism-be-damned example of what can happen if you dream big and believe in yourself. About the only person who wasn't overwhelmed by what he'd done was Jamie himself. When a thrilled teammate asked him what was going through his head as the medal ceremony neared, Jamie shrugged: "I thought I was gonna win."

As each of their careers took a turn after the Olympics, it dawned on people that maybe they weren't as inseparable as everybody thought. Tom didn't return to Yale—though he was one class short of graduating—and eventually ended up back in D.C. Jamie turned his intensities to his studies, eager to address the issue of what he was going to make of himself. He continued to paddle, but not year-round as the U.S. athletes he'd inspired did. He stayed on at Yale as an admissions officer. His wife, Sandra Boynton—a struggling artist when the two met in college—became a hyper-successful author and illustrator with her whimsically drawn animals that soon appeared on everything from pillowcases to sippy cups. Jamie stayed in Connecticut for good, living near the Housatonic and taking a larger and larger role (as Sandy's wildly prosperous career became more demanding) in looking after their four children. In 1992, twenty years after Munich, he made a remarkable Olympic comeback at age thirty-nine. For those who knew him best, his startling fourth-place finish at Barcelona in the two-man whitewater canoe competition simply reaffirmed what they'd always known: He was unstoppable when he wanted to master something.

Yet the Barcelona Games, his last major competition, wasn't really the high note he'd hoped. He'd been featured as the gold-medal favorite in a pre-Olympics article in *Sports Illustrated*. Finishing a few tenths of a second out of the money wasn't how he wanted to end up (in fact, a controversial judging error denied Jamie and his partner, Lecky Haller, a bronze medal). He'd had a nice career at Yale, had gotten the opportunity to be a hands-on dad, and had written a children's book and an unpublished novel, but sometimes he regretted that he hadn't let paddling consume his life during his prime. In 1975 he was the top-ranked boater in America but elected not to compete in the World Championships, a surprising decision especially since he was a favorite for gold. With the arrival of a new generation of U.S. talents, the bypassed 1975 Worlds amounted to his last shot at a solo championship. "I had the attitude that paddling wasn't real life. It was just a game," he told a newspaper reporter about his haste to immerse himself in a more refined, serious realm. "But since then I've discovered real life is just a game, too."

Tom and Jamie, along with their older sisters, Mary and Evelyn, *were* products of a kids' outdoor fantasy: They were raised on a creek-bordered, thickly wooded swath of family inherited land in Colesville, a section of Silver Spring, Maryland. Their father, Roger, was a grade-school teacher at Landon private school in Bethesda. Their mother, May, played polo from time to time on the all-men's team at George Washington University (where she earned graduate and post graduate degrees) and founded her then all-girls Valley Mill camp in 1956. Beautiful, keenly observant, and a little awkward in crowds, May McEwan introduced her energetic, eldest son to kayaking in the early sixties, electing to take the course with Tom and in the process getting nearly as taken away with whitewater as he. Along with Tom, and later Jamie, she built her own fiberglass boats at camp and well into her forties began to challenge the steeper rapids on the Potomac. "Mom used to tell this story about Jamie, then ten, and one of the early times he flipped his boat," says Evelyn. "He'd poke his head up and say, 'Mom,' then he'd get sucked back under. After about three or four times—Mom was apparently busy—Jamie finally screamed, 'Mom, do you want me to drown?'"

In 1973 she accompanied a U.S. women's whitewater junior slalom team to Europe as a coach but raced as well. The influence she had on Tom and Jamie was obvious to all—and she was there in 1972 when Jamie stepped atop the podium to collect his Olympic bronze—but in 1975, May McEwan took her own life, her death a shattering tragedy for the family and many in the

Potomac area community. "She lived such a beautiful life," says Evelyn. "It's hard, hard to understand." The impact on Jamie and Tom—then twenty-two and twenty-nine, respectively—is impossible to quantify, but her passing certainly left a massive hole in their lives.

Among the Potomac tribe there were always two schools of thought about Tom's enigmatic path since then. There were those who weren't sure what he had done with his life. And some of those same people—many of whom graduated to successful careers, families, and big homes—glumly reflected that they weren't really sure what they'd done with theirs. Said Norm Bellingham, a "red shirt" student of Tom's who won a gold medal in the 1988 Olympics: "You can't imagine how addictive Tom and that group were. I made a conscious decision to break from that group. Back then it was just really hard to understand where it was gonna go at the end of the day." Bellingham, who now studies mental toughness in potential medal-winning athletes for the U.S. Olympic Committee, still wonders why he splintered off, whether it says something about him or Tom—or both. Bellingham was aware that Tom seemed to be teaching a way to live life, not win races. At the time he thought it was more important to win races. The career track followed. "Look at where a lot of us have ended up," he says. "Our lives are nauseatingly traditional. Tom pursues excellence in a way that is so nontraditional and pure, it's hard to know what to do with it."

Many of Tom's students, and Jamie, too, asked some of the same questions, wondering about their past selves and present incarnations, wondering if Tom was merely an incurable Peter Pan or a model of unblemished integrity. Naturally, Jamie half muses, as he has always on trips of these sorts, if he'll measure up. Not that Tom is out to test him or judge him, but it's hard for anyone to be entirely at ease when his big brother never, ever flinches. Tom was still as hungry, fearless, and committed as ever. Jamie always figured he'd write a book about him someday. Every week it seemed he was going to some river somewhere, missing the rendezvous with the pickup shuttle van, and spending another night out in wet clothes without food, just a hair or two ahead of hypothermia or worse. On the river he slept either in the open or in an old threadbare sleeping bag fit for a junior camper. "How come the older I get, the more I accumulate?" a client once asked, "and the older Tom gets, the less he accumulates?" Just last winter, so the story goes, Tom was leading a group of clients on a river trip in Mexico. They came up to a waterfall where the plan was to rope up and rappel into their boats below, something that in and of itself isn't an everyday occurrence on a commercial trip. Instead, Tom took a stroll out of sight of his clients, and leapt. It was a seventy-five-foot drop into uncharted water. You could call such stunts silly, reckless even, or you could call it training. Tom was always training for something bigger, wilder. The Tsangpo Gorge, it occurs to Jamie, is it.

Less clear is what this is all about for him. Is he here to have fun, or to go after another Olympic-quality milestone? Or should he even be here? He certainly prepared with his hallmark intensity and thoroughness, taking expeditionary trips with Doug and others, and training himself in advanced river rescue and rock climbing. He used a kitchen scale to weigh caloric sources, and, finding fat to be the least heavy, tested himself on a new meal plan enriched with heaping tablespoons of pure canola and olive oil. His chiseled physique, bright smile, and tousled mop of brown hair seemed bequeathed to him for life. Arriving in Kathmandu on September 24—coincidentally his forty-sixth birthday—he'd been awestruck by the countryside, soon exchanging

"Wow, look at that!" gasps with Roger on the truck ride through the Himalaya. But given the events of the past few hours, it's hard to imagine the Tsangpo was meant to be. Even on the first day, he was involved in a mix-up looking for Paulo and missed most of the paddling. No, nothing has gone quite according to plan. There is a strong sense that if anyone has taken the good and proper road to this place, it's his brother, or maybe Doug—not him.

≋

BACK AT THE BEACH CAMPSITE, THE REST OF THE TEAM WAITS AND wonders for news of Jamie. Their route here hasn't been easy, either. The trio worked its way down two large rapids, taking lines around the corners of things, as Tom put it. Both Tom and Roger, eager to exercise some control over the river, are extra conservative. Doug is more his normal self, carving a line or two out near the hole-studded middle. On a couple of occasions he gets flipped, but each time he rolls up quickly. Whatever problems Doug had with his roll—or, more accurately, his boat—seem gone. Doug's back to being Doug, thinks Tom. Here to run the river, he's finally getting a chance to do it. He looks pumped.

Around camp, Roger tells Tom and Doug that he thinks Jamie's episode is a real wake-up call. The most innocuous mistakes—Tom not telling Roger and Doug what he was up to, Jamie sliding off the rock—turned into life-threatening situations in a matter of moments. The exposure on this river was unbelievable. "We can't split up like we did," he says, pointing out the fact that half the team was out of position, or at least unaware of where the others were. "Doug and I were three hundred feet up. We couldn't scramble down fast enough if we had had to help. Next time we split up, let's be in radio contact," he adds. As for the future, nobody knows what's up. Roger isn't feeling too enthusiastic about continuing the whitewater trip with Jamie out. They'd arrived at four as the minimum party size, thinking that two could look after each other in case they had to find help for a seriously injured team member. The final team member would be needed to stay with the victim. Three seemed to tempt fate. Like fishing trawlers that operate hundreds of miles offshore with a skeleton crew, they'd be fine if everything went according to plan, but stretched dangerously thin if a disaster struck. A smaller team worries Tom and Doug less, but they don't press the topic. They hope he'll change his mind.

The final, somewhat ill-timed task of the day is a satellite phone link-up with a National Public Radio reporter in Washington, D.C. The team is calling in weekly to report progress for broadcast. In the interview Tom is upbeat and informative, but gives no hint he's discouraged or that the trip is hanging together by a proverbial thread. He explains that they're bound for the inner gorges, and hope to paddle as much as they can. They're paddling the margins of the river, scouting for long, arduous distances, and trying to "stay out of the huge power of this river." If you are successful, will you be the first group to travel the full length of the Tsangpo, the NPR reporter asks. "Well, yes, we certainly would be the first to travel the full length of the Tsangpo," Tom replies, sounding like a second baseman being asked at season's start if it's true he'd hold the record if he smashed seventy-one home runs. "You know we have quite a distance and still a huge project ahead of us."

The next morning Harry Wetherbee, heading up the Gyala-based support team, radios the river team that Jamie is okay. Tom assumed he'd overnight somewhere, then finish up the hike in the morning. Instead they learn that Jamie kept going for ten hours straight, finally to be met at 2:00 A.M. by Pemba Sherpa and a team of porters searching with headlamps. "I finally found the path," says Jamie. "If I hadn't, they never would've found me." Two more hours of difficult hiking got them to the riverbank and the ferry, where Harry—and daybreak—awaited.

At Gyala is old friend Lukas Blücher. He'd seen the blue boat with the red tip floating down the river as he trekked toward the village, and immediately feared the worst. At the village he learned that Jamie was okay, but the boat was missing. Upon meeting Jamie in the morning, Blücher tells him he's sorry, but adds that maybe not all is lost. Downstream from Gyala is a huge kind of flat texture, he said, and an eddy a kilometer by a kilometer and a half wide. He knew, he'd scouted it. "Maybe it's not all bad. Maybe you have luck and it got trapped there." Maybe, but the two of them are doubtful. Between the time Blücher saw the boat and the time of the accident was only a few hours. In that time the river had managed to shoot the empty boat eighteen miles. Blücher is on his way out today, he adds, bound for Lhasa and then his home in Germany. He probably was never really close to reversing himself and calling in his kayaking team, but the events of the past few days have confirmed his decision. It was tempting to get caught up in the "race to Shangri-la" hype, but clearly a race was not only stupid but also deadly. He didn't think the boaters were under that spell, but he wasn't entirely certain why they persisted either. "It is just no use," Blücher E-mailed his partner Doug Ammons. "I don't have to go any further. This amount of water just won't fit in the gorge together with us."

On October 9 in Gyala, the day after Jamie's arrival and Blücher's departure, a relieved river team glides onto a sandy beach and shoulders their boats for the steep half-hour hike up to the village. There are a handful of villagers, including a visiting monk in a flowing crimson robe, who have come down off the hill to get a closer look. As Roger, Tom, and Doug step out of their boats and stretch to shake the feeling back in their legs, it's fairly obvious that the arrival has been highly anticipated. The monk twirls Roger's doubled-bladed, break-apart paddle and looks quizzically inside the boat's cockpit, where watertight bags of food and gear are crammed into the shallow spaces fore and aft. The extent of the monk's possessions, for what is to be a weeks-long pilgrimage into the gorge, is a small satchel and a rolled-up, ruglike mat to sleep on. There's alpine-style for you, jokes Roger, who is elated to have landed, but is increasingly self-conscious since nobody seems to be doing anything but staring at them. Wouldn't it be nice to slide into this place unobtrusively, like a true pilgrim, he thinks. Things are shaping up differently for them. Without a doubt, they're going to be a sideshow.

It has taken them the better part of two more days to get here. Yesterday they'd backed off a sweeping bend where a spit of land pinched the river into a series of crushing holes. The portage of several hundred vertical feet pushed everyone's heart rates to the brink—and to get back to river level they'd used climbing ropes to lower their boats in a series of eighty-foot rappels. Earlier today the canyon began to open again, the foamy wild water and the low-pitched, decibel-rising rumble of 'round-the-bend rapids giving way to a last, long, boulevard-like stretch. For the past two miles into the beach, the purring river ran as flat as a carpet.

Jamie actually sees them arrive—they and the river appear to be a good five hundred feet below—but he's occupied. A couple of hunters have apparently found the kayak in exactly the area the German described. They'd dragged the boat off the river and stashed it in a tree somewhere on the opposite shore. The villagers, Jamie, and Harry are embroiled in protracted negotiations to arrange a retrieval mission. One of the villagers has a small motorboat—typically used for crossing the river for visits to a monastery and a pilgrimage shrine—but the cost for salvaging Jamie's boat is obviously exorbitant. Two thousand *yuan,* they want. The team counters with five hundred. Amid the back and forth, Doug arrives. "You found your boat!" Not me, gestures Jamie, these herders did. "And I don't have it *yet.*" Ultimately the two groups settle on the reward: For about one hundred dollars and a tarp, the hunters will go get the canoe.

There's much to hammer out regarding the trip's future—the true guts of the journey are coming up, and the first four days haven't been smooth—but the feeling for Jamie is that of a second life. Miraculously, his trip is back on.

The credit belongs to the man who is actually in the arena, whose face is marred by dust and sweat and blood; who . . . at the best knows in the end the triumph of achievement and who at the worst, if he fails, at least fails while daring greatly.

—THEODORE ROOSEVELT

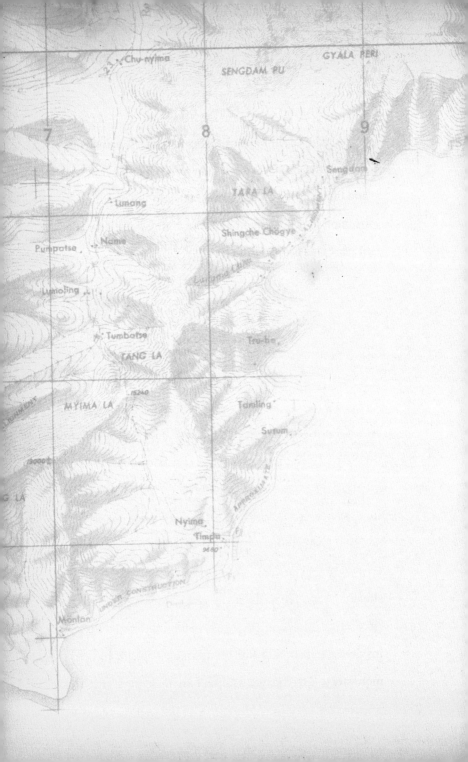

Gyala, Tibet, October 10

On a wide plain above the river, Gyala (pronounced *Gee-ala)* is a tiny village of stone houses under walnut trees. The hothouse air is sticky sweet, the gorge serving as a conduit through the Himalaya for tropical currents borne from the south. At river level, a short walk downstream, is a paradisiacal white sand beach bordered by bluffs and teeming tropical forest. Across the 100-meter-wide river is the deserted Gyala monastery, Sinje Chogyal. A frail skiff, powered by an even more frail one-cylinder smoking diesel, shuttles brave pilgrims on the dicey bank-to-bank journey. According to legend, the deity Sinje Chogyal is chained inside the stream that hurtles down a steep cliff next to the monastery. The image, sculpted in rock in a small cave behind the waterfall, is veiled now by the rushing waters. It is the exact same cascade that Kintup saw (sparking the grail-like hunt for the Lost Falls of the Brahmaputra). The Sinje Chogyal torrent slackens in the winter and early spring, lifting its misty plume for ritual observations and long meditations. The bluff-top monastery of Pemakochung, where Gyala Peri and Namche Barwa's summits brush within a mere thirteen miles of each other, is a difficult four- or five-day bushwhack down the right bank. Right now the trek is nearly impossible, since parts of the track remain buried by the Tsangpo's high water.

Stirring as their physical setting is, the poor village seems barely afloat. There are maybe a dozen homes inhabited by farmers, with a few beleaguered yak herds roaming nearby. There is no school, no running water, or much in the way of apparent food—in fact, Roger, noticing no signs of crops anywhere, wonders whether the harvest season has come to a close or simply never got under way to begin with. The spiritual veneer of the place seems a little rough around the edges. Prior to the river team's arrival, Harry broke the ice with the headman, not with smoky Buddhist ritual, but by joining him in a little .22 target practice. Harry's ability to hit the fifty-yards-away bottle on first shot earned him, and by extension the expedition as a whole, some initial celebrity, but the hard negotiations for Jamie's boat turned relations unavoidably tense. Paulo wonders if Gyala's precocious location at the narrowing entrance to the inner gorge has altered the normally charitable mood of a Buddhist hamlet. Gyala is the last village in the upper gorge, and in recent years the residents have seen a growing number of needy foreign expeditions. The stupendous amount of money floating through the gorge—in the way of fancy gear, clothing, and electronics—is impossible not to notice, and for villagers, who often know the terrain best, it's impossible to ignore. With each passing expedition the divide between what the determined visitors expect and what the hosts expect probably grows deeper. Jamie would pay anything to get his boat back, but Paulo is alarmed by an attitude he characterizes as mercenary and unprofessional. "It just feels like it's their mission to rip us off," he'd say later.

The close proximity in which everyone lives seems to aggravate both parties: The team has politely declined the lodgings—an abandoned one-room wooden shack—and is instead quartered in its geodesic-domed tents (and is using the shack for its gear and for group map sessions). The base-camp setup offers no privacy—Roger is right, they are the show. Meanwhile, the terrific amount of gear and influx of people leave some of the villagers justly unsettled. How long do they plan to stay? There is no outbreak of hostility, but the vibe isn't smooth. Tom mitigates some of the damage by paying a cordial evening visit to the headman's house, accompanied by a translator the team hired in Lhasa. In the smoky, flickering light produced by a stone hearth's taper, Tom gamely accepts a near continuous service of yak butter tea and outlines the expedition for his incredulous counterpart. The river is not a friendly place, the headman emphasizes. Do they understand how dangerous it is? Tom nods but quickly deflects the conversation toward questions about Gyala and other areas within the gorge. According to the headman, there used to be a regular, well-used trail network between Gyala and the villages downstream. But in recent years that flow has slowed to a trickle, the result, Tom gathers, of a massive earthquake in 1950 and the Chinese assault on Tibet's monasteries during the Cultural Revolution. There is no school for the children, he explains, because they haven't been able to keep a teacher.

Tom is sympathetic, but the headman isn't the sort of leader he can summon much respect for: If his lackluster day-to-day routine is any measure, he seems resigned to the village's ruin and what little industriousness he shows seems mostly to do with plucking more money out of them. Tom says goodnight after an hour, assuring him they aren't going to stay forever. But he can't say exactly how long, either, since the hunters haven't returned to Gyala with Jamie's boat yet. That they've been gone so long—over a day—isn't helping anyone's peace of mind. If the reunited boating team was banking on a restorative interlude at Gyala, it isn't getting it.

To avoid obsessing over the whereabouts of Jamie's boat, Roger, Tom, and Doug go off on a reconnaissance, eventually finding a runnable rapid a mile downstream from Gyala. With their boats unweighted and little danger of getting swept around the bend into the bigger stuff, the trio get an opportunity to rip into the whitewater, pounding through the towering waves in the momentarily benign heart of the river. They're so far out that the signal for a remote-controlled camera won't cover the distance from shore, so Doug rigs up a system where he duct-tapes the remote to his paddle and tags behind Tom and his deck-mounted camera, firing pictures as they crash through the watery barrier. The paddle-like-hell catch-up game feels like a race, no gates, the arena formed by a ring of blindingly white snow peaks. After each run of "video rapid" they carry back up the shore and do it again and again and again. The tension release—hell, the pure fun—is almost profound. For the first time since they started, they are, as Jamie had hoped, coexisting peacefully, getting along with their Goliath-sized ring partner.

That night the debate heats up about their immediate future: What's next? Should this be their quitting point? Or should they hazard on, continuing their catch-as-catch-can approach as far as it will take them, maybe all the way to Pemakochung, twelve miles downstream, and maybe farther, to Rainbow Falls (twenty-six miles)? Or should they ditch the boats and start working their way downstream on foot, plunging into rain-forest terrain no westerner has visited before? As it has been from the beginning, the team's viewpoint is not unanimous. Roger, relieved to make it this far, wonders if they shouldn't call it quits and go somewhere altogether different. "How about the Caribbean?" he half-jokes.

During the several days of discussion at Gyala, Jamie and Doug favor continuing with boats. They're here; their boats are here. Tom says they're unlikely even to get to Rainbow Falls, but Jamie and Doug, never having been here before, can't believe things won't open up. At the very least, Jamie says, they should try to reach the deepest point within the gorge. Roger likes the idea, too, but isn't sure he knows why. They have nothing to be ashamed of, no need to go out of their way to save face. The river is huge—river people understand that. Really, Roger is looking no further than not getting himself killed, and yet he's not hard-line—he's certainly not delivering any ultimatums. As long as he feels nobody is intent on doing anything that'll get him killed, he's willing to trudge on. He doesn't want to be the one to pull the plug on the expedition. Maybe—heck, probably—they'd continue on without him, but Roger is convinced that four, and only four, is a safe number. If something bad were to happen, without him it wouldn't be easy to deal with.

Tom appears relatively neutral, but likes the exploratory advantage the boats give them (for crossing the river). He recaps in his log that the size of the rapids is "intimidating, imposing, trepidacious" but that they seem able to maintain a comfort zone amid the outsized terrain. "It could be really hairy," says Jamie. "Well, what do we do? Think about it or take a vote?" Think about it, they decide. There are obvious reasons to turn back: their fatigue, the near-disastrous accidents, the squeezing canyon walls, and their own uncertainty. The high water has turned away two other teams now, Lukas Blücher's and Steve Currey's. The latter, who was due to arrive in a few weeks with clients, catarafts, and kayakers, is convinced that the river is a minefield and that the Walker-McEwan team, if they proceed, is a tragedy waiting to happen.

But after a playful day in the boats and a dramatic shift in tactical strategy, the tide changes in camp. The team opts to push forward. Because they need much more time to safely and slowly negotiate the stretch between Gyala and Rainbow Falls, they'll load up with more provisions. Much more. They'd originally envisioned the passage taking eight days; now they think the more realistic figure is fifteen. The extra food—some forty pounds against the planned-for twenty—is insurance against long bouts of scouting and maybe being stopped cold near Pemakochung, where the river regathers yet again for a steeper, more lethal stretch. On the left bank the topo maps show an apparent overland escape route up a steep ravine (eventually to the tiny confluence villages), but the multi-day ascent and traverse promises to be difficult and to necessitate extra food. "We're going to go ahead and bite off this next chunk and who knows what's gonna happen," says Jamie, announcing the decision to Paulo. Jamie got his boat back hours ago (apparently out of curiosity, the hunters who retrieved it had unnecessarily gutted the boat of everything in it, including its glued-on outfitting and flotation bags. All the parts have been returned, but rerigging the boat amounts to another half-day delay). "We may need to be rescued," he continues. "The fifteen days of food is gonna make our boats very heavy, but we feel we have to allow that much time for all the unknowns and the height of the river."

Part of the momentum to proceed comes from Wick's progress. He's en route to the heart of the Great Bend after all, having finally reached road's end at Pailung and begun his monster hike. The well-worn, roller-coaster-like trail along the Po Tsangpo to the confluence is spectacular. The slim, exposed footpath sometimes faintly reminds him of the northern Appalachian Trail, the Eastern classic that briefly darts across his old Dartmouth campus en route to the White Mountains. Of course, the AT doesn't skip across wide rivers, as this trail does, using primitive steel cable crossings and trip-trap hanging bridges clinging to cliffsides. The rope-and-pulley Tsangpo River traverse, near the confluence, is arguably the most scintillating heart-thump. With steel cable paid out several hundred feet (and bowing toward the main channel at its midpoint), the crossing can strike anyone with terror. "When you are halfway along the cable," according to a local guide in the lavish pictorial book *Brahmaputra*, "you have to muster all your strength to climb back up towards the other bank, exerting every single muscle in your arms and legs. The sound of the water is deafening and the whirlpools beneath you can make your head spin. It is at this point that you may be overcome with nausea and you may become immobilized, unable to go forwards or backwards, a prisoner of the river until, overcome with tiredness, you fall into the waters which draw you to certain death."

Fortuitously perhaps, Wick's itinerary keeps him on the north bank and doesn't require a main river crossing. At Sengchen and Medung, small neighboring villages near the confluence, he completes the easiest leg of his trek and hires a dozen

Monpa porters for the trackless journey to come. Meanwhile the other support team, headed by Harry, will stay in Gyala, ready to help out if need be until the river team decides it can get downstream and commit for good to either Rainbow Falls or at least Pemakochung. The satellite phone links the three teams' movements, with prearranged calling and listening times enabling everyone to know of on-the-go changes. Though the river team is having trouble contacting Wick directly, it can patch through Harry, who can get him. Wick is keeping his communications short, since he's about to descend into the abyss and needs to conserve battery power. The river team, however, is paired with Harry in Gyala, and since Harry can count on the truck in Pe as a regenerative power source, the members avail themselves a little more freely of the ship-to-shore wonders of the Immersat satellite phone. Several call home. Roger has checked in multiple times with Nancy, the no-more-than-ten-minute conversations ranging from the pragmatic (Roger filling in his wife about some esoteric and unexplained part of the Gauley operation) to borderline emotional. "A fair bit of the water is pretty crazy," he told her from Pe, "but we're being as careful as we can." The calls "made things real bearable," Roger remembers, with each team member's ration getting more valuable by the minute. "The phone was expensive and battery time pretty precious," he adds, "so we started bartering with each other, you know, it was getting like, 'I'll give you two chocolate bars for one of your phone calls.'" Roger held off making another call at Gyala, figuring he'd save his time for wherever they were October 22, the couple's fourth wedding anniversary.

In a brief talk with Connie near Gyala, Doug sounds neither alarmed by what he's seen so far, nor unrealistic. "The river is a lot higher than any of us want it to be," he says, "but we're fine."

The next call might not be for a while, he adds, since they're going deeper and will have to save the phone's battery for emergency use. He'd call when he could. The crispness of his voice is almost disorienting—he sounds as if he's calling from school, not from the edge of the world.

As they ready themselves to get back on the river, the team checks their Global Positioning System readings against the maps. Their handheld receiver device, another commercially available gizmo originally developed for the military, uses a series of overhead satellites to triangulate on their position. They can keep precise track of their progress, both in miles traveled and in vertical feet dropped. With latitude and longitude positions plotted against their assortment of maps, they know where they are and are reasonably certain what's coming next. Using the team's original topo maps, Doug has already computed the average feet-per-mile steepness by measuring the distance between two elevations. (Though the exact locations of the drops are inaccurate on the original topo, the general gradient is not.) Scribbling the numbers into the margin of the team's enhanced "sky" map, they've delineated the sections alphabetically, beginning at Pe and continuing well past the confluence into the lower canyon.

In general, the steepness increases radically in severity, from only thirteen feet per mile near Pe to fifty, one hundred, and more than two hundred feet per mile. A two-hundred-feet-per-mile stretch is suicidally steep on a big-volume river, but what the number doesn't say is precisely where the drops occur. Rarely is the fall line steady. Much of the team's hope for running stretches of the inner gorges was based on the supposition that the drop might be concentrated at Chu Belap and Rainbow Falls, making some of the in-between stretch within the ballpark of Class VI boaters (if it could be reached). The team's first glimpse of the aerial maps back in McLean put much of that discussion to rest, showing the chunk downstream of Rainbow Falls as a death plunge. There might be a brief doable run on the straightaway upstream of Chu Belap (the area Tom had seen on his scout the year before), but according to Doug's calculations, that stretch averages well over two hundred feet per mile. Another intriguing section is a lower canyon stretch below Payi that they descriptively identify as the "7." On the aerials there is a gash of white (a major falls) followed by discernible ripples (a wave train made up of twenty-five-foot-plus giants, they think). Hardly boatable, but the riverine tsunamis are something everyone wants to see with their own eyes.

In the best of all worlds, the team sees an outcome in which they reach the deepest point in the gorge, somewhere just downstream of Pemakochung. Taking out soon thereafter (presumably aided by Wick) for an exploration of the inner-gorge stretch, they'd continue to portage around the waterfalls, then drop down into the straightaway stretch before yet another and even longer portage past Chu Belap, all the way to the confluence. Wick and/or Harry would lend support and technical hiking gear for that march. If time permitted, they'd boat a part of the lower canyon below the confluence before winter closed in. In practical terms the best they can probably hope for is to paddle past the deepest point in the gorge, followed by a decent foot exploration where they might get a look at Rainbow and the Crease. Though nobody really talks about it, the emphasis is no longer on a first descent at all—no longer kayaking as much as they can. In Tom's and Roger's minds there is a sort of subtle shift to "doing our job, gaining ground." Their view is increasingly turning away from the river and toward the uncharted landscape surrounding it. Jamie and Doug remain hopeful that the whitewater part of the trip isn't entirely dead. It's no secret that hiking isn't as easy an option for them.

At noon on October 11 the team finishes packing. After one more bit of awkwardness concerning what they're willing to pay for use of the storage quarters, the river team sets off on the steeply dropping path to the beach. As Jamie line-drags his boat and a hundred pounds of gear across the bony terrain, there is a look of outright astonishment from those who've retrieved it. After being dropped off by the ferry where the rapids start, they'd trekked to the eddy, then carried the boat the entire distance back to the village—an intensely tough, two-day bush trek on sloping muddy trails. Because they were concerned that any rough handling, like dragging it, might crack the thing in two, they never let it touch the ground. In a few days the river team will find itself battling the same terrain and marveling that the men didn't get fed up and ditch Jamie's boat off one of the many promontories.

There is some relief in being in motion again, but for the first time in the trip there is no immediate safety net downstream. This is the last village they'll see for weeks, and these may be the last people they'll see, too. Any pilgrims that might be headed to Pemakochung—and many do, to trek the well-marked *khora* circuit—usually come in the spring and from another direction. What the core of the canyon possesses isn't entirely a mystery, but how they'll push through it is one. With soggy, low-hanging cumulus clouds overhead, they slip into the river and wave goodbye to Harry, his wife, Doris, and their travel-agency chaperon. With repeated assurances that everything will be all right, they've persuaded the chaperon to let the team off completely on their own. The man looks nervous but relieved. The Chinese government requires all foreign visitors to restricted areas in Tibet to be accompanied from the start of their journey to completion. If something were to go wrong and he had to fess up that he wasn't there to witness it or, better yet prevent it, he'd get in serious trouble. Nasty as the consequences might be, however, there's even more motivation to let them paddle away: Who would want to go where they're going?

Tom's boat feels sluggish as he sets out—with the weight he's carrying, he's powering the whitewater equivalent of a barge—but he's relieved to push off and put the tense delibera- tions of the past few days behind them. There's actually a sense of lightness; what he's long imagined he's actually going to do. A short time later he confidently approaches "Video Rapid," the same wave train they'd done countless times a couple days ago, and strokes for the now-familiar line. But as he drops into the first trough, he realizes the water level has dropped just enough to mutate the big rollers—they're now collapsing on themselves, the grabby turbulence exactly what pummeled Doug back at Pe. Tom smashes into the breaker as fast as he can, figuring he'll still crash through, but the river doesn't give an inch, the blasting wall of water seemingly charging as fast upstream as downstream. The collision feels like a knee-buckling punch to the gut, and moments after impact, he and his boat are sprawling backward end over end. Stunned but together, Tom recovers quickly, rolling back up, and riding out the last waves. He isn't banged up, or coughing up river water, but he is struck that the Tsangpo just delivered another message—and this one, well, it's somewhere between beware and a cross-this-line-if-you-dare ultimatum.

A few miles downstream (beyond the recycling eddy where Jamie's boat, and a swirl of river debris, was trapped), they are stopped by a major forty-to-fifty-foot drop at a sharp right-hand bend. Walking through the shoreline woods, they find that the rapid continues for some distance. They deploy to scout both sides of the river, Jamie and Doug taking the left side, Roger and Tom the right. Cliffs block the left-side route—one of the long, river-pinching spurs of Gyala Peri. They might be able to get around it, Tom and Jamie think, but it won't be easy. Tom and Roger march more than a mile down the right side, counting off some ten drops and choreographing an intricate dance in which they run the smaller drops, portage others, and skip from eddy to eddy. When the team regathers, it elects to work down the right side of the river. The members return to their boats, dragging, carrying, and paddling the rest of the day. The next day is worse. Working downstream another arduous mile, they run out of shoreline, the slim margin of boulders disappearing and a cliff barring the way. Nobody sees a possibility for crossing the unceasing rapid—the river is too wide, the water far too turbulent—and yet the portage is equally daunting, a sheer, 2,000-foot vertical ascent followed by a sketchy rappel back to the riverbed. They have no option but to retreat and grind their way back upstream. They are at it almost two days, hacking away trails through thick bramble and bush and tugging along their ungainly, ninety-pound Arctic-like sledges. "The next two days are devoted to making negative progress," Tom despairs in his trip log.

It's unclear what if any communication the team has with its sponsor, National Geographic, but on October 12, the same day the team is backtracking, the Expedition Council's Rebecca Martin sends out a fax to Ian Baker informing him they've funded his upcoming trip for $38,000. Baker is surprised by the news—they've actually tracked him down to a hotel in Lhasa, where he's leading a cultural tour for the Smithsonian Institution. Though Baker had always planned to return to the Hidden Falls with Hamid Sardar and Ken Storm, he'll now be joined by Bryan Harvey, a Geographic videographer. The plans haven't changed much;

the team will hike back to the falls they saw in the spring, and document the height of the cascade using a laser range-finder. For the film's dramatic purposes, Baker and his cohorts need to behave as if the exploratory and the unveiling of Hidden Falls are occurring for the first time.

Back on the right bank, the team is nearing the "lake," the large, flat-textured spot below Gyala, where they can recross. In normal instances retreating a few miles might not be so hard. They'd all been on trips where the route-finding had been complex and time-consuming. In British Columbia, Jamie, Doug, and E.J. McCarthy had spent a heinous day climbing up and out of a canyon in order to avoid what they wrongly figured to be an unrunnable stretch. But in that case there was always the motivation that they would finish the river. Here the goal is more elusive, and given how little progress they've made, Jamie finds it hard not to get frustrated. To his surprise, Doug seems to be managing much better. "You know, one thing that makes all this portaging and hiking worthwhile is just the great smell of these herbs." Jamie—hot, tired, disgusted—shoots him a look. Herbs? Jamie pauses. Indeed, there is a remarkably strong smell. He later reflects that some people sort of marginalized Doug as this super-analytical entity. He *was* very analytical, but he didn't just think his way down the river. He probably experienced it more fully than most people ever do.

In that way, Doug was more the scientist-explorer, similar to Britain's renowned flower hunters early in the century. Francis Kingdon-Ward, the most famous of them, used to travel with two strings to his bow, his book publisher once wrote. "And it was hard to say whether exploration or botanizing has the first claim upon him." As an explorer, he went to determined and exceedingly risky lengths to solve one of the last great problems of the nineteenth century: unveiling "the Lost Falls of the Brahma-putra." As a flower hunter, he painstakingly and anonymously collected. In his celebrated tramps he snipped, cataloged, and carted seed back to England by the trunkload. Doug wasn't a naturalist, but he possessed the same skill set: He was a meticulous, well-trained observer with a beaming fascination for places of intrigue. Like the flower hunters, he seemed to revel in a budding, prolific landscape that rose out of one of the most cataclysmic landscapes on earth.

On the banks downstream, where the rain-bearing winds breached the Himalaya and completed the gorge's transition from high plateau to verdant oasis, there were not only such collectibles as madonna lilies, silver fir, and the cedarlike Tsuga, but a thousand kinds of animals, including snow leopards, Bengal tigers, pandas, long-tailed langurs, white-lipped deer, golden cats, and Assamese macaques. Given Doug's work in the lab, he wasn't uncomfortable with, or easily beaten down by, the grinding stages of *process* (of which this portage was an extreme example). On the other hand, Kingdon-Ward hadn't had to shoulder a hundred-pound kayak on his journey. In roughly the same section they're walking now, Kingdon-Ward had with him twenty-three porters, several companions, two dogs, and one sheep.

On October 12 they finally make it back to the flat stretch below Gyala and flirt briefly with the idea of calling the expedition off. They know they're in for an equally formidable approach on the left side. The mistakes grind at all of them. In eight days on the river, they're merely twenty miles along—about two miles a day. Everything is so painfully slow: the driving, the boating, the walking. It took them four days to reach Gyala, instead of the usual two. Pemakochung is almost as far again, and from what they've seen along the right bank, the stretch is one continuous, almost river-wide rapid. A few weeks later another trekker en route to Pemakochung will get there in only eight days. In some ways their chosen tool for the river exploratory—at least at this swollen water level—seems utterly and dangerously wrong. The inimitable Rick Fisher said as much years ago. Fielding a call from an even-then inquisitive Gordon, Fisher had told him a raft was the wrong exploratory tool and a kayak even more wrong. "It's not in our culture to believe something is impossible," Fisher said. "But taking a boat into the narrows is just the wrong equipment to address the terrain. It's like trying to hammer a nail with a saw. Won't work."

The remarkable fact is that team members are not at each other's throats. Hard, team-oriented expeditions are prone to collapse even under the best conditions, but especially when progress is retarded or the mission changes scope. Living for days on end in a wind-scoured tent is one of the most challenging parts of a Himalayan mountaineering trip. On the Tsangpo the thing itself, the river, was testing their patience, not weather or being stuck in a tent. The sheer quantity of unknowns, the absence of a procedure, put the Tsangpo team under severe mental strain. About the only break they had—and maybe a critical one, as far as team relations went—was that they'd been wise enough to limit media intrusions. Even Paulo, whom they all liked, was allowed to travel with the river team only along the "easy" stretch between Pe and Gyala. After that the team would film itself and Paulo would mostly be tagging along with Harry or Wick. They'd also managed to avoid a Web site, an almost de rigueur element of big-budget expeditioning. The Peeping-Tom presence of the online world is often a mixed bag for expedition members, and sometimes even ruptures a team's fragile dynamic. In one notable case, during an alpine-style climb of a massive Himalayan wall called Trango Tower, the pair of mountaineers began squabbling after reading each other's Internet diary posts.

Though there was plenty that was unsettling about the Tsangpo expedition, and though there were different points of view on the risks they were taking and how they might proceed, there were no thunderous clashes of egos, no mutinous fractures. The almost improbable camaraderie seemed a plain enough reason not to pull the plug. There was no evil, reckless captain. Bad as it was, doomed as they sometimes seemed, nobody came near snapping. Unlike mountaineering trips, the team wasn't stuffed into the same tent at night and tied into the same line in the day. With bivvy sacks they could spread out, their turf anything from beaches to grassy bluffs. Around the hot, ascending flames of the nightly campfire, the talk didn't begin and end with the river. The quartet had opinions to air on religion, family, politics, anything and everything. Strangely, the chemistry grew. "It was never hard for any of us to put aside ego," recalls Zbel. "A big part of that was the river. It was so huge, so obviously the number-one presence. You'd go to sleep at night and you'd hear it roar and wake up and there it was again."

The relative harmony was in stark contrast to another "last great undone" whitewater expedition—the first descent of the Upper Yangtze. Like the Tsangpo, the Upper Yangtze had been closed to exploration, but in the mid-1980s the Chinese, recognizing the growing demand, bid out the river. The race attracted Chinese and American teams, the most notable of the competitors being a rafter named Ken Warren. In a tragic sequence of events, the obsessed Warren—desperate to beat another American team and two exclusively Chinese squads for the coveted first descent—refused to pull off even after team member David

Shippee died from high-altitude illness and several others quit in disgust and protest. The Yangtze race had been an appalling disaster from start to finish. Shippee was the lone American and the only member of Warren's group to perish, but in total, twelve died—half at two rapids, Yela Shoal and Moding Shoal. The whole episode was viewed as a sorry black mark that highlighted the worst that corporate expeditioning had to offer: greed, hubris, and needless death. (Though the 1998 competition for the Tsangpo struck some as a potentially disturbing case of déjà vu, the tone was a good deal different. The competition was much more muted and mysterious, partly in deference to the fact that the Tsangpo was a far harder objective—a moon shot compared with the Yangtze's transatlantic flight—and partly because nobody wanted to be lumped with the notorious Warren nor the kamikaze pilots who leapt into the fray in a misguided attempt to preserve national honor. Obviously the most striking reminder of the Yangtze debacle was the fact that well upstream—several weeks behind the Walker-McEwan team—the heralded boatman Yang Yong, who ran Tiger Leaping Gorge and achieved the Upper Yangtze first descent, struggled on.)

≈

THE BIG PROBLEM FOR THE RIVER TEAM IS THE LEFT BANK'S SPRAWLing Gyala Peri. With its immense southern flanks of black mica gneiss dropping vertically to the river, they need to improvise a way around. If they get past the cliffs, then they can get access to both the river (the map showed that it widened briefly beyond the cliffs) and the valley they'd earmarked for their last-ditch escape route to the confluence villages. They successfully ford an ice-water-cold tributary barreling off the side of the mountain.

From there the plan is to pack two days of food, ditch their boats, and set out on an extensive multi-day hike. They don't want to make the same mistake as before and plow themselves *and* their boats into another impasse. If they can hike their way down the left side, beyond the cliffs that blockaded them on the right side, then presumably they'll be able to locate a river crossing slightly downstream. That would reopen the right-hand side of the river for them—allowing them to continue either by boat or on foot to Pemakochung, while looking for another crossing point downstream. The error they'd made in their obvious eagerness to make miles was neglecting to first make sure of the next place they could cross the river. It wasn't an egregious mistake; again, the Tsangpo was the only river they'd ever encountered where traversing or ferrying was as potentially dangerous as running a major rapid. They simply needed to budget more time to scout "globally." After hiking far downstream and identifying a negotiable stretch of river to cross, they'd return upstream to retrieve their left-behind boats and begin the business of making miles.

On October 13 they bushwhack their way downstream, beginning at 9:00 A.M. and not returning to their tributary campsite, and the boats they've left behind, until almost dark. The marathon ground day is well worth the effort. In pushing beyond the route-barring cliffs on the other side of the river, where the Tsangpo takes a hard right bend, they discover calm water and the "window" they need. Now they can proceed confidently downstream with their boats, knowing they won't get closed out. None of it is easy, however. The following day they carry and haul boats past the first set of cliffs, another all-day affair (and the reason they opted for the right-hand route to begin with). The portage is brutal, but at least they're moving forward with the comfort of knowing they won't soon be retreating.

The next day's cliff, the final one, is more backbreaking work. Sort of surprisingly, Doug and Jamie say they're going to boat around it. They'll put in at the eddy below the rapid and ferry across the ripping current until they're out and around the cliff, then they'll zip back in again. It's only a hundred-yard stretch, but risky given the heavy wildwater. One slipup and they're easily in trouble, since the main current is cranking again. First, however, they help Tom and Roger rope up their boats for the sweaty haul up and over the cliff. Jamie and Doug's dash goes off without incident. Watching from the shore, Tom is pretty impressed. The folks back on the Potomac might have been surprised to see him take the conservative route—more than one thought he'd be the one to overdo it and even Tom is a bit astonished by the role reversal—but he is intent not to make a mistake. He doesn't want to die in Tibet even if some figured it was the perfect blaze-of-glory way for Tom's story to end. He is also aware that, teamwise, it's not a bad strategy to stay closer to Roger's camp than to Doug and Jamie's, who seem to be getting more enthusiastic about paddling—a fact Tom is vaguely concerned about. Roger's a big boy, and not likely to be tempted into anything the three of them might do, but just the same, Tom's keen to set a circumspect tone and make sure nobody feels perpetually outnumbered.

On the evening of October 15 they are camped above the river on a high grassy bluff, twelve miles downstream of Gyala, eight miles past their mistaken "advance" of three days earlier. They aren't free of the heavy rapids yet—the stretch they're on drops a hundred feet per mile—but they're close. A short distance downstream is the final spur of Gyala Peri and the big river bend. Beyond that is a brief section where the river levels off before falling steeply again. They're going to make it after all. During the nightly 7:00 P.M. call between Tom and Harry, Tom gives him the go-ahead to leave Gyala and begin the second stage of their leapfrog support plan. The next morning Harry, Paulo, and the porters will begin hiking back to the truck at Pe, after which they'll head for the confluence and the lower canyon. "We're committing to downstream," says Tom, who is virtually certain they can get to their designated escape route, maybe farther.

After the call Tom and Doug chat about the state of things. The river's freight-train roar makes even a brief casual conversation an effort. Tom must yell into Doug's ear as if he were at a roadhouse tavern, trying to outshout a Lynyrd Skynyrd revival band. By nobody's estimation has the journey gone as expected. Every time they get going, something seems to trip them up. Moreover, the gorge is proving as difficult by foot as by boat. Yet both are optimistic. "We've done our learning," Tom says, and Doug nods. Learning indeed. They know from Doug's near-lethal first rapid the frighteningly deceptive size and power of the river. They know a swim is probably fatal and that unlike many rivers they have run, there is very little possibility of rescuing one another. If you got into trouble, you had to get out of it. Teammates couldn't chase blindly downstream into unknown rapids, nor could they likely get a throw-rope to a teammate, since the middle of the river was too far from shore. As never before in their lives, safety hinged on error-proof judgment and self-rescue. On this river, they agreed, the team wasn't much of a safety net.

But out of their miscues—their gropings, as Tom put it—a "system" seems to be emerging. In some ways it's much like his and Wick's old waterfall-running days: Back then there was no handy blueprint, either. Trial and error had to be part of the process. Then as now, they'd been looking at water they didn't really understand. But in their eleven days they seem to have sussed out a way to tackle the gorge—and their errors haven't cost them; they know the drill to advancing now. They know where to scout from and understand the scale of the landscape. They can answer the question "What can *that* really do to you?" Their boats might seem an ill-chosen tool, but the boats mean they can stay at or near river level. They aren't several thousand feet up, peering between shifting cumulus clouds. They were right on it, and Tom and Doug agree: If they can't run the Tsangpo, they want to go down right along the water's edge where the river can be observed and absorbed. Tom swears he can remember every footstep he's taken on a wild river: what the rocks looked like, how they felt; the texture, formations, smell, taste, and subtle color variations of the flowing water. "It's seldom you can remember every day of your life, but I can remember every step I've taken here—it's like they're imprinted," he will later say. Despite their troubles, he wouldn't trade anything for the intensity and focus that comes with the territory. Clearly, Doug feels similarly. Everybody is working hard and working well together. There is reason to think—with a new system in place and everyone more settled on the level of risk they feel comfortable with—they are ready to break out.

They might get as far as Pemakochung in only a couple more days. And according to Doug's calculations, they are right on the cusp of crossing the imaginary point where the gorge is at its three-mile-plus deepest (the map point is determined by shooting a straight line from the top of Gyala Peri to Namche Barwa and marking where the line transects the river). At first he thinks they may already have passed the mark—"Hey, we can quit now, we've done it," he jokes—but he later corrects himself. Sometime tomorrow they are certain—barring some other crisis—to become the first paddlers to boat through the deepest gorge on the planet.

Wick, in his latest dispatch to Harry, reports he's almost in place. Having been trained in technical rock climbing, glacier travel, and high alpine rescues at the elite Alpini Military School in the Italian Alps decades ago, Wick is getting his refresher course. After much difficulty he is past the hunters' settlement of Chu Belap and nearing the top of a 12,000-foot ridge that Baker pointed out weeks ago. The old-growth forest through which he's traveled is awe-inspiring, like Nepal thirty or forty years ago, he says. Beginning in the lower-elevation subtropical bamboo forest, he's risen through rainforest belts encompassing vast species of flowering rhododendron, massive oaks, and ancient, two-hundred-foot-tall cypress trees. Finally, near the ridgeline, they crest into the icy alpine zone. The rainforest-to-snowline ascent sparks memories of Kingdon-Ward's most soaring prose. The going is insanely hard, but he's traveling over hallowed historical ground. He has passed the village where Kintup was sold into slavery, and is following the same tortuous route Kingdon-Ward took seventy-five years earlier in his last-gasp effort to find the Lost Falls. Moreover, like Kingdon-Ward he is accompanied by a spirited party, including his Vietnam war buddy and trip medic, Dave Phillips, Ankame Sherpa, a Tibetan ex-convict he hired in Lhasa, and a number of Monpa porters who are far more motivated by the prospect of hunting than by crashing down to river's edge in pursuit of a Western geographical obsession.

Wick intends to relieve some of his eleven porters, keeping some with him for the exploratory and deploying others with a cache of supplies at the top of the bluff and sending others back. But none of the porters are keen to split from one another—especially since the hunting in the territory they're covering is superb—and Wick doesn't press. For all of his numbing logistical preparations, there is a certain romance to all of it, even their vaguely rebellious porters. Theirs is a massive step back in time, closer to exploration's Golden Age than to the robotic-led deep-water, deep-space wanderings of the twenty-first century. Characters like he and Tom—their modern route-finding and communication apparatus notwithstanding—probably have far more in common with that era than this one.

He's read practically everything that has been written about the Himalaya. The Shangri-la imagined by British novelist James Hilton was a lost civilization in the high peaks of the Himalaya, a sanctuary where the best of world culture would be preserved in order to reseed a planet bound for self-destruction. Those who arrived did so after a perilous and unintended (but just the same compelling) journey. Shangri-la is the Western myth, Wick knows. Buddhists know no Shangri-la. As the Columbia University scholar Robert Thurman says, the Buddhist version of Shangri-la isn't some "dinky place" in a remote chasm; he defines the utopia they envision, not as a place, but as "revelation and planetary happiness on a cosmic visionary scale."

Yet within the vast Buddhist journey to enlightenment, the Tsangpo Gorge has long been identified as one of Tibet's most sacred *bayul*s, or Hidden Lands, the alternately punishing and beneficent landscape where the pious find reward and others find trouble. "[Buddhists] envision the entire river as it flows through the Great Bend and into Pemako as the central energy channel of the tantric deity Vajrayogini," explains Ian Baker in his widely read Explorers Club article of a few years back. "Gyala Peri is the goddess' head, while the peaks of Namche Barwa and Kangla Karpo represent her breasts." The river is her spine. They also believe, adds Baker, that the way is fraught with dangers, both real and imagined, and local spirits are believed to continuously test pilgrims' motivations. Waterfalls are reserved for particularly high regard, since they believe them to be guarded over by duplicitous nature spirits. As Baker continues, if the journey is undertaken purely for self-advancement, the sacred nature of the land will never be revealed and Pemako's innermost regions will remain forever out of reach. It is provocative stuff, and within the landscape and splendor and crushing remoteness of the Tsangpo, with the Monpa porters stringing prayer flags from precipices and waking most mornings in prayers and smoky offerings, the aura of the place grows rather than diminishes. Wick is a realist, hardly prone to the sometimes comical transformations that befall westerners in the spiritual grip of Tibet, but he is sure of one thing: "We are as out here as we can get," he says.

Ascending the ridge on October 15—a few miles west of where the river wraps back on itself and begins its northern Great Bend loop—Wick and his party are a day from the bluff top. From there he'll strike out for Rainbow Falls, the Crease, and whatever else lies in the gorgiest stretch of the gorge. Both teams are making it up as they go along, but both are also right in the thick of it. From the bluff Wick may be only three days' hike from the same gap that has eluded everyone from Bailey to Kingdon-Ward. The river team is a stone's throw from sweeping through the deepest point in the world's deepest gorge. They are poised to unravel the riddle once and for all—Tom, Jamie, Doug, and Roger following the unknown course of the river; Wick Rambo-ing his way in by unknown land. As the crow flies—an unhelpful measure of distance in Pemako—they are no more than a handful of miles apart.

Conway went to the balcony and gazed at the dazzling plume of Karakal; the moon was riding high in a waveless ocean. It came to him that a dream had dissolved, like all too lovely things, at the first touch of reality; that the whole world's future, weighed in the balance against youth and love, would be light as air. And he knew, too, that his mind dwelt in a world of its own, Shangri-la in microcosm, and that this world was also in peril. For even as he nerved himself, he saw the corridors of his imagination twist and strain under impact; the pavilions were toppling; all was about to be in ruins. He was only partly unhappy, but he was infinitely and rather sadly perplexed. He did not know whether he had been mad and was now sane, or had been sane for a time and now was mad again.

—James Hilton, *LOST HORIZON*

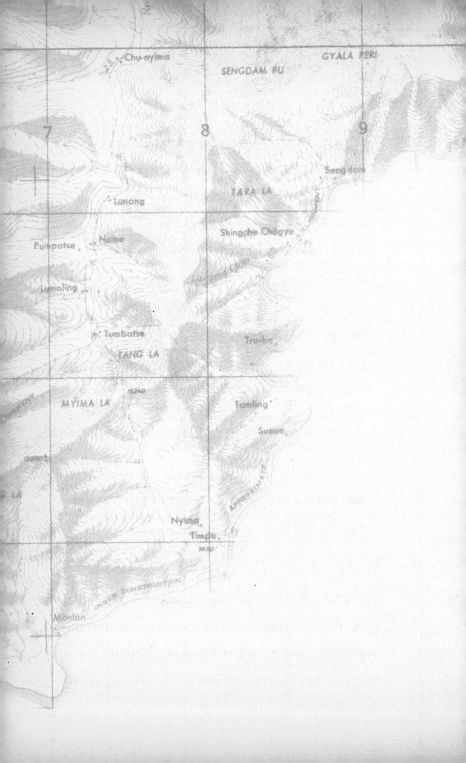

Near Gyala, October 16, 1998

THE TEAM SETS OUT NOT LONG AFTER DAYBREAK—ABOUT 7:00 A.M. in this part of the gorge. Part of the plan discussed last night is the need for earlier starts. The weather is auspicious, the warm sunshine slotting through cottony, peak-blotting clouds. From their bluff-top perch a few hundred feet above river level, they're easily able to scan three or four moves down the gorge. They are looking at more carries along the low, lushly vegetated embankments, but the final move looks more promising—maybe they'll run some whitewater after all. Beyond that the walls appear to close in and the rapids intensify. Given the choice weather and the fact that they're anticipating more walking and more rain in the days to come, Tom tells the others he's going to focus on filming today.

Uncharacteristically, Doug suffers a few bobbles in the usual eddy-to-eddy paddle-and-portage routine. He mistimes an eddy surge—not hard to do, given the all-at-once maneuver, in which he must fling his paddle ashore, pull the spray skirt, and leap onto a rock with his boat. Instead the wave breaks early and swamps his boat, forcing him to scramble to recover. Later he's almost dragged out into the seething main current when he misses another move. Whether he's tired, distracted, or just having one of those days, he's not on the flow train. Shaking his head, Doug tells Roger he's not sure what's going on. "That's the second weird thing to happen to me this morning. I gotta get with it," he says.

At 11:00 A.M. they're upon the fourth move, the one they'd spied from camp. The river is humping here, bordered by a massive slide of pulverized gray rock and mist-glistening, egg-brown boulders the size of buildings. On the map Tom scribbles "very wild water" for this stretch, especially the midchannel portion, where the holes are among the biggest he's ever seen. Along the left bank, however, there are possibilities: two or three cheat routes (the easiest paths on a particular rapid) along the shoreline and one direct but exposed shot off the lip of an eight-to-ten-foot waterfall. The main drop is borderline—it's certainly the riskiest thing they've considered so far, since it feeds fearfully near the accelerating main current—but there's room for backup. In other words, if someone blows the move, he has time to roll up before getting swept into the middle of the river. Jamie, Doug, and Roger scout for several minutes. Running through everyone's mind is the long portage to come. The run is tempting. Clearly the number of opportunities to run hard stuff is dwindling. In a few more days they'll be upon the narrows, and in a few after that they'll be in the twisted, innermost sections of the gorge, where 1,000-foot-

xpect, Doug decides on the side chute, then hikes off to retrieve
is boat to get under way. But in the interim he changes his mind.
assing Tom, he says he's going to run the exposed main drop. It's
ore straightforward, he explains. Tom doesn't try to talk him
ut of it—for one thing, he hasn't been a part of their discussions.
or another, Doug is their obvious leader—and his comfort level
ith the river, whether in carving lines between midriver holes or
n yesterday's gutsy cliff ferry, is clearly a cut above everyone
se's. If Doug thought he could run the line, and didn't—well,
om knew how that felt. Anybody who ran hard whitewater did.
could gnaw at you. They'd probably never be back, either.
esides, it's not as if he were being grossly negligent. The drop
elf is no bigger than Valley Falls, the place in West Virginia
here they all learned to falls-jump. Of course, the riverwide haz-
ls make the move a "must make," but the drop isn't radical.

Yet the business of questioning another expert boater's judg-
ent is awkward. Reading juicy whitewater is an academic
ercise; the decision to proceed, however, is purely personal judg-
ent. Observations are swapped, evidence considered, but rarely
high-caliber teammates bluntly and aggressively intercede. The
ea is to see things for what they are—the credo of Tom and Wick
d countless other elite river runners—not for what your fears
someone else's) tell you. But sometimes the process becomes
erudite, so seductively hypothetical, that one can backdrop the
k factor to a place where perhaps it doesn't belong. E. J.
Carthy has seen Doug and Jamie and others look at
unnable rapids before, eventually working themselves into a
ve-by-move sequence where it sounded for all the world as if
y actually might be contemplating the run. "What are you, stu-
?" Some didn't appreciate E. J.'s candor—he didn't conform to

plus walls rise off the thrashing waterline. The trip's w
component, whatever is left of it, is nearly done.

Roger is not going to run it—why bother, they'll b
shortly, he reasons. The others aren't surprised by Ro
though he seems much more settled in recent days,
inclined to walk. Still, none of the options speak to hi
boulder separates the comparatively slow current that
the chutes. The upside to the chute "cheat" routes is th
close to shore, well clear of the main current. The probl
technical nature—the pulsing reaction waves, the ha
surges, an assortment of water-glazed rocks. A diffi
made still more difficult by what Roger thinks is ar
sieve at the base. Rock and tree strainers in fast water
the current strains through, but boaters don't—are th
more fatalities than anything else in whitewater. "
around to the point where I'd watch other people run t
if it looked really straightforward and okay, then I
'Well, yeah, okay, I'll go ahead—it's easier than walkin
one, when I got up to it—Doug was already there lool
options—I said, 'Nah, I'm just gonna walk.'"

Tom is undecided. The main flow of the river isn't
over the falls, just a fraction of the overall volume, re
not a big-water move where you ride the V-shaped tor
racing main current and hope to God you punch tl
abyss. It's more of a technical route, really, he thinks,
the cumbersome amount of weight in their boats, he
how he feels about a technical route. But as the others
rapid, Tom isn't much a part of the discussion, e
upstream of the others, filming them.

Doug is going to make the run; Jamie's not sure,
freely admits, to see what happens to his pal. As Roger

a hushed plebe status—but Doug wasn't one of them. Recalls McCarthy, "He'd say, 'E.J., don't worry, we're not serious.'"

Tom bids Doug good luck and swiftly sets up at the bottom of the rapid with the video camera and a rescue throw rope. Though the team talked earlier in the trip about having two boats in the water at all times—such as in the eddy, for instance, at the base of the falls—the drill is skipped. As they know, the chances of a teammate getting in trouble are far greater than the odds of being able to come to the effective aid of anyone. Paddling out midriver from the eddy to offer a bow to a flipped teammate (a common rescue procedure for teammates who cannot roll up) is out of the question. It was Roger who'd originally suggested the tactic earlier in the trip, but he's aware that even on easier stretches of the Tsangpo, it's probably more a psychological crutch than a safety boost. You simply can't give team protection. The other disincentive, he adds, is that "none of us are eager to admit, even to ourselves, our roll might fail."

Backup is moot, however; Doug never runs the new plan past Jamie and Roger. He's not going center, as far as they know. Minutes earlier he warned Roger about the backwash at the base of the big drop. "If you're thinking about running that main drop, go downstream and look at the backwash for yourself," he said. Doug is careful not to describe what he sees, but what Roger sees is a nasty reversal. Now, watching Doug warm up, however, Roger gets his first inkling that he's changed his mind. Instead of edging close to the chute to gauge the slot's irregular surge (something he'd need to time just right to ride into shore), he looks like he's preparing for a fast, several-boat-length charge. "I think he has his eye on the big drop," Roger tells Jamie, the two standing on rocks to the side and slightly upstream of the main drop.

The change in plan isn't unusual—Doug often switched up if he got a better read from his cockpit. But Jamie can't believe Roger's right. Given the morning slipups and his obvious concern with the backwash, he figures Doug has conceded the line. The approach isn't entirely straightforward, either: He'll need to angle right to left with good speed and glance off a slightly submerged rock ramp at the lip to kick up his bow and prevent penciling in. If the boat sails more or less horizontally over the drop, he'll need to punch through a portion of the curling backwash, then prepare for the jolt of the main current. The final part of the "out and back" sequence will be a hard right sweep to get him out of the main current and back into a protective eddy. "I had also heard Doug say, twice, that the problem with the big-drop route was that if you flipped or something happened to you in the hole at the bottom, you would be carried out into the main current," recalls Jamie. Indeed, the feeder eddy to the left of the backwash feeds upstream current back into the backwash pile, which will cause the hole to kick a "held" boater left to right, away from shore. Downstream, Doug has also directed Jamie to the most obvious and nightmarish consequence of all: a one-hundred-foot-wide hole, the first of five or six in the welter of the main current.

For all those reasons, Jamie figures—even as he sees him stroking hard to build up speed—Doug will peel off toward him and Roger and set up for one of the near chutes. But he doesn't. "When I saw him lining up for the middle drop, I was bewildered," admits Roger. "I didn't know why he decided to do what he did, I just said, 'Oh God, he's going for the middle, and you know I just had a real bad feeling . . .'"

As he draws closer, Roger and Jamie (watching through the lens of his still camera) can see that Doug's approach is off. He's angling right to left, but his speed is down and he doesn't get far enough left. He never gets to his launch rock, never fully buries the last critical right-side stroke—the "boof" stroke meant to sweep against the rocky outcropping at the falls' lip for extra push-off. Perhaps the boat is too heavy to maneuver, or perhaps the current is too quick, but instead of planing over the abyss, Doug is dragged over the brink in the main flow, his boat free-falling almost sideways. The bow plunges deep into the pile, killing much of his momentum. Still, he's almost out of the back-wash—on the bubble, surfing upright for a few seconds, Jamie later recalls—when it inexorably pulls him back and to the right, drawing his stern under the thumping flood of the main cascade. The force of the falling water, coupled with the now extreme downward pull of the foaming hydraulic, stands his twelve-foot boat on end. Doug is half out of the river for a suspended moment—though upside down and staring directly at the face of the waterfall—then he flips backward and the world becomes a watery whir. For ten seconds, maybe more, Doug is sideways in the hole, getting spun repeatedly in the maw, all the time getting kicked right, all the time closer to the humping main channel. Roger blasts his whistle three times—the emergency distress call—to alert Tom downstream, but Tom is right on it. Incredibly, Doug almost rolls all the way up, his spray skirt still on, only to have his edge snagged by the hole's warring currents. He flips again.

Finally his boat is spit out. He's moving slowly, sweeping right past the large boulder dividing the eddy from the main cur-rent. Now he's on a patch of fast but smooth water—here's his Plan B, his chance to recover in the event everything else has gone to hell. Doug's got maybe fifteen seconds before, as Jamie puts it, the river begins to slide, as if down a ramp. Tom is gripped—he's dropped the video camera and has his throw rope ready if he can get some eye contact—but he's sure Doug is going to roll up.

"Keep your head down!" Zbel screams, but to his horror, Doug can't seem to roll up. "Keep your head down!" But Doug's roll is unaccountably sluggish, labored. There's no hip-snap, and his head is coming up. As even a beginner knows, the head should be the last thing up. The head and neck muscles aren't nearly strong enough to yank upright a submerged torso and a ninety-pound boat. Hips are. With beginners the mistake is common: The brain's instinctive response is to rush the head above water for a gulp of air. The kayaker's learned response is to override nature's preservationist hard-wiring. Doug, like any Class V boater, could easily do that. The only explanation for the lapse, thinks Zbel, is that Doug *can't* roll. Maybe the last flip dislodged him from his housing, and that's killing his roll. Given the first day's episode, Zbel is sure Doug realizes what's going on and is in the several-seconds-long, below-the-waterline process of pausing, wrapping his arms around the hull and wedging himself back in tight.

The second and third rolls are weaker than the first. Obviously, something is terribly wrong. Maybe he blew out his shoulder on the flip—who knows? But each time it's the same awful thing: Doug's yellow helmet, briefly . . . and nothing. He's nearing the first big hydraulic now—a gaping hundred-footer stretching nearly across the river. Here's Doug's moment, Jamie thinks, the time when he pulls off the move from out of nowhere, as he did the first day, the first rapid. As he'd done a million times. He isn't gonna give in, he knows—he's not going to swim, either. He can't. He's methodically working on Plans C, D, E, and F, Jamie knows. In the hole he'd undoubtedly done that, taken his pounding, then, at the first sign of daylight, he'd nearly righted himself. He probably worked himself out of the hole by extending his paddle as a probe, finding the tongue of water that flushed out, and levering his paddle against it. Most kayakers can't get their boats to go where they want to go when upside down and getting trashed in a hole. Even the best ones swim if they are overturned long enough. But Jamie knew Doug's mental rigor: He believed the best judgments were made right side up. Foremost among them was the simple credo: If he flipped, he rolled up. He mentally eliminated the other options. Choice hampered performance, especially in combat situations. If he tenaciously committed everything to the roll, he'd roll. What was more rational than that?

After the third missed roll, Doug is drawn into the driving current, then avalanched seconds later into the first big hole. It's twenty seconds before Roger and Jamie see his boat pop up—but it's upside down in the backwash, and neither can tell whether he's in or out. Because there's no sign of the paddle floating, Roger figures he's still in the boat, still doing something, but his lungs have got to be bursting, and moments later he's washed into the next hole. If he's not connected to his boat, the only thing he can do is ride it out and hope the boat gets flushed out and he gets another breath. With almost a minute gone by, there is still hope, but what hope there is has to do more with the whim of the river than anything he can do with the boat.

More seconds pass. Jamie desperately scans but sees nothing. Doug is out of Tom's view. Roger is the last one to spy him—he's washing into yet another massive terminal hole. "What do we do, Jamie?" asks Roger. "Do you have a throw rope?"

"No. I'm going to my boat and get a rope."

"Tom's got a rope. I'm gonna get with him."

Tom is already scampering like a billygoat downstream, and Roger races across the bouldery shore to catch up. Jamie, hampered by bad ankles, can't keep pace with Roger and Tom, so he empties out his boat, grabs his paddle, and carries the rapid. He'll paddle to catch up. The trio all know the chances of anyone surviving the holes are slim—nobody needs to say anything—but in the backs of their minds is the sense that this is Doug. They'll find him downstream, tucked in behind some rocky refuge, his hand wiping across his brow as if to say, "Wow, that was a close one." But there's a twin thought, too, nearly as vivid: Maybe they'll never see him again.

Don't give up. Stay calm. More than anything, that was the underwater drill. Fear and panic—utterly understandable, natural—were also lethal. The more energy you expended, the more your body screamed for air. You needed to get oriented, find top from bottom. Light. Bubbles. Surface.

Doug was prepared for this. He studied and marveled over this. He and E.J. and Jamie used to stroke into micro-eddies on big rivers, little dollops of soft water bordering gnashing holes, and they'd all peer down and feel the pull, all equally fascinated and horrified by their proximity to something so gorgeously raw. In the deepest, most unforgiving holes, the primeval power of the flowing water took on pure form, dwarfing everything, engulfing everything. But there was structure and reason to it—like the pure, perfectly formed crystalline molecules he forged from the torch of a 1,500-degree flame—and fierce, fierce life.

Now to be bound to it. After several minutes the vital signs grow faint—the body's defense mechanism against the extreme stress of cold and oxygen starvation. In some cases the cold water is a lifesaver, not a killer—sending the body into a conservation mode, giving more time. But the brain begins to trade thought for sensation—sometimes keen, sometimes drifting, dimming. Where are you? Rising, falling, tumbling. Don't give up. Roll. But now the pile of water deepens, darkens. Water on water on water.

≋

AFTER A MILE AND A HALF OF PORTAGING AND PADDLING, JAMIE catches up with the others. They are blocked at river level by cliffs. It's 3:00 P.M. and there's still no sign of Doug. Was he held somewhere—drawn by the current under a huge boulder and pinned? If so, and only for that reason, he would've swum if possible. Or had he simply been flushed downstream, faster than they could possibly keep pace with? In the two or three hours they've been searching, he could easily be far downstream, beyond the ten-miles-away falls section and already into the looping lower canyon. Tom and Roger take off ahead of Jamie, again, scaling a high, steeply exposed cliff to see around the corner. Nothing. They decide to return to their boats back at the site of the accident. The one place likely to hold someone—a large eddy after a sweeping bend in the river—is empty, too. As they march downheartedly back upstream, numbed by the events and the unrelenting artillery sound of the river, they realize there is no sign of Jamie. Had he ferried across the river and continued the search down the other side?

Near the accident site is Jamie's gear. Figuring he'll be returning to it, they set up camp on a nearby bluff and hang a flashlight as a beacon. Jamie stumbles in at 11:00 P.M. No Doug, no gear, nothing, he reports. A part of Jamie tells him Doug is gone; a part of him won't let go: "The cold, analytical part of me says it's over, he isn't coming back, but there's a part that says somehow, by some miracle, he got out." As it turns out, Jamie had searched down the left bank, just as Tom and Roger had done. As they retreated and Jamie pressed forward, the two parties actually passed one another. The fact that they never saw Jamie (or his boat, which he ditched late in the day in order to make better time on the steep terrain) offers a little hope. If they missed Jamie—the maze of boulders lining the bank were towering, easily obscuring anything human-sized—maybe they could've missed Doug somehow. Everybody is torn up, Jamie especially, but the decision is made to continue the search in the morning, and to alert Harry and Wick so they can figure out a way to get down to the river and start searching, too.

Nobody sleeps much. The accident sequence replays over and over again. They stay up for some time, talking it over, trying to find an explanation in the details of what each saw. The feeling they can't shake is the helplessness of watching and not being able to do anything but scream and yell and put their heads down and run. They second-guess every moment, and the biggest second guess isn't about the run at all: "It plays over and over in my mind," confesses Zbel, thinking about Doug's earlier uncharacteristic bobbles upstream. "If only I'd said, 'Doug, don't do that.' Or something like that."

In the morning they begin retracing their steps back down the left shore. At the comparatively calm stretch—well before the cliffs they'd reached yesterday—the three ferry to the right-hand shore. Even here the crossing is risky. The support teams are now in motion, too. Harry's team is headed for the main road near Pe, where he'll set up a communications base and coordinate logistics between the other two teams. Atop the bluff, poised to drop down to Rainbow Falls, Wick is instead heading due south, straight down his 12,000-foot perch to the near shore, opposite the old Pemakochung monastery. With any luck—and after strenuous negotiations with the reluctant Monpa porters—Wick thinks he can be down in two days and begin searching up- and downstream.

By the end of the second day, October 17, the river team has combed virtually the same stretch it did the day before, but this time with its boats in tow. Whatever hope they had at the dawn of the day is gone. They begin to shift their thinking to both coping with the loss and figuring how they're going to get out. "You know," says Roger, turning to Jamie on a portage, "if I could get on a 747 right now, I'd do it in a heartbeat." They still haven't come across anything of Doug's. For all trace of him to have vanished is incomprehensible. When the river took Jamie's boat days ago, they'd found several items adrift in eddies or washed up on sandbars. They all expected to see something—a paddle, at least. Nothing.

Their plan is to search the river up to the point of the escape ravine—the same one Wick is supposed to march down—but the five or so miles to cover is by no means a given. In their haste to get downstream yesterday, they had stumbled on the best way yet to deal with the river. Formerly they'd tear ass downstream on foot, then return to retrieve their boats. From here on in, they'd load up as much gear on their backs as possible for their one- and two-day hikes downriver, then create a forward base camp. And then they'd double back for their half-again-as-light boats. Not only would the boats be easier to carry, but they'd perform better in the whitewater. In the next two days they follow the same pattern: On the eighteenth, they march to a sandy beach almost directly across from their intended escape ravine, and set up camp; the following day they retrieve their boats, carrying and paddling most of the same distance. On October 20, four days after the accident, they are back at their advance base camp.

Across the river on a wide, sandy expanse, Wick and his Monpa troop are waiting, having been in place and searching since Sunday the eighteenth. Late in the afternoon the packed-up river team makes the wicked ferry across, hazarding fifteen-foot standing waves. Still separated from Wick's camp by a final rapid and a sheer cliff, Jamie entertains the idea of running the stretch. The portage is an obvious ball-breaker. "There's a couple big holes to deal with, and if you miss the move you're gonna be swept out into the middle," says Roger. "I don't think it's for me." Earlier Wick had radioed the team his own read: "From where you guys are, it's Class III all the way to the beach," but he'd been mistaken. As he watched them disappear into bottomless wave troughs on the bruising ferry across, he began to get a sense for what the river guys had found out on Day 1: The river was not as it appeared. With Wick's encouragement, Tom, Roger, and Jamie decide not to chance the Tsangpo's final rapid, and rope up for the extreme cliff portage instead. It's almost dark when they finally reunite with Wick.

For the first time, Wick gets a full accounting of what happened. Heretofore, he'd known almost none of the blow-by-blow. "Up on the hill I was hopeful, all I had was a few words," he recalls. "Doug had been lost and washed downstream, let's go looking—that was about all I had. I knew he was well equipped and how capable he was. I held out much more hope than the rest of the guys, who'd actually seen everything."

Upon being briefed, everyone agrees there's nothing more to do. In addition to the river team's eight-mile search, Wick has bushwhacked a few miles downstream and a mile upstream on the river-left shore. Wick opts not to call in any additional rescue help—such as a Chinese military helicopter—believing an SOS is both futile and dangerous. "Rainbow Falls was about ten miles downstream, then Hidden Falls. The chance of anything coherent being recovered after that was nil. I suppose in theory you could fly a helicopter through the gorge looking for a body, but the weather was bad and we'd be risking more lives. I didn't make the request," he says. Hours after meeting up, on October 20, the team telephones Harry to make their decision official—Doug is presumed dead. The search is over. Even though the GPS unit was with Doug in his boat, the river team had in fact crossed the deepest point in the gorge—Doug somewhere in the throes of his accident, the others as they raced downstream to rescue him. The day he vanished, October 16, is the same date that the gorge claimed Hiroshi Onishi, the Japanese mountaineer on the inaugural Tsangpo expedition seven years before.

≋

OVER THE NEXT TWENTY-FOUR HOURS, THE FULL WEIGHT OF WHAT they've been through takes hold. Stunningly wild as their beach camp is—they dub the place Panther Beach after spying tiger tracks and piles of goat bones—they are six, seven, maybe eight days from any roadhead. Because they weren't prepared for their major portage here, Wick's hauled-in supply includes only food— not hiking shoes or rugged, internal-frame packs. They'll have to climb thousands of feet out of the gorge, through sheer technical terrain, in nothing more than their floppy river shoes. The task ahead is daunting under the best of circumstances, but the team is hurting, suffering both the emotional and physical trauma of four nonstop days in crisis. Jamie is in the worst shape: He's violently ill, unable to keep any food down. Yesterday he called his wife, Sandy, with instructions to contact Connie's mother, who would in turn deliver the news about Doug. The team would wait to make an official report to the State Department or the Chinese until they had return confirmation that Connie knew. Jamie added that he'd call Connie directly as soon as he was able. Dave Phillips, the team medic, treats Roger and Tom for extreme exhaustion. On the morning of October 21, Wick makes the decision to take a rest day. Jamie is in no condition to go anywhere. Roger sits down for a short nap and doesn't wake up until late in the afternoon. "Everything just caught up to us," he says.

Late the same day the entire team, the Monpa included, gather near a towering mound of blue-gray boulders for memorial rites. With the charged river booming into the same tangle of rocks, the mist and whitewater hurtling high in the air, the words rise softly. Both Tibetan and American songs are sung. *Shoo Yarlung Tsangpo* . . . *O chay nay dintay ympam umpee ny yay samnang yongwee* . . . You like fast, don't go . . . in my heart or mind a great request . . . come back. . . . You have run away and I miss you. . . . Tom writes Doug's name on a square stone, and one of the porters showers it with barley, Pemako's holy grain. The stone is cast into the river according to local custom.

After the service, there is brief discussion about whether they should indeed quit the gorge or stay. Personally, Tom is in favor of continuing the exploration. He has struggled with the conclusion but come to it nonetheless. Doug had said it himself back in Kathmandu: He'd want the others to continue if something happened to him; he had no problem with that. From Tom's perspective they are in a place he has dreamed of all his life: a beautiful wave of sand at the precipice of raging wilderness. The last four days the stuff they were searching for all along, the thing he and Doug had talked about the night before the accident, has truly fallen into place.

They had a system of travel—a confidence and a rhythm and an expertise. In many ways Tom can't shake the feeling that they are at the beginning of the trip, not the end. To be right in the heart of it—to truly understand what it takes—and have to say good-bye seems a shame. Doug's exploring spirit—the value and sacrifice he'd invested in the trip—had undeniably carried them through the toughest, most unknown segment. Not everything was lost.

But Tom hardly says any of it. He certainly doesn't argue with anyone. He knows how despondent Jamie feels, knows there are practical and personal reasons to evacuate as soon as possible. The topic is closed in minutes. They're quitting. They'll leave the boats behind and, starting tomorrow, "return home by the most direct route."

There are different options for getting out. Conceivably the team could get back to Pe, but the Monpa say they can expect an extreme twenty-day trek as they work their way around the shoulders of Gyala Peri. Besides, if they want the Monpa's support they'll have to go back the way Wick and Dave came, through their villages. Another possibility is for the river team to ferry back across the river and hike up to Pemakochung, continuing out along the river-right trail (which may or may not be partially submerged). Wick and Harry can't join them, however, since they can't get across the river. Stressed out as everyone is, nobody's eager to split up again. They decide to climb up the ravine with the Monpa.

On October 22, the day they're to set out, the Monpa headman informs Wick and Tom that they will carry loads only if their wages are doubled. The renegotiation attempt strikes Wick as blatant extortion. He says no. They are exploiting the fact that his team is highly vulnerable. The headman tells Ankame Sherpa, who is interpreting, that without the wage increase they will abandon the Americans and all their gear immediately. An aggravated Wick refuses. Early in the afternoon the Monpa party begins packing, and at 2:00 P.M. they walk out of camp and begin the long gully ascent out of the gorge. Watching them go, Zbel gets a sinking feeling; if they don't come back, the team will have no choice but to leave almost all the gear behind. It's gonna be an epic, warns Wick, adding that they're damn sure gonna chuck their $6,000 worth of gear in the river so the porters won't end up getting it.

An hour later, a few Monpa return. Then the rest straggle in. An uneasy truce is struck: The rest of the day will be spent eating up the extra stores of food to gain strength for the hike out (and lighten loads). They'll also get more money, though not as much as they'd demanded. As he planned almost two weeks earlier in Pe, Roger takes the satellite phone out of the dry-bag and calls Nancy. Dialing up tiny Friendsville from a beach in the Tsangpo Gorge seems to mock the survival game they're living. But Nancy's voice, while a balm, is also a reminder of how far Roger's got to go. Nancy knows about Doug and is desperately relieved to hear that the whitewater part of the expedition is over. "We're all together now and we'll be out in a few days," says Roger. "I love you. Happy anniversary."

On Friday, October 23, the team departs, quickly ascending high above the river. Sneaking repeated glances downstream, Tom sees the steep, rapid-filled pitch beginning right around the corner from their encampment. Farther down is a mellower stretch—maybe a place to cross the river. On the river-right side, if he can barge his way downstream, perhaps he'll eventually (and unknowingly) bump into the network of hunters' trails Ian Baker learned about in the spring. From what he sees, Tom is certain they would have pushed very close to Rainbow Falls—how low they would have been able to stay, and what, if anything, they'd be able to do with the boats were the questions. Somewhere beyond, out of view, of course, lie Hidden Falls and the Crease. A few miles below that, maybe they can drop down to the river again along a little streambed and paddle some more. Then, at Chu Belap, where the river turns terminal again, they can make the longer portage to the confluence. The higher he climbs, the more the ridge-steepled topography unfolds before him. Nearing the pass, he can make out the clearing where the old Pemakochung monastery and a few houses sit. As with so much of this trip, the more he sees, the farther away things get.

The hike to the pass is plenty rugged enough to keep everyone's mind focused. Rising up through the dense lower understory, they ascend into the leafy wet silence of the primary rainforest. Where there are footpaths, they are faint—more game trail than anything—and each foot placement is consequential. On several occasions they rope up rather than chance steeply exposed cliffs and landslide-prone mud slopes. It rains almost every day, the porters building huge fires at night to dry out, then taking cover in caves and deeply undercut boulders. On the first night out, a sleeping Zbel awakens to the rumble of thunder passing overhead. Then he feels the ground shake. An earthquake. It's a modest temblor, but more than enough, thinks Zbel, to collapse the thirty-ton piece of rock he and everyone else is sleeping under. He picks up his bivvy sack, abandoning the stone roof for a wet sky.

Over the next four grueling days the expedition will rise up and over a blur of fog-drenched ridges. They'll scramble across glacial streams and rappel down to overhangs with tantalizingly brief vistas to the river thousands of feet below. Near Natang, a small village in the Bend, they'll encounter a large herd of takin,

causing the Monpa to set out on a wild impromptu hunt. Ultimately they'll track down and kill five of the thirty or so herd.
This isn't a happy-go-lucky tourist hike—there are numerous
places where falls would be deadly—but the landscape continues
to awe, continues to pull. At the small villages where the Monpa
live, the porters offer their apologies for the attempted walkout. If
the Americans are to return—and Wick and Tom say they
might—they hope they can join on future journeys. Tom isn't
rude, but he's firm: Their actions stung. The next time they come,
he says, they'll be bringing their own help.

On October 30 they finally make the roadhead and board a
hired truck for the long overland drive west to Lhasa. In the early
evening they find the road victimized by another landslide, this
one having occurred just minutes earlier. The team takes up shovels and begins the tedious business of digging out. On the other
side of the landslide, shoveling in the opposing direction, is
another American team—Ian Baker, Ken Storm, Bryan Harvey,
and Hamid Sardar. Of course, the latter four are beginning their
trip, not ending one. They are also in hurry-up mode since the
Chinese teams, both rafting and trekking, are close to the inner
gorge. Baker is already aware of Doug Gordon's fate, having been
informed by the National Geographic Society while awaiting a
flight connection in Bangkok. Baker tells the others he's sorry,
and that he'll look and ask questions for any clues to Doug's
whereabouts while he's in the gorge.

As the Walker-McEwan team loads back into the trucks for
the long trip home, Sardar is struck by the expressions on their
faces. "They looked shellshocked," he recalls. "You know, they'd
had this great adventure—the exploration of theirs down the left
bank, the death of their friend, the walk out where they were

feeding off slaughtered takin. Death, horror, beauty—it all showed in their eyes. They'd experienced everything. There was still this glimmer of innocence about them, but the landscape had been a complete initiation. I left them thinking this place is simply not meant for everyone."

It's a different world over there, past the edge. . . . I've paddled a lot of rivers. Kayaking has shown me a lot of fun, a lot of seriousness, and a simple fact: life is full of horizonlines. They come in all shapes and sizes— accidents and jobs, people, marriage, and children. Time is the current that pushes us toward the edges of what we know, usually faster than we can cope. And flowing water is the current of time made real. I know that fear comes from doubt about where those horizonlines lead. I also know that the truths of life, large and small, are what lie beyond each one.

—ACCLAIMED BIG-WATER BOATER DOUG AMMONS,
IN HIS ESSAY "THE HORIZONLINE" from
THE LAUGH OF THE WATER NYMPH

Most kayakers will tell you they are not going to drown. I will tell you I will never drown. I know I could paddle Niagara Falls and not drown. I just can't drown.

—BIG-WATER PIONEER WALT BLACKADAR,
IN THE 1976 MOVIE THE EDGE

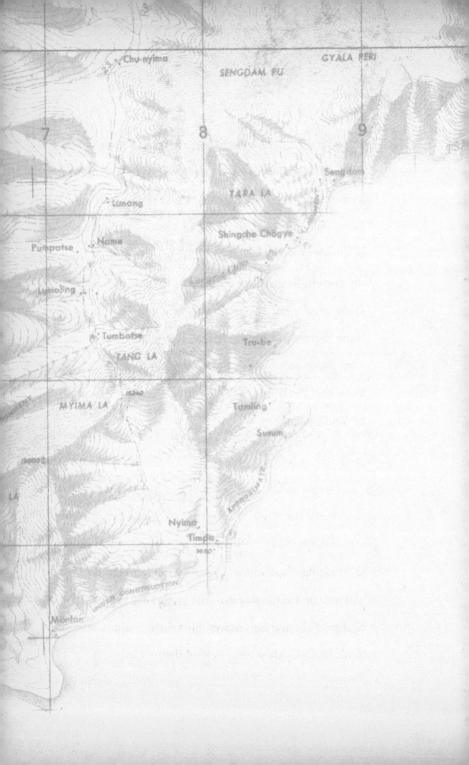

Sera Monastery, near Lhasa, November 3, 1998

LATE AFTERNOON IN THE DUSKY FOOTHILLS NORTH OF LHASA: Wick, Tom, Roger, Jamie, and the others stand on the periphery of a pine-tree-lined courtyard at Sera Monastery. Hundreds of solemn, red-robed monks flood from the maze of chapels and colleges, taking up cross-legged positions on the hard stone patio. Suddenly a lama rises and begins to verbally accost one of the others. He is dancing, gesticulating, herding his seated adversary with his rising, sharply timbred voice and crackling claps of his hands. What's under way is the afternoon ritualistic debate. The withering examination is meant to challenge the novices' knowledge, values, and intellectual stamina—they must defend themselves.

Watching the tranquil, tensionless scene erupt isn't so different from watching a wide, lazy river sweep into a tight, vertical-walled gorge, thinks Roger—and then Tom is motioning. The monks have offered the floor to their visitors, and Tom is rising before Roger, challenging him about his philosophy and happiness and ambition. He's talking about the river. "Was it worth it?" he asks, clapping his hands, as the smiling monks pass them chains of brightly colored prayer beads.

"Did you learn something?" Roger mounts a pretty fair defense, asserting that the trip has "met every one of my expectations and then some" and that he found—in circumstances he never would choose, nor wish on anyone—an unexpected level of strength. "To have tried what we did is better than if we hadn't tried at all."

Surprisingly intense, the exercise would pale in comparison to the grilling the team soon finds itself subjected to.

Published accounts of the team's tragedy reached the States almost immediately. In fact, only days after her mother got word to Connie—and before Walker officially reported the accident to Chinese authorities or the U.S. State Department—a story appeared in the October 23 *Salt Lake Tribune*. "One of the kids in Tyler's school told his father and his father had a contact at the newspaper," says a dismayed Walker, who'd only been informed the day before Connie had been notified. The story, distributed on the wire services, reported that Doug Gordon was missing and presumed drowned and that the remainder of the team had begun the week-long trek out of the gorge.

During the ensuing week (and with the team still in Tibet), a front-page story appeared in *The Washington Post*. Simultaneously, the paddling community launched into a full-on debate about the team's judgment on a popular Internet whitewater news group, www.rec.boat.paddle. Newsgroup devotees are sometimes lumped into the same gossipy category as radio talk-show addicts—the "fellowship of the miserable," in the words of one critic—but the reaction was notable for both its intensity and its conflict. The gut feeling among those making posts fell into two basic philosophical camps: those who thought the risk was justifiable, and those who couldn't remotely understand what the father of two young children was doing on the gnarliest river in the world. In the latter camp, a paddler lamented that "twice now in recent history, two world-class paddlers have died paddling difficult whitewater, leaving behind wives and children. With respect to their skills and their desires, putting themselves at risk—even when the risk is known, calculated, and guarded against—demonstrates a lack of empathy for their families, and possibly a lack of responsibility." Added another: "Maybe ultra extreme paddlers with children should be heavily insured ($1M?) and willing to pay whatever high premiums it takes to cover that sort of death by misadventure. Or maybe trip sponsors should pay for or require such coverage." And another: "We all lose in the death of Doug Gordon. It is more than just the loss of a husband, father or friend. As I read Doug Gordon's bio I could only think what a waste. So much was lost in such a senseless tragedy."

An equally charged subset of the paddling community condemned the commentary as ignorant, insensitive, and too judgmental. "You cannot sacrifice what is beautiful within yourself for anyone, not even your family," wrote a parent. "I have a child. I've made a choice to be involved in the sport. It may add years to my life because at forty-five I'm in better shape than I've ever been both emotionally and physically (perhaps spiritually). It may kill me—it almost did two weekends ago . . . is it not disrespectful to protest the choices made by the deceased?" Added another, "Doug's choice to go on the expedition was between him and his loved ones—who are we to judge?" And another: "What type of lives would we lead if we never followed our dreams and our adventures?"

On November 3, as the team was just arriving in Lhasa, *The Washington Post* gave broader, more mainstream airing to the rampant second-guessing. Rumors were flying around that more than a half-dozen teams had given up on the Tsangpo—the Walker-McEwan team being the only one that elected to go forward. Andy Bridge, one of the paddlers who'd been asked to go on the trip and a close friend of Wick, Tom, and Jamie, seemed to question the group's judgment in the article, recalling his shock at their post-scout thumbs-up verdict a year earlier: "I was surprised when they said it was runnable. Everything I'd seen suggested it wasn't." Other paddlers wondered if sponsorship had affected the team's judgment, the paper reported. Nobody was eager to go on record, but some paddlers speculated: Had they felt obligated to run the river because of their backers? Had the money and prestige associated with the trip corrupted their vaunted decision-making?

The debate went back and forth. One expedition paddler said that if he were in their shoes, he'd tell the world the sponsorship had nothing to do with anything—and maybe even believe it. But he also wondered how such a financial investment couldn't be a factor. Yet the *Post* article (which Geographic asked to see in advance in return for a statement—a highly unorthodox arrangement that the *Post* refused) rallied others to the team's defense. "All this says much more about your paper than about Tom McEwan, who is an anomaly in the Washington area with respect to his concern (or lack of it) for the importance of money," fumed a backer on the op-ed page. "McEwan has always been motivated by challenge, by the thrill of discovery and the adventure of engaging in nature."

On November 6, after several drafts, Tom McEwan E-mailed Sarah Park, his significant other and the team's D.C.-based spokesperson, a summary "trip report" with instructions to forward it to National Geographic Society public affairs officer Barbara Moffet. "I will recommend that we send it to our list of family and friends, but Wick has not consented to that," Tom wrote, adding that he hoped NGS would agree to forward the report to the *Post*. Given the amount of misinformation in circulation—especially among the newsgroup crowd—the report was long overdue. Basically it covered in detail the condition of the river at put-in, Jamie's accident, their rationale for progressing downriver, and Doug's death. It concluded, "The expedition members deeply regret the death of loyal friend and teammate Doug Gordon, an expert kayaker who lost his life in this challenging undertaking."

Upon finally arriving home on November 8th, however, Tom and Jamie quickly realized the depth of the controversy. They submitted a brief addendum to NGS and asked that they be allowed to distribute it within the paddling community. (According to the team's standard expedition contract with NGS, they needed permission to speak publicly about trip details.) The report, which Jamie wrote and NGS signed off on, was titled "Were We Foolish to Be on the River at That Level?" "In light of what happened to Doug, it's easy to say yes to the question above," he wrote. "At this point, knowing the consequences to him, naturally, I wish we had never put on. And yet, take away the benefit of hindsight, I believe I would make the same decision, if I were again in the same situation." He convincingly explained the team's rationale for putting on and their motivation for pressing ahead:

> We had all been in places on other rivers, above unrunnable waterfalls, huge holes, or rock sieves, where a missed eddy or a swim would have sent us into situations of great danger, even of probable death. This, in itself, was not new. The difference was not in degree, but rather in constancy of the danger. . . . However, we felt that by taking the same sort of precautions we always took, we could only tackle those risks that we felt we could handle. Even if this meant hiking most of the way. I don't see the flaw in this reasoning. The only way I can imagine that we were affected by the "Tsangpo difference"—by the unusually unrelenting downstream push of the current—was that our healthy fear may have become dulled. We might have become inured to the danger because of its constant nature. Yet, in all, and judging particularly from Doug's comments that morning, including soon before his run [in which he'd remarked on his need to be careful after earlier bobbles], I don't think this was the case. I believe that there is no particular "reason" for Doug's death, nor moral to be drawn, other than that which Doug wrote about in reference to Richie Weiss's death the summer before: that running hard whitewater is dangerous, and that those doing so must accept that danger as the price of pursuing their sport at a high level.

Rather than write anything, Roger decided to take on the entire mess as directly as possible. He invited anyone and everyone in the paddling community to a friend's micro-brewery outside Friendsville, where he explained the trip in detail and answered all questions. "Were there any other teams at the river that didn't put on, Roger?" asked a paddling friend from Confluence, one of about fifty on hand. "Absolutely not," said Roger, putting to rest the most pernicious rumor. He went on to talk about his misgivings, the team's trials, and Doug's last day. Tom, Jamie, and Wick did their explaining more selectively. Jamie told his and Doug's buddy Bruce Lessels that though Doug had made a mistake—that was all—the decisions they'd made as a group were cautious. Tom made some calls to former and current students, people to whom he thought he owed more. "I was sort of surprised he called me," says the then-eighteen-year-old Ryan Bahn, a Valley Mill and Calleva alumnus. "I didn't feel really like he was trying to set the record straight, more like he just needed to talk about it." For everyone it was agonizing to rehash the story, but also cathartic. Many came to agree with Jamie and other team members, that perhaps there wasn't a big lesson to be learned, perceptions to the contrary notwithstanding. Perhaps it was just one of those things that are impossible to see coming.

Several prominent Western expedition paddlers didn't agree—nor were they nearly as forgiving. In E-mails and conversations among them (and later in phone interviews with various magazine reporters) they all concurred that the team put on at the wrong time of year. Why did they start in early October—a time of year universally considered early but especially premature given the extreme high-water conditions? Why didn't they wait for the river to recede? Western kayakers obliquely suggested the team was overanxious, compelled to move ahead for reasons they weren't being forthright about. The team countered that their plan had been to depart comparatively early so they could exit the high downriver passes before winter snows. Yet early on they conceded they weren't going to run the entire river, so why continue to rush forward? Were they concerned about other competitors? The Chinese teams, Baker's, others that never materialized? The Walker-McEwan team said they weren't racing anyone, that they moved ahead because they believed they could while being cautious. They'd minimized their expectations, figuring they could get a piece of the exploration done, leaving the rest to others, whoever they might be.

Still, the Western gang (some relying on their returning pal, Paulo Castillo, for unpublicized trip details) had doubts. And two months later there rose a general I-told-you-so reaction after National Geographic issued a long-withheld press release announcing Ian Baker's discovery of Hidden Falls. What raised eyebrows was the timing: The gap was a mere ten days between Baker's discovery and when he'd run into the boaters on the Lhasa-Chengdu highway. "The [McEwan] team was dreaming of climbing over the ridges river left and rappelling into the very hairpin we are now reading about," said Lukas Blücher in an E-mail. "So no wonder they were in a hurry! Guys sponsored by the same mag were hot on their tails." Some even suspected that Geographic had intentionally obscured the timing in order to remove any suspicion of an unseemly race, but a spokesperson said that the story was held because the nation was in the grip of the Monica Lewinsky scandal. They were simply waiting for a slower, more-bang-for-their-buck news cycle.

Why had they put on at all? Jamie seemed to have adequately addressed the second major criticism, but some thought the explanation lacked logic, and likened the ensuing expedition to a slow train wreck. The river was huge—two to three times the volume they'd scouted it at. As they'd acknowledged, high water severely compromised their ability to deal with the river. Doug Ammons, who had conversed with Tom McEwan about a Tsangpo attempt prior to the trip, was particularly emotional about the team's missteps. He made the analogy to a mountaineer on an avalanche-prone slope. "If you're an experienced mountaineer, and you know there's avalanche danger on a slope, do you take one step out and then, if it doesn't slide, take another and another?" He also said deciding to start on a river was the crucial decision: After getting under way, it was psychologically harder and harder to walk away. Your judgment couldn't help but be compromised. The deeper into the gorge you traveled, the more you became committed.

Yet others disagreed with the criticism. How could anyone say they'd walk away from the trip of a lifetime? "We've all been in these situations," says *Paddler* magazine editor Eugene Buchanan, a Western expedition boater. "They came a long way. It's unrealistic to think they'd take one look and turn back. You just say, 'Hey, we can do it. We'll just hug the bank, play it safe, and portage stuff.'" John Weld, one of the boaters initially asked to join the trip, also saw nothing wrong with their decision to proceed. (Nor did Andy Bridge after spending time with the team after their return.) "I think it's very reasonable, what they did," Weld says. "I think at some point when it becomes obvious you say, 'Okay, it's too much, we're bagging out.' But sure, I can understand why they put on."

Others pointed out that the team's racing-heavy background, impressive as it was, might have been the wrong sort of experience; no team member had a cutting-edge big-river first descent on his résumé. Part of that was because there weren't many big-water rivers. On the other hand, several boaters who were considering a run on the Tsangpo, such as Ammons and Scott Lindgren, did have big-water descents, including the Grand Canyon of the Stikine, a sixty-mile gorge in B.C. considered by many to be a must-do qualifier for a river like the Tsangpo. In an early proposal the Geographic team seemed to address the issue, stating its plan for a "team training exercise" at the Clarks Fork of the Yellowstone, a river with renowned big-water rapids in the springtime. Because the Tsangpo expedition didn't get funding until well into summer, the costly warm-up run never happened. "The Tsangpo is still a grade way beyond the Stikine," says Bryan Tooley, a highly regarded Western boater who has run the Stikine, "but I think less than eighteen kayakers have run the Stikine, most of those in the last couple years. It's the only thing currently being done that even comes close." Tooley believes the team had a lot of pluses—Wick's organization and Tom and Wick's ability to "stay calm when the shit hits the fan"—but thinks they might have misread the project in one crucial way. "The reality of doing the Tsangpo is you're going to have to do stupid stuff. It's not a rational place. You must go to a place like that with the understanding, 'I'm going to do stuff I don't want to do.' For that reason a lot of us recognize that it's a young man's river. I was asked to go by another team and I just said, 'I'm too old. I've got two kids. I just can't lay it out that far anymore.'"

The mind-sets of big-water paddlers and technical boaters differed, too. The latter were often exquisite boat handlers who'd set up a move and travel from spot to spot with marksmanlike accuracy. The former were often less deft and nifty but were expert at staying composed when a river offered no letup, bad sightlines, and no smooth ramps (leading into rapids) to set anything up. In a way that was utterly dissimilar from steep, low-volume boating, heavy water violently snatched away the one thing that racers like Jamie, Tom, Doug, and Roger specialized in: control.

The team and its backers acknowledged that they didn't have the big-water experience of some. "It's true most of our paddling has been more technical in nature," says Tom. But they'd it takes is a fluke avalanche for somebody to die and all the second-guessing to start. A death shouldn't automatically indict a team."

And so it went, back and forth. Eventually the furor eased off. Team members, like Tom and Roger, ended up talking and exchanging mail directly with others in the boating community, and a truce took hold. (Tom, for example, sent Ammons an eleven-page letter.) Big differences of opinion remained, but clearly there was more common ground, too. They were good boaters, good people, their former critics relented. Maybe they'd erred, maybe they'd done something they shouldn't have—but who of them hadn't? On extreme occasions they'd all taken chances they probably couldn't reasonably defend. Fortunately, they'd never had to. Nor had they watched a friend drown and been unable to do anything about it. "These guys don't deserve to be pecked to death," reflects Ammons, sounding sort of exhausted himself. "They've been through hell."

≋

NO PARTICULAR LESSON TO BE LEARNED—THE WORDS HUNG AWK-wardly and bothered some. Is that really so? thought Jamie's former slalom coach and whitewater dean Bill Endicott. Deaths among the sport's best suddenly seemed epidemic. In the wake of Richie Weiss's death, Endicott had found himself consoling the mom of a paddler who told him she threw up every time her son prepared to run a course. "Here I was trying to tell her that it was all right, but I realized I didn't understand what was happening in my sport," says Endicott, who himself had looked at the Tsangpo in the early seventies before backing off and passing along his research to Wick and Tom.

been pioneers in almost every facet of the sport—and t
brought to bear a level of planning, sophistication, and all-a
toughness that no Rocky Mountain youngster could t
Moreover, they hadn't really been done in by big-water phe
ena, they argued. Owing to the high water, they'd walked al
everything—and even Doug's last rapid was more technical
big water. They estimated the flow to be a few thousand
feet per second, a mere fraction of the main flow. The holes
big water, but the holes would've shredded anyone.

A final critical (and extremely touchy) undercurrent ha
do with the tone of the trip. Self-proclaimed purists were pu
by the idea of such a modern, goal-driven enterprise in the h
of an ancient, sacred landscape. It wasn't a classic exploration
a sporting competition, they said. Some questioned the tea
humility and respect for the river. Did they truly abide by
ethic that wilderness river runners avowed as fundamental: t
the river called the shots and they were merely granted, if tl
were lucky, a few moments in time to live with it? Did they tr
feel chastened by the grace and magnificence of the last untam
river on the planet? Or had they, as it appeared, charged forwar
motivated by what they might've viewed as an even greater da
ger than the river—the threat of failure?

No, said the team's many defenders. Their ideology wa
beyond reproach: They were precisely the types who wouldn
hesitate to pull the plug on a risky mission, and they wer
respectful of the local culture and of the river. But at the sam
time they were committed to and inspired by the challenge
How else do great pioneering feats get accomplished? Doug
Gordon's death was simply a tragic, isolated accident. It could
have happened anywhere, on any river. "I could take a great
American team to Everest," says David Breashears, "and all

Maybe the tragedy wasn't the result of any one glaring thing, but rather a series of small mistakes that seemed to compound on one another and draw them closer to disaster. It was much like the business model, which posits that operational system failure isn't due to any one failed link in the command chain, but to a string of such failures occurring with neither notice nor comment. Endicott didn't run his theory by Jamie, but he did write him and gently urge him to reassess. "Maybe the trip wasn't a failure," he wrote, echoing Jamie's own appraisal. "Maybe its legacy will be the lessons learned."

≋

OTHERS WONDERED IF ULTIMATELY THE TRIP'S FAILURE HAD MUCH more to do with Geographic than with any team mistake. They'd sent them away underfunded, several believed, "paying just enough to tempt them to go." That was harsh, but the society's decision-makers weren't as familiar with extreme paddling expeditions as with mountaineering trips, for example, and not nearly as surefooted.

At the very least, what was evident was the markedly different relationship that organizations like National Geographic now had with the parties who did dangerous work for them. In the past, old-timers could fondly recall a time when the decision-makers were explorers themselves, well tuned in to the complexities, rigors, and hazards of expeditionary travel. Longtime president Gilbert Grosvenor would fret over each explorer's trip as if he or she were a son or daughter. "Yours is the first expedition we have entrusted to a man as young as yourself," Grosvenor once wrote a then-twenty-four-year-old (and not nearly yet famous) Bradford Washburn. "The ascent of previously unscaled mountains is always attended with considerable uncertainty and peril. . . . The fact that you have, in your few years of active work, made a really remarkable record of achievement in Europe, the United States, and Alaska, which is good evidence of your ability to prepare beforehand, might very naturally lead you to be a little overconfident and to take risk . . ."

It's hard to imagine any sponsor writing a letter like that today. The era is much different. At the extreme end are Hollywood moviemakers who have no idea whatsoever about the difficulties of extreme sports, or much of any apparent concern for the welfare of those pursuing them. After river runner Arlene Burns did rapid running work for the action drama *River Wild,* it struck her that the filmmakers didn't much care whether she lived or died as long as they got their shot. An Italian sports watch company that sponsors daredevil outdoor athletes is famous for its policy after a death: They refuse to release any photographs of the adventurer, since their logo is usually emblazoned on the deceased person.

Geographic certainly wasn't guilty of that level of callousness, but the organization's extreme entrepreneurial makeover (including significant layoffs, a rapidly expanded for-profit division, and a desire to attract a more youthful audience) seemed to embrace the very thing the old institution was famously known for resisting: trendy, marketing-friendly stories. The goals of the Expeditions Council, which awarded the Tsangpo grants, were defined thus: "Council supported projects are intended for a broad audience, they must be highly visual and have great storytelling potential." Such projects as the Tsangpo were considered to be a new model of Geographic assignment: an adventure in untamed territory that all of its media divisions might grab a piece of.

Many noticed a sometimes-frightening gap in expertise between those calling the shots in D.C. and those flinging themselves toward blank spots on the map. Some thought Geographic, given its prestige and respect among skilled explorers, needed to meet a higher (if not the highest) standard, that it needed to understand and consider the risks with more aplomb, and perhaps restraint, than that of just another corporate titan. And yet the society's for-profit TV and film division was in its own pitched battle for cable supremacy with the Discovery Channel and others. The corporate emphasis appeared to be volume, and even longtime contributors lamented that the quality was far more uneven of late.

In fact, when the film of Baker's trip debuted at the Telluride MountainFilm Festival in the spring of 1999, the program's director said the quality was so alarmingly amateurish he regretted he'd included it. Hamid Sardar said the prospect of staging the discovery for Geographic cameras had so bothered him that he'd simply decided to wander off elsewhere in the gorge while Baker and Storm performed. (Ultimately, his might have been the most meaningful expedition, since he and four Tibetan hunters pushed their way through large swaths of the remaining five-mile gap, encountering dense aboriginal forest and a profusion of wildlife, but no more waterfalls.) "They told us we had to act as if we were discovering the falls and finding the route for the first time," says Sardar. "As soon as I found out about it, I said, 'Listen, Ian, you can play it as you want, but for me this isn't really honest, to discover something and rediscover something in this kind of commercial, popularized way. This looks and feels like a bit of a fake.' A much better film could've been made that didn't center on our role as great white explorers."

Another unsettling part of Geographic's controversial role in the 1998 exploration, and one that seemed to further erode their credibility, was the contention over credit for the discovery of Hidden Falls. Upon designation as "the Lost Falls of the Brahmaputra" (something that, in itself, is debatable since the popular myth centered on something far grander), the discovery of the hundred-plus-foot falls resulted in arresting headlines worldwide. Whether the blame rested with Baker for not fully informing them on the sequence of the discovery, or with Geographic's concern that the truth might diminish the wallop of their news event, Gil and Troy Gillenwater were omitted from the society's triumphant press releases. The brothers originally thought it was an oversight—after all, they'd clearly seen Hidden Falls a full year earlier, and had told Baker and Sardar about where they'd seen it from. Later the pair became incensed when they felt they'd been duped by Baker, who had asked them to hold off publicizing the find until they returned to the site with a laser range–finding measuring instrument. (Baker later maintained that the Gillenwaters were paying clients who saw the falls, but would have had no idea of its significance if it weren't for him.)

After some terse exchanges with Baker, the Gillenwaters eventually lost patience with Geographic, too. "National Geographic's claim of 'discovery' by the 1998 return expedition is so egregious that it again forces us to speculate that the 1997 account was intentionally excluded from the story because it wasn't part of a National Geographic Society funded expedition," the brothers wrote in the last of a series of letters attempting to clarify their part. "In other words it appears as though this act of revisionist history is motivated by the greed of selling more magazines and elevating television ratings."

Geographic's claim to the falls discovery also prompted protest from the Chinese. Ian Baker's team wasn't the first to spy the waterfall, said a lead organizer of the 1998 Chinese Academy of Sciences team. Photographs of the same falls were taken from a helicopter overflight of the gorge in 1986, said geologist Yang Yichou, author of numerous academic articles on the Tsangpo. It may be new to Geographic, he said, but it wasn't new to them. He added that the Geographic team wasn't even the first to see the falls in 1998, since his Chinese team, which in fact comprised three teams, had already pushed through the gorge and reached Hidden Falls by the time Baker arrived on the scene. The Chinese scientists reported four multilevel waterfalls from 30 to 35 meters high, all within a 20-kilometer stretch.

Baker vigorously contested Yichou's claim that he'd beat him to the falls, and Wan Lin, a member of the rival Chinese rafting team, seemed to support Baker. Wan's team, led by Yang Yong, arrived at the entrance to the gorge on October 28. Fearing for their lives, they'd proceeded on foot into the inner gorge, but, like the large CAS team, they were unable to access the innermost gorge. Wan paints a portrait of intense rivalry between the private China Youth Travel Service Expedition and the state-supported academics; the two groups were apparently too busy squaring off with each other to much notice Baker. "There were (*sic*) a policy in their team called 'three bans: no contact, no help, no support,'" wrote Wan about the rivalry. "What great shame . . ."

National Geographic's January 7 news release did draw notice, however, and was answered by an article in the *China Daily* outlining Yichou's counterclaims. On the heels of the article came the stunning decision by Chinese authorities to close the gorge to Western exploration. At the time of the announcement, Baker, Sardar, renowned wildlife biologist George Schaller, and a National Geographic filmmaker were in Lhasa, poised to begin a daring winter expedition to document the gorge's rare wildlife. Baker and Storm blamed the ban on publicity surrounding Gordon's death, noting that officials feared a rash of deaths with international kayaking teams and sponsors zeroing in on the alluring first descent. Gordon's death had in fact done nothing to deter boaters from the Tsangpo challenge, and had only enhanced the prestige of conquering the gorge. Even boaters agreed the next season was shaping up to be a circus.

Others, too, thought the kayakers-are-to-blame explanation was self-serving: The Chinese obviously considered the gorge an Everest-like national jewel and its exploration a chance to propagandize its daring adventurers at the dawn of the new millennium. China's Ministry of Civil Affairs officially renamed the gorge the Yarlung Zangbo Grand Canyon, a title befitting the "matchless grandeur" of the "grandest canyon in the world." The 1998 scientific inventory not only established the new Grand Canyon as a global attraction on a par with Mount Qomolangma (Everest), the state news media reported, but confirmed the immense water resources available for a hydroelectric project in the core section. According to Yichou, fellow scientists believed they might construct the world's largest water-power–generating plant and solve energy shortages in arid western China by building a dam at the entrance of the canyon and blasting a tunnel through the Himalaya, harnessing the steepest, most storied stretch of the river. Though such a project would be impossible using standard construction practices, it would be doable, noted a statement by the Chinese Academy of Engineering Physics, with the use of nuclear explosives. Newspapers reported the

Grand Canyon discovery to be one of the top news events of the year and added (ominously, some thought) that the "era for the Canyon is coming." They closed the gorge because of Geographic's credit-mongering and because they didn't "want Americans in their backyard discovering things," said Sardar. The irony, he added, was that the waterfall wasn't that big a deal. It didn't look terribly impressive and wasn't the whole point of the place. "The hype, the whole Western fantasy thing got so far out of hand," says Sardar, sobered by what he describes as his own unpleasant education. "It's a shame, because there's so much more to see."

The myth-chasing and the fevered Shangri-la-ism had snowballed, it seemed, turning allies into enemies and bringing out the worst in everybody. Many thought Geographic had thrown gasoline on the fire by chasing and selling the myth hardest of all. *National Geographic* magazine expeditions ex-editor Peter Miller (who left the Society in 1999 to start his own innkeeping business) characterized the National Geographic Society criticism as "distorted and twisted," but declined to elaborate, saying only, "I haven't seen a lot of good writing coming out of this." Of those who were enraged at the results of the 1998 campaign, Rick Fisher was, not surprisingly, the most vocal. He bitterly spewed out a stream of near-libelous letters to Geographic, charging them with sponsoring a fraud in Baker and a coward in Walker. He suggested they'd sent the river team off, knowing they were in grave danger. Everybody agreed Fisher's accusations were spurious (and probably motivated by bitterness at not being Geographic's anointed one). But most believed he was right about one thing: The movies, the international headlines, and the making of a pinup explorer in the dashing Ian Baker had come at a cost. "When I first saw the canyon in 1992 I thought it was the most beautiful place I'd ever seen," says Fisher. "Its history was clean, virgin. It's not anymore."

≋

TWO EMOTIONAL MEMORIAL SERVICES WERE HELD FOR DOUG Gordon, one organized at Lakeside School by former classmates, the other in Cornwall, Connecticut. Some two hundred attended the Quaker-style service in New England on November 21. It was held in a Grange hall not far from the banks of the Housatonic— the same river where he and Jamie had lived and trained, and where Doug and Connie had met more than a decade before. No one led the service. Instead, those who wanted to speak did so. In the center of the large hall, dwarfed by the building's high ceilings and arched windows, sat Connie and five-year-old Tyler. Ringed around them and facing the pair were their family and friends— past teammates, professional colleagues, high school and college friends. The wave of memories—funny, sad, and searching— lasted two hours. Doug's presence rose so vividly, some thought, the occasion sometimes felt more like a long-overdue visit than a final good-bye.

"Doug was my friend, and Doug had all the virtues that make someone a good friend," Jamie told the gathering. "He was strong enough to be sensitive to other people and to care about them. He was also the most rational person that I have ever known. Not, I hasten to say, 'coldly rational'—no, he was *warmly* rational. Too rational to ever think that his mind should suppress his emotions or that he had to deny what he was feeling. He had fire—he had desire, he had—I don't know how else to put it—he had a 'hot' approach to life. . . . And that's why it's so hard for me, and I think for everyone, to realize that he's not here—he's gone. Because he was more alive, more awake to what was around him; both thinking more about what was around him, and feeling more, all at the same time. That was why he was really a special person and why, when I think of him, I'll hold him not just as a memory, but as a kind of ideal."

But Doug's array of gifts, quirks, and trademark confidence and integrity also underscored a searing question that lasted beyond the memorials at Cornwall and later at Lakeside: What had truly happened? Doug's death seemed the biggest riddle of all. In light of what Doug represented, the whole sequence of events was baffling. He had seemed more cautious than usual earlier in the day, but he went ahead and ran the most exposed line. He'd pointed out the severe backwash on the run to Roger, but chose to take it on. He'd seemed to rectify his roll problems, but then he didn't roll. His closest friends seemed to be searching for some sort of "eureka" moment, some last conversation or eyewitness comment out of Jamie, Roger, and Tom to explain everything, to answer the contradictions with the crap-clearing logic that Doug brought to bear.

David Halpern, his friend from Lakeside who'd learned to race and paddle at the same time Doug did, has rolled the episode over endlessly, too. Prior to their twenty-fifth-anniversary high school reunion—held a few weeks before the team's departure at none other than Bill Gates's house—he and Doug hadn't seen each other for fifteen years. The reunion was notable for a couple of reasons: Bill Gates and Bill Gates's house, and the fact that Halpern and Doug hit it off again, making tentative plans to paddle in the summer. (The kid prodigies Gates and Doug also hit it off, the pair obviously thrilled to be back in each other's company and seemingly picking up where they'd left off back in the old lounge.) Doug talked about the Tsangpo, and David felt he was proceeding with eyes wide open, neither crazy with bravado nor unaware of the risks. Nor hunting fame. Same old Doug. But in reflecting on their last conversation, Halpern returned to an earlier time in his own career, almost twenty years earlier, when he'd paddled the hardest whitewater rivers in the West. "I'd ask people to go do these things and nobody would go. I'd go and wouldn't feel at all at risk. Pretty soon I started to realize if nobody is willing to do what I want to do, maybe it *is* life-threatening. Doug understood risk. But he never got to the point I did. I stopped. Somehow that risk element that he calculated in every river he ran wasn't frightening enough to him, not real enough. Doug was a man of numbers and calculations, and I'm sure he could calculate the risks and knew they were real but they were small numbers.

"In hindsight you say maybe he should've done more to make the boat fit tighter, tape in some foam or something, but maybe not. He went seven more days after that first rapid without having another problem. The drop was reasonable. If he got caught in the curler he still had time to roll up. He had a margin of error. It was only if everything went wrong did he have a problem. Everything went wrong." There was nothing blatantly unsafe about his last rapid except maybe he'd been wagering himself against wicked rapids most of his life. Ultimately, Halpern thinks, the law of averages simply caught up with him. More than two decades of hard whitewater is a long time—especially when the biggest is the last. "I suppose we all wish he would've said, 'Yeah, I can do this, but I've got kids and a wife and maybe it's time to tone it down.' He wasn't able to say that."

Ken Stone, a former coach of Doug's, wished similarly at the memorial service: "Doug had this insatiable desire to be on the edge. He made choices to race—which put his intellectual life on hold; which put his career life on hold; which put his family life on hold—because he had a quest—a burning desire to have that one run 'in the zone.' When I am angry with him, I think that once he had a family, he should no longer have taken chances on dangerous rivers. But then I think river-running, for Doug, must have been the ultimate race. . . . Albert Einstein said that God was in all things that were held sacred and even inspirational by man—from the simplest everyday task to the truly holy. Perhaps the beauty of that one fast and clean run, better than anyone could imagine, was—and is—the racer's connection to God. Perhaps Doug's God drew him to those places where his experience on the river felt almost holy. And perhaps this is where he finally met his God and will be with him for all eternity. I thought about this, and him, more than you can imagine—too much, in fact—and I certainly have no answers. I do know this: Doug is one of my heroes."

E. J. McCarthy, Doug's friend of fourteen years, considered Doug a mentor—not just somebody whom he aspired to emulate because of his intellect but because his values, honesty, and judgment were second to none. The two of them had talked many times about why they paddled, what the payoff was. In some ways it went no deeper than getting away. In other ways the river was a profound touchstone for everything important in life: love, challenge, freedom, mystery. Doug often tussled with the equation of family and what he did, E.J. knew, but believed that he had room for all the passions. He didn't believe it served anyone well if he walked away from the river, if he lived a life insulated from risk. And yet he was cautious, never sloppy—he took calculated risks.

All of which E.J. trusted, admired, and witnessed time and again. But when he saw the video of Doug's final rapid, E.J. found himself mystified. "Doug was my best friend. I love him. But I said to myself, 'What on earth was he thinking?'" Many things trouble him: Why would Doug take on an extreme move with a boat he didn't like? Why didn't his Plan B work out, and where was his Plan C? "Doug always taught me to make a plan and try to anticipate the problems," he says. "'Sometimes you get lemons,' he said, 'but you've got to be able to make lemonade.'" The fact that Doug didn't recover, or couldn't recover, is baffling. But beyond the failed move, what weighs on E.J. is that he can't imagine a damn good reason for going through with it. He's wondering if something on the trip corrupted Doug's vision. Did the presence of the cameras alter his judgment? The thought that the trip was his last big hurrah, a chance to make the kind of milestone achievement in the sport he hadn't made in slalom racing—did that enter in? Would it have mattered if E.J. were there and said, "What the hell are you doing, Doug?" Frankly E.J. is riddled with questions. "I don't know what went on, that's the hard part," he says. "But it's a disturbing image to think of Doug drowning on that river, just flushing endlessly downstream through India and Bangladesh, like so much flotsam and jetsam. It tears me up."

Lukas Blücher, the German paddler Doug befriended on the river, is by no means certain what happened, but wonders if Doug wasn't victimized by something else, a culprit he probably wasn't even fully aware of. In Blücher's read, the most dangerous part of the Tsangpo was the degree of exposure. He defines exposure as one's "distance to safety," and he listed several factors that seemed to affect exposure. A short list included the difficulty of the river, the amount of water, the problem of getting from shore to shore, the distance to shore, the obstacles on shore, the scarcity of easily walked terrain, and the quality of help and support available in villages. "This kind of exposure makes you feel extremely alert, which is what many of us like about [expedition paddling] and what makes us want to repeat the experience," he says. "Quite many kayakers find the super-exposed realm more real than 'daily life.'"

But when paddlers travel in super-exposed arenas for extended periods, he continues, the mental wear and tear add up. Otherwise minor things—like the adrenaline surge you get just looking at a difficult rapid, or the fatigue of a tough, just-completed portage, or the heat at midday on a tropical river—have the ability to produce an overload. In overload the mind sometimes reacts bizarrely: Rather than becoming more vigilant and scared, it seems to relax. "It's almost as if your system drugs itself, you are feeling a natural high," says Blücher, likening the judgment-impairing effect to what mountaineers go through at high altitude. It's like a velvety bolt of adrenaline. In the moment you don't have the feeling of great risk, he says, but the feeling you have "found the tool to make it smooth." In several cases Blücher says he's found himself, or expedition partners—elite, highly analytical paddlers—doing things that had no rational basis and were completely out of character. They even made "rookie" mistakes they couldn't explain, like ignoring parts of their normal checklist for assessing a rapid. Usually these things occurred under a set of super-exposed conditions. "People all of a sudden isolate themselves and run off to attempt the most idiotic lines they would never attempt as their 'normal selves.' But then it may be too late."

The river conditions in the fall of 1998 certainly qualified under Blücher's definition of "super-exposed." Whether Doug was done in by forces he couldn't see coming is a tantalizing but unanswerable question. The fight-or-flight impulse is a scientific given; the specific ability to anticipate or subdue it is not. Blücher and other paddlers who have explored the notion don't really even like to talk about it. That our judgment may be impaired by someone or something else, or snatched out of our hands at the exact wrong time, isn't a comforting thought. On the one hand, being aware of the syndrome might be critical if the river is attempted again; on the other, just thinking about it adds stress and another dimension of risk, one more thing on the Tsangpo that is seemingly beyond human control.

≋

BACK IN THE LAB AT THE UNIVERSITY OF UTAH, DOUG'S LABMATE, Laura Deakin, was as stunned as anyone by the news. Doug was an immensely resourceful and careful chemist, one of the few who had the technical patience to work safely with the most volatile materials. Most couldn't handle either the practical or the intellectual risk of creating pure matter. It was painstaking and rarely successful. Of course, the upside to working with fringe materials was that lightning might strike.

It had never remotely occurred to Laura that he might not come back. The pair had had long talks about Everest and the notorious 1996 disaster. Doug had been absolutely clear that the fatal mistake on Everest, in which several lives were lost, was that everyone's judgment seemed compromised by things that didn't belong on the mountain. Ambition, fame, and other factors had all conspired to muddy clear analysis. It certainly seemed to Laura, though she wasn't a paddler, that Doug must have been the same in the field as he was in the lab: adventuresome and determined, but above all deliberate and controlled.

They hadn't had much time to talk before he left. In a quick blast through the lab to check on his experiments, Doug told

Laura he had some ideas he wanted to talk about with her later. He had just returned from his presentation in France, but was on his way out the door to pack for the Tsangpo trip. One of the last things Doug did, Laura recalled, was to eyeball a series of reactions he was "cooking." At the back of his inert glove box—a large Plexiglas box in which exotic substances are derived absent from the corrosive effects of air and moisture—a flask contained the molecular material Doug had been working with and exploring for some four years.

What Doug was looking for was what he was always looking for: a perfect crystal. In molecular science, salt crystals—with nice clear molecular positions—reveal structure in a proof-positive way that can be seen under a microscope and X-rayed. Doug had cracked the mechanistic code for V-TCNE, the molecular magnet his department chair had discovered ten years ago, but had yet to come up with the crystal evidence to hang his research on. It was important research, too, since working out the structure meant that promising high-tech materials could be routinely made. Over months and months he'd attempted to induce crystallization in the molecular material he suspected to be the core ingredient. Tweaking time, light, and solvents—everything he could think of—he'd tried hundreds of reactions. At group meetings there'd be a general roll call for "new crystals from new materials," and it was no secret that Doug was frustrated to be coming up empty. At the time he left for the Tsangpo, none of his experiments had taken.

Around the time of Doug's memorial service, Deakin had been wandering through the lab when she decided to take a look in his gloved box. In his absence a reaction in one of his flasks had produced a nearly perfect salt crystal. To some degree the 0.1-millimeter crystal was the fruition of everything Doug had worked for. It certainly completed one of his explorations. With the blessing of Doug's wife, Connie, and the support of Dr. Joel Miller, Deakin organized Doug's research for submission to the prestigious *Journal of the American Chemical Society.* In going over Doug's chemistry journals, Deakin says his wide-ranging interests and expertise astounded her. "It really didn't seem to matter what it was," she says. "The scientific process thrilled him."

On January 19, 2000, the journal published his paper posthumously.

Epilogue

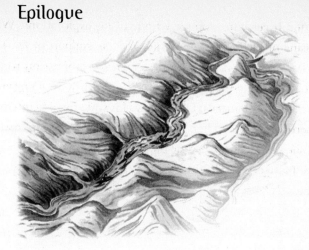

Valley Falls State Park, West Virginia, September 26, 1999

It's early morning, a picture-perfect fall day with temperatures building into the seventies. The riverfront foliage is flaming orange and red, the flowing water blue-green clear. Exactly a year ago, Tom was crossing the border into Tibet. Today he and his four-member team are on the river, peering over the lip of a fifteen-foot drop. The team is made up of Tom's D.C.-area students: a middle-aged woman who is a writer for the *Washington Post,* a twelve-year-old boy, and a real-estate developer and a programmer, both in their twenties. Yesterday they paddled the challenging lower

Yough, then spent the night camped out on somebody or other's front porch. Today, in a kind of graduation ceremony after a summer of Tom's instruction, they're getting their first shot at jumping a waterfall, the same falls Tom and Wick learned on twenty-five years ago.

The starter step is a "seal launch" off this fifteen-foot ledge. To simulate the current, Tom hand-pushes each of them across the raspy, flat-topped rock and out into the void. Each is to hit his or her "boof" stroke at the exact moment the world drops away. The landing zone isn't whitewater but an easy pool. The next runs will be in the actual river current, over a series of increasingly difficult falls. Everybody is nervous but trusting. "You know, Campbell, I can't let you go ahead unless you show me you can do this," Tom says, smiling. He's not pushy, nor too quick to let the twelve-year-old off the hook. Yesterday Campbell took a nasty swim, but he's had them before. Campbell accepts the push-off and sails over the drop with perfect form. "Way to go!" hoots Tom.

Over the next several hours, Tom will orchestrate a vintage outing, leading them into a realm they might scarcely have imagined. At the first big drop he'll traverse into the fast-moving, waist-high current at the lip of the falls, his scrawny, Bermuda-shorted body serving as launch bull's-eye for his upstream charges. Later he'll beckon the others to follow as he paddles hard, straight into the base of the cascade, ushering them through the pounding torrent and past a stiff opposing current. Unseen from shore, and reachable only by kayak, is a becalmed, boat-length chamber undercut into the cliff. The day goes by in a flash. No lunch, no nothing. Five hours and nobody notices anything but the flow of water and their particular place in it. They run through the drops one by one, finishing the rousing day by running the whole sequence top to bottom. Tom is obviously tickled. He caps the day by dropping into the pile of the last drop—the same hole he'd gotten Maytagged in twenty-five years earlier—and pirouetting his boat on its stern tip. It's the boating equivalent, both for its showmanship and skill, of a game-ending slam-dunk.

Tom is, as Tom was—absorbed in flowing water. All summer long, as usual, he bounced from river to river. Out west to Colorado, up north to Canada, throughout the Southeast. The Gauley, the Cheat, the Yough, the Potomac. His Calleva program during the summer. After this weekend the season is more or less over until Christmas, after which he'll guide a three-month-long series of trips in remote canyons of Mexico. On the three-hour drive back to D.C., he says he and his girlfriend plan to take some time off for a few days. What is he going to do? "Ah, probably go paddling," he laughs. "Desperate, isn't it?" But, he adds, it's nice to get on a river when you aren't so overwhelmingly preoccupied with safeguarding others.

The Tsangpo doesn't seem to have changed him much. "When Tom came back, I really didn't know if he'd be bitter, or not talking, or never getting in a kayak again," says his nephew, Alex, who heads up the Calleva camp. "He was hurting some, but really he hasn't missed a beat." He stands by what they did in Tibet. They proceeded reasonably, he says, and developed a good system. Were it not for the accident, they would have probed further than anyone thought possible. If he got the opportunity, he'd go back in a heartbeat. He's eager in part because he's unhappy with the perception that they failed, but also because he knows there's so much more to see. He doesn't think Ian Baker or anybody else got to the biggest falls—the Crease—and nobody's been downstream of the confluence in the section of the river they dubbed "7." With low water levels, more of the river would open up. They could portage less and run more. The problem is that to get low water, somebody is either going to have to get lucky and blunder into the right year, or be on the scene waiting and watching. Of course, neither scenario is currently possible since the area is closed. But not all of Tibet is shut down, and Tom hopes he'll be allowed back to run rivers somewhere—perhaps he'll even lead a commercial trip for some of his D.C. clients.

Doug's death remains hard to explain. Tom thinks the soft "boof" stroke at the top of the falls hurt his launch and that he fell out of the housing, preventing his roll. He feels that he set the right tone for the trip, but that Doug needed to do more. "He's a whitewater paddler and he was there to run the river," says Tom, in a way that's not critical but is, especially to him, perfectly understandable. "Truthfully, I think that was a big part of it." In some ways Tom seems less mystified by Doug's death than others do—maybe because their river personas were a lot alike. He was rational, reasonable, but he had a fiery hot desire to see things for what they were.

Doug's loss hit Tom hardest as he thought about Doug's two young children, Bryce and Tyler, and wondered if they'd ever understand what he was truly about. Tom's own two children were adults now—once disinterested, Andrew, twenty, is now among the top wildwater paddlers in the United States—but there'd been a time in Tom's life when he could have vanished on a river, and what would his children have known? Most of his river exploits, given his penchant for keeping them to himself, he would have taken to the grave. The river experience—any river experience—was personal for Tom, and like the prototypical whitewater hero, he didn't much care to broadcast to those who hadn't been there themselves. But Tom relented and talked publicly and in great depth about the Tsangpo. Perhaps it was cathartic; perhaps he had changed. Or perhaps he reflected on something his nephew Alex observed: "It was almost like it happened to the wrong person," he told Tom, half-seriously. "If it had happened to you, it would've made sense."

≋

LIKE TOM, ROGER ZBEL HAS PICKED UP WHERE HE LEFT OFF. HE AND Nancy continue to run their popular whitewater business in Friendsville, and Roger continues to good-naturedly drub all comers, including Tom's son, Andrew, in the annual Upper Yough downriver race. In November of 1999, he, Nancy, their daughter, an old black Lab, and a newly acquired yellow Lab, Canyon, had just moved into a beautiful, log-constructed A-frame on a wooded ridgetop plot high above town. With the season over and the move still only a month old, they're still living out of boxes and taking long exploratory walks along the winding creek that passes the property. The new setup is going to give them space and more separation between home and their river business.

In the next few years Roger and an architect friend plan to build custom vacation homes in the off-season; Nancy is hoping to get her real-estate license—each side job a hedge against the slim margins of the whitewater trade. Though he seasonally asks himself "why I don't do something else and make a lot more money," he isn't tired of the river running. Months later, on one of the early spring runs, he'll drive the shuttle bus to a sunny, Upper Yough put-in, caretake for three rafts full of clients, rope-rescue a kayaker's pinned boat, and grin knowingly when one of his raft guides goes overboard in a rapid but refuses help. "He wouldn't take the rope," says Roger, darting about in the same fire-engine-red kayak he took to Tibet. "Guides just hate to owe somebody."

In putting down deeper roots in Friendsville, he seems to have put a lot of distance between himself and the Tsangpo experience. Yet he continues to be riddled with differing emotions. Foremost is the haunting memory of Doug's last rapid. "I mean, hardly a day goes by when at some point I don't think if only I'd said, 'Doug, don't do that.' Or done something that could've prevented what happened." Roger has watched the video many times and doesn't see any real technical error on Doug's part. "He lined it up okay, fading left in order to land in the weaker point of the backwash," he says. Doug just underestimated the difficulty of the line. Roger had been in situations where he'd get himself in the flow by *not* backing off. On the other hand, the river was utterly unforgiving for even slight error. "You can second-guess all you want, but, yeah, it plays over and over in my mind and it's not a pretty picture," he says. "I don't know if I'll ever get over it, and I can only imagine how Jamie must feel because they were so much closer."

At other times Roger sounds almost fatalistic, softly wondering if maybe "things happen for a reason," and what if Doug's death had prevented all of them from vanishing? Roger says he probably won't return to Tibet, but there's also a sense that he hasn't entirely sold himself on the no-go, either. As the trip wore on, especially during the search and evacuation, Roger took on a more prominent and vocal role. Tom called Roger's transformation through the course of the trip a "neat evolution," adding that he became "stronger and more settled within himself." In trips like this, explained another expedition paddler, you find your weak points but also maybe discover some strengths. So it had seemed with Roger. And he can't disagree with Tom that ultimately they did arrive at a pretty good system for squeezing themselves through the gorge.

"The whole time I was there, I was feeling like I don't want to leave my wife and child behind," he says. "But I had a positive feeling about my risk assessment and the way I was managing the conditions. I think I can put myself in that same situation and be equally as strong, but to put myself in that situation again after what has happened and realizing how quickly things can change, I don't know. I don't think it really hit home to me until we got off the plane and I got my first hug from my little girl. I would love to go back and do that trip again, but I don't know if I could, just because I realize what I stand to lose."

≋

WICK WALKER HAS RETURNED TO SEMIRETIREMENT BACK ON HIS horse farm outside Pittsburgh. Up the creaky backstairs of his rambling nineteenth-century house, the walls are lined with handsome photographs from his travels in Pakistan. The second-story study itself is heaped with the quirky odds and ends of a well-traveled warrior: a gilded samurai saber here, a host of rare clothbound travel books there. This is not the antiseptic place of a military planner but the literate, full-bodied quarters of a Victorian-era wayfarer in midstride. Back-burner as the Tsangpo is for Tom and Roger, Wick is still active. He's got photos he wants to show potential sponsors, and a half-hour slide show is on the carousel, ready for viewing. By default and out of his own interest, he is the trip archivist.

If anyone asked, he'd surely go back to Tibet, he says. Like Tom, he stands by their approach and is sure the descent can be done. "The thing you find hopeful is that every step of the way they had these boulder fields [on the river margins]—it was not a bank-full flood, and they had a zone that was growing day by day." In hindsight he thinks they should have started the trip a few weeks later, but he says all the people who have talked about going in midwinter "haven't ever been midwinter." The only person who was in the gorge in winter months was Francis Kingdon-Ward, he adds, and "he didn't describe it as fun." Doug's accident was horrible and tragic, he says, but he's also convinced it could happen "stateside or in any big rapid anywhere." For both sporting and personal reasons, he continues to keep close tabs on the political situation in Tibet, trying like many others to get a fix on when (and for what price) the area might reopen.

The coverage of the trip irked him, especially the reportorial feature in the premier issue of National Geographic's *Adventure* magazine, a new, hip spin-off of the yellow-bordered eminence. Wick seemed stunned that the magazine wasn't more gracious or, to his mind, more accurate about the expedition. He also didn't like the slick magazine—at least in comparison with the august original. According to Wick, the original plan—to publish an entire issue of the *Geographic* about the Tsangpo, featuring the Walker, Baker, and Breashears expeditions—was scrapped when the Falls controversy erupted and the Chinese prevented Baker, Schaller, and Sardar from entering the gorge to complete their wildlife inventory. "I was crushed," half-kids Wick, describing his reaction when expedition editor Peter Miller told him he'd relinquished his rights to the story for Old Yellow and relegated them to the start-up.

Originally, Jamie had intended to write a book about the trip. But after Doug's death, he passed on it and Wick decided to take on the project. Telling the story, he decided, had a certain challenging appeal. He could set the record straight, but, maybe more important, he could place them on the Tsangpo's historical map. Didn't his intrepid pal Tommy remind anyone else of Kintup? Wick asked.

≈

OF ALL THE PRINCIPALS ON THE TRIP, JAMIE McEWAN IS THE ONLY one to state categorically that he wouldn't go back. Doug's death made him wonder if he was being as safe in big whitewater as he thought he was. "I have a certain way I looked at things and certain things I believed in, and that's just gone," Jamie told Paulo shortly after they got out of the gorge. "I don't think I'll ever do anything anywhere near that challenging, or put myself in a risky situation again."

Months later, in what he called a period of reassessment, he continued to reflect on his assumptions, his close calls. Years ago he'd missed a ferry move on the Homathko and would have washed into a lethal hydraulic had Doug not grabbed his bow loop and pulled him ashore. "My wife asked me how I would quantify an acceptable paddling risk," he recounted in a *Canoe and Kayak* article titled "Why Are Great Paddlers Dying?" "After I thought about it, I told her that it's acceptable if the risk is one in a hundred that I'll blow it, and then one in a hundred that even then I'll die. 'Okay,' she said, 'that's one in 10,000. Where are you now?' It made me really think. One in 10,000 seems so remote. But you know, I'll bet I'm just about there." In other words, the odds were perhaps no longer in his favor after years of risk-taking.

He, too, was disappointed by the trip's depiction in the media. The trip failed, he insisted. The only reason anyone is interested, he told friends, is that Doug died. The *National*

Geographic Explorer movie, which aired in spring 1999, had left the impression that the pair were sort of free-spirited and boyishly arrogant, almost courting tragedy. He said he would keep his thoughts to himself; he especially didn't want to grieve for his best friend in public and feed the demand for Everestian drama.

What he did say was that he wished they'd trained more. They'd counted on the first eighteen miles being a warm-up, not an extreme trial in and of itself. "We weren't really searching that hard for Tsangpo-like rivers to train on," he says. "In hindsight I wish we had done more and Doug had done more, too." Of the four, Doug and Jamie had consistently taken on the most challenging Tsangpo runs, not because of some competitive need to push one another, but because they'd paddled a lot together and often saw eye-to-eye on the lines. Besides, they both knew they weren't equal, he said. "On the trips we took, we often shared leadership, but when it got really tough he'd be the first down," he says. "I knew and was comfortable with the fact he was probably a little more daring and just a little better than me."

In devoting such a large portion of one's life to amateur whitewater racing, Jamie had once explained the inducement as the "fascination of what's difficult." The line, borrowed from Yeats, probably went a long way in defining their friendship as well. Around the one-year anniversary date, Jamie went to visit Connie and her kids. The trip went well, and he returned certain he'd write something about Doug and the trip after all. Around the same time Jamie began training again, racing as a two-man team with his son, Devin. Remarkably, the pair qualified for the 2000 U.S. Olympic whitewater slalom trials on the Ocoee River. "When I raced with my brother, there's a bond that I could never explain to you—I can't even explain it to my wife," says Lecky Haller, a close friend and former Olympic partner of Jamie's. "I'm not surprised Jamie's back. For Devin and him, just like it was for me and my brother Fritz, it's about much more than racing, it's about love."

≋

It's months earlier, Memorial Day weekend, when I meet Connie Gordon. She's understandably reluctant to get together, confused and skeptical about the hubbub of attention focused on the Tsangpo trip. "I don't know whether to beat them or join them," she says—whether to share a part of her husband or tell everybody to get lost. Five weeks ago, she and the boys left Salt Lake's high desert and moved to an historic mountain town in southern Colorado. She's taking a chance, she says, starting anew in a town where she barely knows a soul. Maybe it'll be a bad fit and she'll be back east near Jamie and other old friends before she knows it. On her plate in the coming months are a dizzying array of things, from getting her architectural business up and running to getting the kids situated in school and day care. Even the Utah house sale, which seemed a cinch, is now in jeopardy twenty-four hours before closing because the buyers want another $1,000 off. She doesn't scare easy but sometimes she's daunted. Nothing seems easy. And sometimes she's pretty sure things are going to be okay. Her kids are kids, so upbeat. And her fast, hard runs, when she can squeeze them in, remain a sanctuary—a time of clarity and quiet.

Part of her reason for getting together is obvious: to decipher what somebody who didn't know her husband might want to say. Like Jamie, she thinks the popular interest in Doug and his trip isn't about him or about it, but about America's late-twentieth-century fascination with fatal adventures. The questions that were asked by others months ago offend her. Was he a daredevil? Should a responsible parent undertake a risky expedition? Did his judgment desert him? Whose business, ultimately, was it but theirs and theirs alone? As she points out, his interest in whitewater didn't come out of nowhere. She knew it was there when she married him, and she accepted that.

She didn't, of course, think he'd die on the Tsangpo or any other whitewater river. He died because some things went wrong, not because he was foolish. The falls he died on was an ordinary expert rapid and not an extreme monster. "Doug wouldn't have done it," she says flatly about the last rapid, "if he'd thought it was dangerous." Some might read denial into those words, but others might note that she and several others who have thought about what happened don't disagree: At that moment he didn't think it was dangerous. What other conclusion could one come to, given the trajectory of his life? As Blücher said, "Your personality is proven over time, not in a split second."

Many months later I venture out to the Ocoee River in Tennessee and the U.S. Whitewater Slalom Team Trials, where hundreds of boaters are competing for a handful of Olympic berths. It's an admittedly late-in-the-game attempt to understand a particular period of Doug's life, but even a brief study of the bibbed racers weaving "fast and clean" between gates and windmilling across the flat finish-line stretch is memorable. Their ability to control sliver-thin boats through gnashing whitewater seems to defy accepted landlubber logic: that which says a small craft in big water loses every time. The frigid, gusty day with intermittent snow showers is also remarkable—the worst weather in trials history, say some—and a few of Doug's contemporaries are reminded of those wintertime workouts on the Housatonic. (Jamie and Devin have decided not to compete this time around due to the strong field.) Not surprisingly, forty-two-year-old Cathy Hearn, who trained with Doug in Connecticut, shines in the gray drizzle, winning the day's heat. She has personal ties to almost everyone on the Tsangpo team—she grew up on the Potomac, worked as a counselor at Valley Mill, and considers Tom, Jamie, and their mother, May, one of her first coaches, mentors. Long after everyone's gone home to warm up, she sits on the stony riverbank, not preoccupied with the troubling particulars of Doug's death so much as with the transcendent power of his life. The image of him boating beneath a lush tropical rainbow—an icon in Buddhist reincarnation belief, she's heard—is never far away. "I dream about Doug, and in the dreams we have these conversations, we go paddling, we have these adventures," says Hearn, who knows rationally he is dead but keeps thinking of him as being very much alive. "I don't think it's my attachment to wanting to have a body found or anything; I just feel like when they went on that expedition they entered another realm, and maybe it's human nature to mythologize people like Doug, but it feels like he's still with us somehow. At least I hope so."

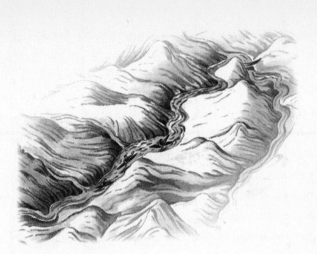

Author's Note

In the early nineties *Outside* magazine asked me to research a story about the last great unexplored places on the planet. Though I arranged things in no particular order, the editors quickly placed Tibet's Tsangpo Gorge atop the "What's Left Out There" list. I'm fairly certain it was the first modern-era mention of the gorge in a major U.S. publication. At the time I didn't have any real misgivings about publicizing the Tsangpo, which was then a kind of unlikely fantasy shared by a small band of river runners and trekkers. But by the end of the decade, when the hype reached epic proportions and everybody and his brother seemed pointed in the direction of southeast Tibet, I began to reassess. By that time I was well aware of the most tragic development of all: the disappearance of whitewater expert Doug Gordon on a first-descent bid.

I agreed to write about the trip for *Men's Journal,* only to soon wish I hadn't. The piece went through an endless number of drafts, ballooning up to ten thousand words and then back down to half that, and each one kind of missing the heart of the story. Part of the difficulty was the length of the article (ultimately only three thousand words), but a bigger reason for my thrashings was that I was unable to talk with any of the team members directly. Their contract with the National Geographic Society, a primary sponsor, restricted them from speaking with competitive periodicals such as *Men's Journal.* I reported what others had to say and attempted to interpret the constrained public statements the team issued about what happened. In almost every way imaginable the process was frustrating and the result unsatisfying.

My initial desire to write a book was surprisingly strong: I felt like I wanted to understand what they did and why, and yet I did fence-sit for quite a while. Anybody who regularly writes about expeditions and adventure, as I do, is well aware of the popular interest in cutting-edge mountaineers, paddlers, and others who are willing to "pay the ultimate price." However, most surviving friends and families suspect that whatever occurs in the media will be inaccurate, sensational, and will wrongly portray the deceased as someone who callously and obsessively pursued their kicks at the expense of those left behind. The cynicism is both abundant and frequently just, and I wasn't sure I might not be snagged in the bottom-feeding cycle myself.

Some exploratory conversations with team members changed my mind. (Wick Walker, the overall trip leader, thought I'd done a fair and nonbiased job in the *Men's Journal* story and paved the way for the interviews.) I became convinced there were solid reasons—not the least was their extraordinary friendship and their shaping role in a sporting culture few understood—to take a closer look. The puzzling spike in fatalities among expert paddlers was another. The ever-expanding annual accident report published by safety experts for the American Whitewater Association is a process that strikes some as grim and objectionable—the after-analysis is often extremely detailed. But those who compile the reports say objective accident analysis is the only way to learn and hopefully prevent future deaths. Unappealing as the process is, I agree.

And yet what's missing in those technical accountings are the emotional, interpersonal, and cultural factors that also affect judgment on high-risk whitewater endeavors. The Tsangpo expedition team—men with families, careers, and philosophy—seemed to billboard one of the most important, if underscrutinized, topics in the sport: What are the limits of rationality?

A word about the reporting: I visited and interviewed all the river team members with the exception of Jamie McEwan, who chose to keep our contact to telephone and E-mail. In some instances their versions of what occurred (and mostly where they occurred) do differ. I've attempted to cross-check any way that I can—with others who were in the gorge at the same time, for example—and where there are discrepancies, I've simply gone with the most plausible sequence. They all kept journals, but given the brevity and arduousness of the trip, some are more complete than others. Tom McEwan offered me a handwritten journal describing the major daily events, and the others chose to keep more personal and less factually concerned accounts private. I was also given access to the expedition's maps and different versions of trip proposals. Connie Gordon, Doug's wife, was also cautiously helpful after I explained in a series of letters and conversations what I was doing and why. In short, I was graciously given an unusual amount of access with no restrictions on editorial content.

Glossary

Big Water: refers to large-volume rivers with massive hydraulics

Boof: launching a boat over a rock or shallow ledge; derived from the sound the hull makes when it hits the water's surface

Boof Stroke: the final prelaunch paddle stroke that sweeps against a rock or ledge lip to help propel the boat horizontally

Booties: treaded, socklike whitewater shoes made of an insulating rubberlike material

Boulder Garden: a rapid that is densely cluttered with boulders

Breaking Wave: a standing wave that collapses upstream

Broach: when fast current pins a kayaker's boat sideways against a rock or other stationary obstacle

Broach Loops: handles made of nylon webbing mounted near the cockpit. If the boat is pinned against an obstacle, a rope can be fed through the handles for a rescue attempt.

Cartwheel: flipping a boat end for end in a hydraulic

Cfs: cubic feet per second; measures the current's velocity past a fixed point in the river

Class I–VI: the international standard classifications—ranging from flatwater to extreme, life-endangering whitewater—used to rate the difficulty of rivers and rapids

Clean: describes a route free of major hazards

Cockpit: entry hole in the deck of a whitewater kayak

Confluence: the point where two rivers meet

Correction Stroke: any paddle stroke used to correct one's course in a rapid

Downriver Racing: a timed, top-to-bottom speed event (like downhill skiing) with no gates on an expert-level whitewater course

Drop: a steep, sudden change in the riverbed grade

Dry Suit: a one-piece, cold-water garment of specially coated nylonlike fabric that uses rubber gaskets at the neck, wrists, and ankles to seal out water

Eddy: comparative calm spots found on the downstream sides of rocks

Eddy Fence: a high water condition in which the eddy becomes dramatically elevated or depressed in comparison to the main current. The turbulent zone where the opposing currents collide is extremely hazardous.

Entrapment: getting stuck (either boat or swimmer) on an obstacle in moving water

Eskimo Roll or Roll: the technique used to right the boat after a flip

Expedition Paddling: a multi-day, self-supported wilderness trip

Exposure: proximity to hazard

Falls: a major drop where the river plunges steeply over rocks or broken riverbed

Ferry: a paddling technique used to propel a kayak back and forth laterally across the river

First Descent: boating a whitewater river that has never been boated before

Float Bags: air-inflated bags placed within the interior of a whitewater boat to aid buoyancy and prevent sinking if swamped

Flush Drowning: a boater who is caught in a series of terminal holes and is unable to swim to safety

Forward Stroke: a powerful, speed-generating stroke

Grab Loops: deck-mounted handles at the bow and stern that are used for rescues and transport

Gradient: the steepness of a river bottom. Low-gradient rivers drop less than twenty feet per mile. High-gradient rivers drop in excess of one hundred feet per mile.

Haystack: a big, unstable standing wave

High-Volume Boat: refers to the amount of water that will fill an empty boat to the top; an exceptionally stable, well-tracking design typically preferred by downriver and expedition paddlers

Hole: also known as a hydraulic or a reversal, usually forming on the downstream side of good-sized rock. Fast water passing around the obstacle and headed downstream is pulled back to fill the vacuum behind the rock. Generally the bigger the drop and faster the current, the more violent the "infilling" action.

Horizon Line: the point atop a drop in which the river visually disappears

Keeper: an extremely deep, violent hole that can keep and hold a boat or swimmer for a dangerously long period of time

Line: a preselected path through a rapid

Low-Volume Boat: high-performance whitewater boat preferred by slalom racers and advanced "play" boaters who specialize in performing acrobatic stunts in river holes

Pfd: personal flotation device—a vestlike, zip-up nylon-covered garment lined with slender foam slats for buoyancy

Pogies: cold-water, paddling-specific gloves

Portage: to haul on land a kayak around a rapid

Pourover: the current pouring over the top of a boulder and then dropping vertically, often into a treacherous hole—particularly dangerous because they appear from upstream as benign, modestly humped waves

Probe: a team's lead paddler in heavy whitewater

Rapid: a section of the river with increased gradient, fast water, waves, holes, and other obstacles

River-Left: the left side of the river as you look downriver

River-Right: the right side of the river as you look downriver

Rodeo: an extreme whitewater discipline where the "arena" is a powerful hydraulic (in which boaters perform an array of boat-spinning tricks)

Roller: a large, curling wave that falls back upstream on itself

Scouting: stopping to preview the possible routes through a whitewater rapid before running it

Scrapey: describes shallow, rocky rapids

Sieve: a "strainer" created by a pile of rocks in which a boat is easily entrapped

Slalom Racing: paddlers navigating through a twenty-five-gate course suspended over hazardous stretches of whitewater rapids. Time penalties accrue for touching or missing gates.

Sneak Route (also Cheat Route): easiest path through a rapid

Spray Skirt: a stretchy girdlelike garment around the boater's waist and fastened to the cockpit's rim to seal out water

Standing Wave: a stationary river wave

Stopper: a powerful breaking wave or hole that kills forward momentum

Strainer: any obstacle on the river that allows water to pass through but not boats and people. Most common obstacles are downed trees, logjams, and boulder piles.

Surf: to ride a wave on its upstream face or to get stuck in a hole

Sweep Stroke: the primary turning stroke. The paddle is extended perpendicular to the cockpit with the blade sweeping arclike to the stern.

Terminal Hole: a lethal hydraulic

Throw Bag: a rescue rope coiled within an open-ended, easy-to-toss sack

Tongue: a smooth V-shaped runway of water that usually offers the cleanest, most deep-water line through a rapid

Undercut: an overhanging rock with water flowing underneath it; often the cause of fatal pinning accidents.

Vertical Pin: one of the most serious hazards of running a big drop. The boat's bow gets snagged between rocks or other river debris.

Waterfall: a big vertical drop, usually six feet or higher

Wave: a hump in the river's flowing water

Wave Train: consecutive standing waves

Index

About the Author

TODD BALF, a former senior editor for *Outside* magazine, writes for *Men's Journal, Fast Company,* and other publications. His cover story in *Men's Journal* on the Tsangpo and the Walker-McEwan expedition appeared in March 1999. He lives in Beverly, Massachusetts, with his wife and two children.